P9-CEC-045

CompTIA Security+™
Certification Practice Exams, Second Edition

(Exam SY0-401)

CompTIA Security+™ Certification Practice Exams, Second Edition

(Exam SY0-401)

Daniel Lachance and
Glen E. Clarke

McGraw-Hill Education is an independent entity from CompTIA®. This publication and CD-ROM may be used in assisting students to prepare for the CompTIA Security+™ exam. Neither CompTIA nor McGraw-Hill Education warrants that use of this publication and CD-ROM will ensure passing any exam. CompTIA and CompTIA Security+ are trademarks or registered trademarks of CompTIA in the United States and/or other countries. All other trademarks are trademarks of their respective owners.

New York   Chicago   San Francisco Athens
London   Madrid   Mexico City Milan
New Delhi   Singapore   Sydney   Toronto

McGraw-Hill Education books are available at special quantity discounts to use as premiums and sales promotions, or for use in corporate training programs. To contact a representative, please visit the Contact Us pages at www .mhprofessional.com.

CompTIA Security+™ Certification Practice Exams, Second Edition (Exam SY0-401)

Copyright © 2014 by McGraw-Hill Education. All rights reserved. Printed in the United States of America. Except as permitted under the Copyright Act of 1976, no part of this publication may be reproduced or distributed in any form or by any means, or stored in a database or retrieval system, without the prior written permission of publisher, with the exception that the program listings may be entered, stored, and executed in a computer system, but they may not be reproduced for publication.

All trademarks or copyrights mentioned herein are the possession of their respective owners and McGraw-Hill Education makes no claim of ownership by the mention of products that contain these marks.

1234567890 DOC DOC 10987654

ISBN: Book p/n 978-0-07-184129-0 and CD p/n 978-0-07-184130-6
of set 978-0-07-183344-8

MHID: Book p/n 0-07-184129-6 and CD p/n 0-07-184130-X
of set 0-07-183344-7

Sponsoring Editor	**Technical Editor**	**Composition**
Stephanie Evans	S. Russell Christy	MPS Limited
Editorial Supervisor	**Copy Editor**	**Illustration**
Jody McKenzie	Kim Wimpsett	MPS Limited
Project Manager	**Proofreader**	**Art Director, Cover**
Charu Khanna, MPS Limited	Paul Tyler	Jeff Weeks
Acquisitions Coordinator	**Production Supervisor**	
Mary Demery	Jean Bodeaux	

Information has been obtained by McGraw-Hill Education from sources believed to be reliable. However, because of the possibility of human or mechanical error by our sources, McGraw-Hill Education, or others, McGraw-Hill Education does not guarantee the accuracy, adequacy, or completeness of any information and is not responsible for any errors or omissions or the results obtained from the use of such information.

For my family and friends—nothing else matters.
Daniel Lachance

ABOUT THE AUTHORS

Daniel Lachance, CompTIA Cloud Essentials, CompTIA A+, CompTIA Network+, CompTIA Security+, MCT, MCSA, MCITP, MCTS, is a technical trainer for Global Knowledge and has delivered classroom training for a wide variety of products for the past 19 years. He has developed custom applications and planned, implemented, troubleshot, and documented various network configurations. Daniel has worked as a technical editor on a number of certification titles, and he authored *CompTIA Security+ Certification Practice Exams, First Edition (Exam SY0-401)*.

Glen E. Clarke, CCNA, MCITP, MCT, CEH, CHFI, SCNP, CISSO, Security+, Network+, A+, is an independent trainer and consultant, focusing on network security and security auditing services. Glen spends most of his time delivering certified courses on Windows Server, SQL Server, Exchange Server, SharePoint, Visual Basic .NET, and ASP.NET. Glen also teaches a number of security-related courses covering topics such as ethical hacking and countermeasures, computer forensics and investigation, information systems security officers, vulnerability testing, firewall design, and packet analysis topics.

Glen is an experienced author and technical editor whose published work was nominated for a referenceware excellence award in 2003 and 2004. Glen has worked on a number of certification titles including topics on A+ certification, Windows Server certification, Cisco's CCENT and CCNA certification, and Network+ and Security+ certification.

When he's not working, Glen loves to spend quality time with his wife, Tanya, and their four children, Sara, Brendon, Ashlyn, and Rebecca. He is an active member of High Technology Crime Investigation Association (HTCIA). You can visit Glen online at www.gleneclarke.com or contact him at glenclarke@accesswave.ca.

About the Technical Editor

S. Russell Christy is a trainer for New Horizons Computer Learning Center of Memphis, Tennessee, delivering traditional and online classroom learning for adults, covering a wide variety of products. He specializes in web and print design;

Microsoft Office applications; and computer maintenance, network, and security. For more than 18 years he has deployed new desktops and operating systems, servers, and network hardware and software, while simultaneously troubleshooting various hardware and software issues.

Russell holds a bachelor's degree in business administration from the University of Memphis. He has additionally gained industry certifications in CompTIA A+, CompTIA Network+, CompTIA Security+, Microsoft Office Specialist Master 2007, Microsoft MCAS Word 2013 Expert, Microsoft MCAS Excel 2013, Microsoft MCAS PowerPoint 2013, Adobe Certified Expert Dreamweaver CS6, and Adobe Education Trainer.

CompTIA Approved Quality Content

CompTIA®

It Pays to Get Certified

In a digital world, digital literacy is an essential survival skill. Certification demonstrates that you have the knowledge and skill to solve technical or business problems in virtually any business environment. CompTIA certifications are highly valued credentials that qualify you for jobs, increased compensation, and promotion.

LEARN → **CERTIFY** → **WORK**

IT is Everywhere	IT Knowledge and Skills Get Jobs	Job Retention	New Opportunities	High Pay-High Growth Jobs
IT is mission critical to almost all organizations and its importance is increasing.	Certifications verify your knowledge and skills that qualifies you for:	Competence is noticed and valued in organizations.	Certifications qualify you for new opportunities in your current job or when you want to change careers.	Hiring managers demand the strongest skill set.
• 79% of U.S. businesses report IT is either important or very important to the success of their company	• Jobs in the high growth IT career field • Increased compensation • Challenging assignments and promotions • 60% report that being certified is an employer or job requirement	• Increased knowledge of new or complex technologies • Enhanced productivity • More insightful problem solving • Better project management and communication skills • 47% report being certified helped improve their problem solving skills	• 31% report certification improved their career advancement opportunities	• There is a widening IT skills gap with over 300,000 jobs open • 88% report being certified enhanced their resume

CompTIA Security+ Certification Helps Your Career

- **Security is one of the highest demand job categories** growing in importance as the frequency and severity of security threats continues to be a major concern for organizations around the world.
- **Jobs for security administrators are expected to increase by 18%**—the skill set required for these types of jobs maps to the CompTIA Security+ certification.
- **Network Security Administrators** can earn as much as $106,000 per year.
  - **CompTIA Security+ is the first step** in starting your career as a Network Security Administrator or Systems Security Administrator.
- **More than 250,000** individuals worldwide are CompTIA Security+ certified.
- **CompTIA Security+ is regularly used in organizations** such as Hitachi Systems, Fuji Xerox, HP, Dell, and a variety of major U.S. government contractors.
- **Approved by the U.S. Department of Defense (DoD)** as one of the required certification options in the DoD 8570.01-M directive, for Information Assurance Technical Level II and Management Level I job roles.

Steps to Getting Certified and Staying Certified

1. **Review the exam objectives.** Review the certification objectives to make sure you know what is covered in the exam: http://certification.comptia.org/examobjectives.aspx.
2. **Practice for the exam.** After you have studied for the certification exam, review and answer sample questions to get an idea of what type of questions might be on the exam: http://certification.comptia.org/samplequestions.aspx.
3. **Purchase an exam voucher.** You can purchase exam vouchers on the CompTIA Marketplace, www.comptiastore.com.

4. **Take the test!** Go to the Pearson VUE website, www.pearsonvue.com/comptia/, and schedule a time to take your exam.
5. **Stay certified!** Effective January 1, 2011, new CompTIA Security+ certifications are valid for three years from the date of certification. There are a number of ways the certification can be renewed. For more information, go to http://certification.comptia.org/ce.

For More Information

- **Visit CompTIA online**   Go to http://certification.comptia.org/home.aspx to learn more about getting CompTIA certified.
- **Contact CompTIA**   Please call 866-835-8020 and choose Option 2, or e-mail questions@comptia.org.
- **Connect with CompTIA**   Find CompTIA on Facebook, LinkedIn, Twitter, and YouTube.

Content Seal of Quality

This courseware bears the seal of CompTIA Approved Quality Content. This seal signifies this content covers 100 percent of the exam objectives and implements important instructional design principles. CompTIA recommends multiple learning tools to help increase coverage of the learning objectives.

CAQC Disclaimer

The logo of the CompTIA Approved Quality Content (CAQC) program and the status of this or other training material as "Approved" under the CompTIA Approved Quality Content program signifies that, in CompTIA's opinion, such training material covers the content of CompTIA's related certification exam.

The contents of this training material were created for the CompTIA Security+ exam covering CompTIA certification objectives that were current as of the date of publication.

CompTIA has not reviewed or approved the accuracy of the contents of this training material and specifically disclaims any warranties of merchantability or fitness for a particular purpose. CompTIA makes no guarantee concerning the success of persons using any such "Approved" or other training material in order to prepare for any CompTIA certification exam.

CONTENTS AT A GLANCE

CONTENTS

ACKNOWLEDGMENTS

I would like to make known the stellar team that contributed to this book's existence. All of the following people were given raw materials that were forged into a refined product, this book.

The dedication of the skilled staff at McGraw-Hill Education cannot be overstated: Tim Green, Mary Demery, and Stephanie Evans from the acquisitions team; Jody McKenzie for her editorial supervision; Kim Wimpsett's work as copyeditor; and Charu Khanna's work as production project manager. These professionals exhibited saintly patience with me, and I thank them.

I would like to thank my friend and colleague Glen Clarke for his guidance in crafting a meaningful body of text and for never running out of interesting things to talk about. To the technical editor, Russ Christy, for catching even the minutest problematic detail in the text—thank you for making me look better.

Finally, to Trinity, Stacey, and Raylee for enduring my and Roman's endless techno-babble.

Daniel Lachance

PREFACE

Welcome to *CompTIA Security+ Certification Practice Exams, Second Edition*! This book serves as a preparation tool for the CompTIA Security+ exam (exam SY0-401) as well as for your work in the IT security field.

The objective of this book is to prepare you for the CompTIA Security+ exam by familiarizing you with the technology and body of knowledge tested on the exam. Because the primary focus of this book is to help you pass the test, we don't always cover every aspect of the related technology. Some aspects of the technology are covered only to the extent necessary to help you understand what you need to know to pass the exam, but we hope this book will serve you as a valuable professional resource after your exam as well.

In This Book

This book is organized in such a way as to serve as an in-depth review for the CompTIA Security+ exam for both experienced IT security professionals and newcomers to security technologies. Each chapter covers a major aspect of the exam, with practice questions to test your knowledge of specific exam objectives. The SY0-401 exam will present you with some performance-based questions where you will be tested on your ability to carry out a task to solve a problem. This could be in the form of typing in a command, placing network devices in the correct positions on a network map, or matching terms with definitions.

In Every Chapter

Each chapter contains components that call your attention to important items and reinforce salient points. Take a look at what you'll find in every chapter:

- Every chapter begins with **certification objectives**, a list of the official CompTIA exam objectives covered in that chapter.
- Practice **questions**, similar to those found on the actual exam, are included in every chapter. By answering these questions you'll test your knowledge while becoming familiar with the structure of the exam questions.

- The **Quick Answer Key** section follows the questions and allows you to easily check your answers.
- **In-Depth Answers** at the end of every chapter include explanations for the correct and incorrect answer choices and provide an opportunity for reviewing the exam topics.

Pre-assessment Test

This book features a pre-assessment test as Appendix A. The pre-assessment test will gauge your areas of strength and weakness and allow you to tailor your studies based on your needs. We recommend that you take this pre-assessment test before starting the questions in Chapter 1.

Practice Exams

Of the 800+ questions included in this book, 300 are included in the customizable test engine on the CD-ROM. You can create practice exams by objective or by chapter, or you can take full-length practice exams. Like the questions in the chapters, these practice exams also include detailed explanations for the correct and incorrect answer choices.

On the CD-ROM

For more information on the CD-ROM, please see Appendix B.

Exam Readiness Checklist

At the end of the introduction you will find an exam readiness checklist. This table has been constructed to allow you to reference the official CompTIA Security+ objectives and refer to the order in which these objectives are covered in this book. This checklist also allows you to gauge your level of expertise on each exam objective at the outset of your studies. This will allow you to check your progress and make sure you spend the time you need on more difficult or unfamiliar sections. The objectives are listed as CompTIA has presented them with the corresponding book chapter and question number reference.

The CompTIA Security+ Exam (Exam SY0-401)

The CompTIA Security+ exam is a vendor-neutral exam validating skills in risk identification and management, the application of physical and digital security controls for devices and networks, disaster recovery, and the adherence to rules set forth by legal and regulatory bodies. This certification is aimed at individuals with a minimum of two years of experience in IT administration focusing on security.

The CompTIA Security+ exam consists of six domains (categories). CompTIA represents the relative importance of each domain within the body of knowledge required for an entry-level IT professional taking this exam.

1.0 Network Security	20 percent
2.0 Compliance and Operational Security	18 percent
3.0 Threats and Vulnerabilities	20 percent
4.0 Application, Data and Host Security	15 percent
5.0 Access Control and Identity Management	15 percent
6.0 Cryptography	12 percent

Your CompTIA Security+ certification is valid for three years from the date you are certified, after which you must take the most current version of the exam to keep your certification. Detailed information regarding the CompTIA Security+ certification and exam is available at www.comptia.org.

Organization and Design of This Book

CompTIA Security+ Certification Practice Exams, Second Edition (Exam SY0-401), is a battery of practice test questions organized by the official exam objectives. The 19 chapters contain more than 500 questions that cover all the objectives for the SY0-401 exam. Additionally, the accompanying CD-ROM contains 300 questions in a customizable test engine that allows you to take three full practice exams in a simulated testing environment or customized exams by chapter or exam domain.

This book was developed and written in conjunction with the *CompTIA Security+ Certification Study Guide, Second Edition (Exam SY0-401)*, by Glen E. Clarke. The order the objectives are presented in is identical, as are the chapter titles. These books were designed to work together as a comprehensive program for self-study.

Strategies for Use

There are a variety of ways in which you can use this book, whether simultaneously with the *CompTIA Security+™ Certification Study Guide, Second Edition*, or as a stand-alone test prep tool.

With the Study Guide: Taking a chapter-by-chapter approach, you can opt to read a Study Guide chapter and then practice what you have learned with the questions in the corresponding Practice Exams chapter, alternating between books throughout your course of study.

The Practice Exams book alone: Using the Practice Exams book after you have read the Study Guide, or as a stand-alone test prep tool, you can work through the book cover to cover and take the three practice exams as the final step in your preparation.

Alternatively, by means of the following exam readiness checklist, you can gauge your level of expertise and determine which objectives to focus on and work through the book by objectives. The exam readiness checklist notes which questions pertain to which objectives, allowing you to tailor your review.

Exam Readiness Checklist

Official Objective	Ch. Nos.	Question Nos.	Beginner	Intermediate	Advanced
1.0 Network Security					
1.1 Implement security configuration parameters on network devices and other technologies	1 3 8	1, 4, 6, 9, 15, 19, 35 2, 5, 6, 7, 9, 10, 13, 15, 19, 21, 23 5, 6, 7, 8, 12, 18, 22, 23, 28, 30, 32, 33, 34, 35, 36, 37			
1.2 Given a scenario, use secure network administration principles	1 8	4, 5, 20, 30 2, 5, 6, 9, 10, 13, 15, 18, 21, 25, 28, 30, 31, 32, 33, 34, 35, 36, 37			
1.3 Explain network design elements and components	1 5 7 8 10	2, 3, 19 15 6, 12, 13, 14, 17, 18, 29, 30 1, 2, 3, 4, 5, 6, 11, 13, 14, 15, 18, 22, 23, 24, 26, 32, 33, 35, 36, 37 4, 5, 6, 10, 23			
1.4 Given a scenario, implement common protocols and services	1 8 12	5, 6, 7, 8, 9, 10, 11, 12, 13, 14, 15, 16, 17, 18, 21, 22, 23, 24, 25, 26, 27, 28, 29, 31, 32, 33, 35 9 2, 3, 4, 5, 18, 19			
1.5 Given a scenario, troubleshoot security issues related to wireless networking	9	1, 4, 8, 12, 13, 17, 19, 22, 26			
2.0 Compliance and Operational Security					
2.1 Explain the importance of risk related concepts	3 11 15	10, 11, 12, 13, 20, 22, 26, 27, 28, 29, 30, 34 29, 30 1, 2, 5, 6, 7, 8, 10, 11, 12, 13, 14, 15, 16, 17, 18, 19, 22, 24, 25, 27, 28, 29, 30			
2.2 Summarize the security implications of integrating systems and data with third parties	15	3, 9, 26, 31, 32			
2.3 Given a scenario, implement appropriate risk mitigation strategies	3 15	16, 17, 18, 19, 31, 33 4, 20, 21, 23, 33			
2.4 Given a scenario, implement basic forensic procedures	17	2, 3, 4, 6, 7, 8, 9, 10, 11, 12, 13, 14, 15, 16, 17, 18, 19, 20, 21, 22, 23, 24, 25, 26, 28, 29, 30, 31			

Exam Readiness Checklist

Official Objective	Ch. Nos.	Question Nos.	Beginner	Intermediate	Advanced
2.5 Summarize common incident response procedures	17	1, 5, 27, 32, 33, 34, 35			
2.6 Explain the importance of security related awareness and training	3	1, 2, 3, 4, 5, 15, 16, 22, 23, 24, 25, 30, 32, 35			
2.7 Compare and contrast physical security and environmental controls	11 3 14	22, 25, 31, 35 8, 9, 14, 32 2, 3, 7, 8, 9, 10, 12, 16, 21			
2.8 Summarize risk management best practices	2 16	12, 16, 34 1–33			
2.9 Given a scenario, select the appropriate control to meet the goals of security	2 14	1, 2, 3, 4, 5, 6, 7, 8, 9, 10, 11, 13, 14, 15, 17, 18, 19, 20, 21, 22, 23, 24, 25, 26, 27, 28, 29, 30, 31, 35 1, 4, 5, 6, 11, 13, 14, 15, 17, 18, 19, 20, 22			
3.0 Threats and Vulnerabilities					
3.1 Explain types of malware	4 5	24 1, 2, 3, 4, 5, 6, 7, 8, 9, 13, 16, 19, 20, 22, 23, 24, 25, 26, 27			
3.2 Summarize various types of attacks	2 3 4 5	32 15, 16, 21 1, 3, 4, 5, 6, 7, 8, 9, 11, 12, 13, 14, 15, 16, 17, 18, 20, 21, 22, 23, 25, 26, 30 10, 11, 12, 18, 28			
3.3 Summarize social engineering attacks and the associated effectiveness with each attack	4	2, 14, 20, 23, 27, 28, 29			
3.4 Explain types of wireless attacks	9	2, 3, 4, 5, 6, 7, 8, 9, 10, 11, 12, 14, 15, 16, 17, 18, 19, 20, 21, 22, 23, 24, 25, 26, 27, 28, 29, 30, 31, 32, 33			
3.5 Explain types of application attacks	4	3, 4, 5, 7, 8, 10, 12, 13, 15, 16, 19, 30			
3.6 Analyze a scenario and select the appropriate type of mitigation and deterrent techniques	3 5 6 8 14 19	34 17, 21, 27, 29 2, 4, 5, 6, 7, 9, 10, 13, 30 3, 4, 11, 12 6, 9 1–34			

Exam Readiness Checklist

Official Objective	Ch. Nos.	Question Nos.	Beginner	Intermediate	Advanced
3.7 Given a scenario, use appropriate tools and techniques to discover security threats and vulnerabilities	15 18	1, 2, 6, 7 1, 2, 3, 4, 5, 6, 7, 8, 10, 11, 12, 13, 14, 15, 16, 18, 19, 20, 22, 23, 24, 25, 28, 29, 30, 31, 32, 34, 36, 37, 39			
3.8 Explain the proper use of penetration testing versus vulnerability scanning	2 18	33 9, 17, 21, 26, 27, 33, 38, 40			
4.0 Application, Data and Host Security					
4.1 Explain the importance of application security controls and techniques	6 7	1, 2, 3, 4, 12, 13, 15, 16, 19, 20, 21, 22, 23, 24, 25, 26, 35, 36 24			
4.2 Summarize mobile security concepts and technologies	3 6 7	6, 7 9 10, 23, 31, 32, 33			
4.3 Given a scenario, select the appropriate solution to establish host security	6 7	17, 27, 28, 29, 33, 36, 37, 39 1, 2, 3, 4, 5, 7, 8, 9, 10, 11, 14, 15, 16, 17, 18, 24, 25, 26, 27, 32, 34, 35			
4.4 Implement the appropriate controls to ensure data security	6 7	8, 18, 30, 31, 32 6, 8, 9, 10, 12, 13, 20, 21, 22, 23, 28, 34, 35, 36, 37			
4.5 Compare and contrast alternative methods to mitigate security risks in static environments	6	5, 6, 7, 10, 11, 14, 37, 38, 39			
5.0 Access Control and Identity Management					
5.1 Compare and contrast the function and purpose of authentication services	10	1, 3, 4, 5, 6, 7, 10, 16, 17, 23, 25, 31			
5.2 Given a scenario, select the appropriate authentication, authorization or access control	10 11	2, 8, 9, 11, 12, 13, 14, 15, 18, 19, 20, 21, 22, 24, 26, 27, 28, 29, 30 1, 3, 4, 5, 6, 7, 11, 12, 14, 15, 16, 17, 18, 19, 21, 23, 24, 26, 27, 32			
5.3 Install and configure security controls when performing account management, based on best practices	11	2, 8, 9, 10, 13, 20, 28, 33, 34			

Exam Readiness Checklist

Official Objective	Ch. Nos.	Question Nos.	Beginner	Intermediate	Advanced
6.0 Cryptography					
6.1 Given a scenario, utilize general cryptography concepts	12	1, 6, 7, 8, 9, 10, 11, 12, 13, 14, 15, 16, 17, 20, 21, 22, 23, 24, 25, 26, 27, 28, 29, 30, 31, 32, 33, 34, 35, 36			
	13	1, 3, 6, 17, 25			
6.2 Given a scenario, use appropriate cryptographic methods	9	32			
	10	28, 31			
	12	1, 2, 6, 7, 8, 23, 25, 31, 33, 35			
6.3 Given a scenario, use appropriate PKI, certificate management and associated components	13	2, 4, 5, 7, 8, 9, 10, 11, 12, 13, 14, 15, 16, 18, 19, 20, 21, 22, 23, 24			

1
Networking Basics and Terminology

QUESTIONS

Secure networks are the result of applying security principles to network devices and resources in accordance with a security policy. Familiarity with switches, routers, and other devices is required before you can apply security settings.

Internet Protocol version 4 (IPv4) and the newer IPv6 are the protocol foundation on which network services are available. Network services such as Domain Name System (DNS) and Simple Network Management Protocol (SNMP) use different port numbers that uniquely identify them. Clients connect to these unique port numbers when accessing network services. Because firewalls could block this traffic, you must know which port is used by which network service.

1. Which network device transmits data between different networks by examining the destination network address in a packet?

   A. Load balancer

   B. Layer 2 switch

   C. Router

   D. NIC

2. You have been asked to implement a solution that separates a large busy network into many smaller collision domains. Which device should you implement?

   A. Load balancer

   B. Layer 2 switch

   C. Router

   D. NIC

3. A busy web site has not been responding well because of the large volumes of HTTP connections to the web server. Which solution would increase web server performance?

   A. Add more RAM to the web server.

   B. Install two web servers hosting the same content. Configure a load balancer to distribute incoming HTTP connections between the two web servers.

   C. Place a router between the web server and the Internet to throttle incoming HTTP connections.

   D. Enable SSL on the web server.

4. Your network consists of customers who connect to the Internet using their Wi-Fi mobile devices as well as employees who use their wired desktops for company business. You must ensure customer traffic and corporate network traffic are kept isolated. What should you do?

    A. Install and configure a load balancer.

    B. Use a separate network switch for customers.

    C. Upgrade the desktop NICs to 10Gbps.

    D. Place the wireless access point on a separate VLAN.

5. Your company's networks and devices were recently migrated to IPv6, although there are still a small number of IPv4 hosts online. You are asked to verify that a server named hq-01.acme.us is reachable on the network via IPv6. Write the command(s) you would use to verify this:

    ping -6 hq-01.acme.us

6. Your network consists of routers and switches, as well as a variety of other network devices. You are configuring a wireless router, as shown in Figure 1-1, and need to allow network management traffic through. Which protocol should be removed from the blocked list?

    A. SMTP

    B. SNMP

    C. IKE

    D. None

FIGURE 1-1

A protocol blocked list on a wireless router

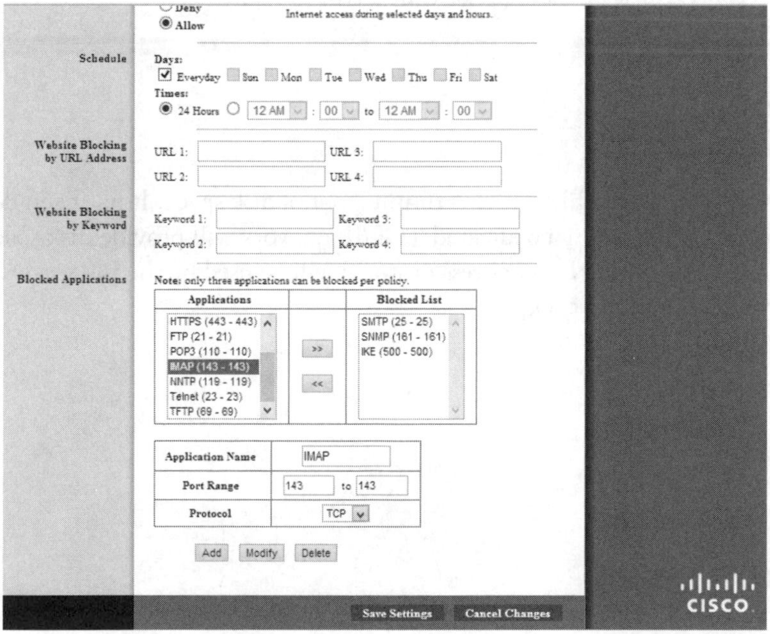

7. Which protocol suite uses 128-bit IP addresses?

   A. IPv4

   B. IPv5

   C. IPv6

   D. Network interface cards

8. Your newly configured SMTP mail server is not receiving mail from the Internet. You realize you did not configure any DNS records for SMTP mail transfer. Which type of DNS resource record must you create?

   A. CNAME

   B. MX

   C. PTR

   D. A

9. While troubleshooting connectivity to your remote file server, you realize that a firewall is preventing you from pinging the server. Which type of firewall rule should you create to allow ping traffic?

   A. UDP

   B. IGMP

   C. TCP

   D. ICMP

10. 199.126.19.71 is an example of which type of address?

   A. IPv4

   B. Port

   C. IPv6

   D. MAC

11. Your Linux virtual file server is running out of disk space. It has been decided that a network storage appliance on a dedicated TCP/IP network will provide disk space to your file server. Which type of SAN disk access protocol will be used by the file server?

   A. Fibre Channel SAN

   B. SMB

   C. iSCSI

   D. TCP/IP

12. Your SAN solution uses optical technology designed solely for high-speed connectivity from servers to disk storage. Which type of SAN is this?

 Ⓐ Fibre Channel SAN

 B. SMB

 C. iSCSI

 D. TCP/IP

13. How do FCoE and iSCSI differ?

 A. FCoE uses TCP; iSCSI uses UDP.

 B. iSCSi uses TCP; FCoE uses UDP.

 C. FCoE uses TCP/IP; iSCSI does not.

 Ⓓ iSCSI uses TCP/IP; FCoE does not.

14. Which TCP/IP protocol uses TCP ports 20 and 21?

 A. SNMP

 B. DNS

 C. HTTP

 Ⓓ FTP

15. Which TCP/IP protocol does not have authentication configuration options?

 Ⓐ TFTP

 B. FTP

 C. SNMP

 D. SMTP

16. Which of the following is Telnet used for?

 A. Verifying routers in a transmission path

 B. Performing encrypted remote command-line management

 Ⓒ Performing clear-text remote command-line management

 D. Forcing the retrieval of operating system updates

17. Stacey, your assistant, has captured network traffic on your LAN for a 24-hour period, as shown in Figure 1-2. You would like to view network traffic related to users connecting to web sites. Which protocol in the protocol column should you filter by?

 Ⓐ HTTP

 B. DNS

 C. TCP

 D. SSDP

FIGURE 1-2 Captured network traffic

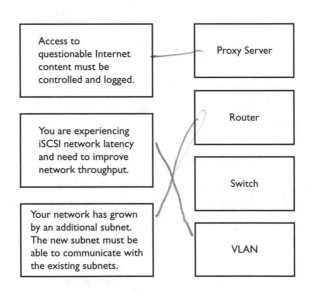

18. Which network protocol is not routable?

A. HTTP

B. DNS

C. NetBIOS

D. Telnet

19. In Figure 1-3, match each stated requirement with its appropriate network device.

FIGURE 1-3

Network requirements and devices

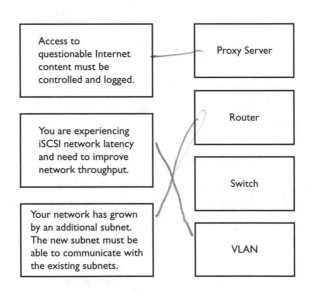

20. Your wiring closet consists of three 24-port Ethernet switches all linked together. Computers from the Accounting department are plugged into each Ethernet switch, as are computers from the Research department. Your manager asks you to ensure computers in the Accounting department are on a different network than computers in the Research department. What could you do? (Choose two.)

A. Replace the Ethernet switches with Ethernet hubs.

B. Configure all Accounting computers on the same TCP/IP subnet (e.g., 192.268.2.0 /24) and configure all Research computers on their own TCP/IP subnet (e.g., 192.168.3.0 /16).

C. Configure an Accounting VLAN that includes the Accounting computers and a Research VLAN that includes the Research computers.

D. Configure all Accounting computers on the same TCP/IP subnet (e.g., 192.168.2.0 /24) and configure all Research computers on their own TCP/IP subnet (e.g., 192.168.3.0 /24).

21. What type of address is fe80::dca6:d048:cba6:bd06?

A. IPv4

B. IPv6

C. MAC

D. DMZ

22. Which of the following statements regarding DNS are true? (Choose two.)

A. It resolves NetBIOS computer names to IP addresses.

B. Client-to-server queries use TCP port 53.

C. It resolves FQDNs to IP addresses.

D. Given an IP address, DNS can return an FQDN.

23. Which protocol uses TCP port 443?

A. FTPS

B. HTTP

C. HTTPS

D. SSH

24. You are troubleshooting TCP/IP settings on a workstation. The workstation IP address is 10.17.6.8/24, the DNS server setting is set to 199.126.129.86, and the default gateway setting is set to 10.17.5.6. The router has a public IP address of 199.126.129.76/24 and a private internal IP address of 10.17.5.6/24. This workstation is the only station on the network that cannot connect to the Internet. What should you do?

A. Change the DNS server setting to 10.17.5.6.

B. Change the router private internal IP address to 10.17.6.6.

C. Change the workstation IP address to 10.17.5.8.

D. Change the default gateway setting to 199.126.129.76.

25. You need a server to store router configuration files. The server must not require a username or password. Which type of server is the best choice?

   A.   Windows file server

   B.   FTP

   C.   TFTP

   D.   FTPS

26. Which TCP/IP protocol is designed to synchronize time between computers?

   A.   SNMP

   B.   Windows time sync

   C.   NTP

   D.   SMTP

27. Which TCP/IP protocol gives administrators a remote command prompt to a network service?

   A.   POP

   B.   ARP

   C.   UDP

   D.   Telnet

28. While capturing network traffic you notice some packets destined for UDP port 69. What type of network traffic is this?

   A.   FTP

   B.   TFTP

   C.   SNMP

   D.   IMAP

29. Which TCP/IP protocols use encryption to secure data transmissions?

   A.   SCP, DNS, SSH

   B.   SSH, SCP, TELNET

   C.   HTTPS, FTP, SSH

   D.   SSH, SCP, FTPS

30. Which of the following network connectivity devices function primarily using computer MAC addresses? (Choose two.)

   A.   Router

   B.   Bridge

   C.   Hub

   D.   Switch

31. Which of the following are considered TCP/IP transport protocols? (Choose two.)

    A. HTTP

    B. TCP

    C. Telnet

    D. UDP

32. Your Vancouver users cannot connect to a corporate web server housed in Seattle, but they can connect to Internet web sites. The network technicians in Seattle insist the web server is running because Seattle users have no problem connecting to the Seattle web server. From the Vancouver network, you ping the Seattle web server but do not get a reply. Which tool should you use next?

    A. tracert

    B. ipconfig

    C. Telnet

    D. HTTP

33. A workstation has an IP address of 169.254.46.86. The server administrators realize the DHCP service is offline, so they start the DHCP service. What command should be used next on the workstation to immediately obtain a valid TCP/IP configuration?

    A. ping -t

    B. tracert

    C. netstat -a

    D. ipconfig /renew

34. Which of the following is a security best practice for configuring an Ethernet switch?

    A. Disable unused ports and assign MAC addresses to enabled ports.

    B. Disable unused ports and configure enabled ports for half-duplex.

    C. Disable unused ports and configure additional VLANs.

    D. Disable unused ports and configure enabled ports for full-duplex.

35. You are attempting to connect to one of your user's computers using RDP but cannot get connected. A new firewall has been installed on your network. Which port must be opened on the firewall to allow RDP traffic?

    A. 143

    B. 389

    C. 3389

    D. 443

QUICK ANSWER KEY

1. C	**9.** D	**18.** C	**27.** D
2. B	**10.** A	**19.** See Figure 1-4.	**28.** B
3. B	**11.** C	**20.** C, D	**29.** D
4. D	**12.** A	**21.** B	**30.** B, D
5. ping -6 hq-01. acme.us	**13.** D	**22.** C, D	**31.** B, D
	14. D	**23.** C	**32.** A
6. B	**15.** A	**24.** C	**33.** D
7. C	**16.** C	**25.** C	**34.** A
8. B	**17.** A	**26.** C	**35.** C

FIGURE 1-4

Network requirements and devices—the answer

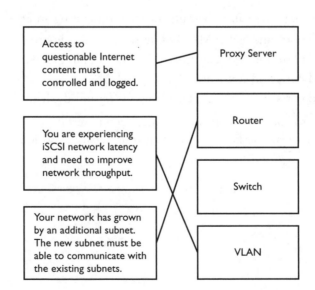

IN-DEPTH ANSWERS

1. ☑ **C.** Routers examine the destination network address when receiving inbound traffic to transmit packets to different networks.
   ☒ **A, B,** and **D** are incorrect. Load balancers distribute network traffic among multiple servers offering the same service. Layer 2 switches are used as physical network connectivity points for wired stations. Network interface cards (NICs) allow a system to communicate on a network; they do not route packets by themselves.

2. ☑ **B.** Layer 2 switches treat each switch port as a separate collision domain.
   ☒ **A, C,** and **D** are incorrect. Load balancers distribute network traffic among multiple servers offering the same service. Routers determine the best path to be used when transmitting data between networks. They are used to create multiple broadcast domains. Network interface cards (NICs) allow a system to communicate on a network; they do not control the number of collision domains.

3. ☑ **B.** Configuring multiple servers behind a load balancer allows the distribution of incoming network traffic among those servers.
   ☒ **A, C,** and **D** are incorrect. Adding more RAM can sometimes improve the performance of a computing device, but the problem here is network performance based. Routers determine the best path to be used when transmitting data between networks. They are not used to increase network performance to a web server. Secure Sockets Layer (SSL) secures network transmissions and is not related to improving network performance to a web server.

4. ☑ **D.** Placing the wireless access point on a separate VLAN will isolate wireless customer network traffic from employee network traffic.
   ☒ **A, B,** and **C** are incorrect. Load balancers distribute workloads across multiple devices. Customers are using wireless devices; therefore, they will not be plugging into a switch. Using faster network cards will not isolate customer and employee network traffic.

5. ☑ **ping -6 hq-01.acme.us.** The -6 option specifies that ping should use the IPv6 address to communicate with the target host. There must be an IPv6 AAAA record in DNS for hq-01.acme.us to be resolved to the correct IPv6 address.

6. ☑ **B.** Simple Network Management Protocol (SNMP) is used to retrieve configuration data and usage statistics from network devices configured for SNMP, such as computers, servers, routers, switches, and so on.
   ☒ **A, C,** and **D** are incorrect. Simple Mail Transfer Protocol (SMTP) is used to transmit e-mail messages between mail servers. Internet Key Exchange (IKE) is a protocol that governs how security keys are exchanged between two communicating parties.

7. ☑ **C.** IPv6 addresses are expressed in hexadecimal and are 128 bits long.
☒ **A, B,** and **D** are incorrect. IPv4 address are only 32 bits long. IPv5 does not exist. Network interface cards are not protocol suites.

8. ☑ **B.** Mail eXchanger (MX) records are required for Internet SMTP mail to be transferred correctly.
☒ **A, C,** and **D** are incorrect. CNAME records are alias records. PTR are reverse zone lookup records. A records are forward lookup records.

9. ☑ **D.** Internet Control Message Protocol (ICMP) is the transport used by the ping command.
☒ **A, B,** and **C** are incorrect. User Datagram Protocol (UDP) is a best-effort transport protocol. Internet Group Management Protocol (IGMP) is used for multicast applications. Transmission Control Protocol (TCP) is a reliable connection-oriented transport protocol.

10. ☑ **A.** IPv4 addresses are 32-bit addresses expressed in decimal form with each octet separated with a period.
☒ **B, C,** and **D** are incorrect. Port addresses represent a network service and do not use periods to separate address components. IPv6 addresses are 128-bit hexadecimal addresses where each hextet is separated by a colon. MAC addresses are 48-bit addresses representing the physical, or hardware, address for a network card.

11. ☑ **C.** iSCSI is a network disk storage protocol where SCSI disk commands are transmitted over an IP network.
☒ **A, B,** and **D** are incorrect. Fibre Channel SANs do not run on TCP/IP networks. The Server Message Block (SMB) protocol is used by Windows file and print sharing networks, but it is not related to disk access. TCP/IP is a protocol suite and not a disk access protocol.

12. ☑ **A.** Fibre Channel SANs use optical technology on a dedicated disk network.
☒ **B, C,** and **D** are incorrect. The Server Message Block (SMB) protocol is used by Windows file and print sharing networks, but it is not related to disk access. iSCSI is a network disk storage protocol where SCSI disk commands are transmitted over an IP network. TCP/IP is a protocol suite and not a disk access protocol.

13. ☑ **D.** Internet Small Computer Systems Interface (iSCSI) sends SCSI disk commands over a TCP/IP network; Fibre Channel over Ethernet (FCoE) allows Fibre Channel traffic to traverse an Ethernet network.
☒ **A, B,** and **C** are incorrect. These do not correctly reflect how FCoE and iSCSI differ.

14. ☑ **D.** File Transfer Protocol (FTP) uses TCP ports 20 and 21.
☒ **A, B,** and **C** are incorrect. SNMP uses UDP port 161, DNS uses UDP 53, and HTTP uses TCP port 80.

15. ☑ **A.** Trivial File Transfer Protocol (TFTP) is used to transfer files, but it does not support authentication.

☒ **B, C,** and **D** are incorrect. File Transfer Protocol (FTP), Simple Network Management Protocol (SNMP), and Simple Mail Transfer Protocol (SMTP) have authentication configuration options.

16. ☑ **C.** Telnet uses TCP port 23 and is used for clear-text remote command-line management.
    ☒ **A, B,** and **D** are incorrect. The tracert command is used to verify routers in a transmission path. SSH can be used for encrypted remote command-line management. Windows systems can be configured to retrieve operating system updates on a scheduled basis.

17. ☑ **A.** HyperText Transfer Protocol (HTTP) network traffic results from web site traffic.
    ☒ **B, C,** and **D** are incorrect. Domain Name System (DNS) traffic normally results from client queries (looking up a name such as www.independent.co.uk and returning the IP address). Transmission Control Protocol (TCP) is a connection-oriented transport protocol. Simple Service Discovery Protocol (SSDP) is a self-managing network service discovery standard.

18. ☑ **C.** NetBIOS is not a routable network protocol. NetBIOS over TCP/IP (NBT) is a Microsoft protocol used in the past for purposes such as file and print sharing over port 139.
    ☒ **A, B,** and **D** are incorrect. HTTP, DNS, and Telnet are OSI model higher-layer protocols that rely upon the OSI Layer 3 IP routing protocol; thus, their traffic is routable.

19. Proxy servers sit between a user requesting a resource, such as a web page, and the server hosting that service. As such, the proxy server can examine requests for Internet content and, based on configured policies, allow or deny the request while logging the transaction. Virtual local area networks (VLANs) are used to isolate network communications for network throughput or security reasons. Routers forward traffic between networks. See Figure 1-5.

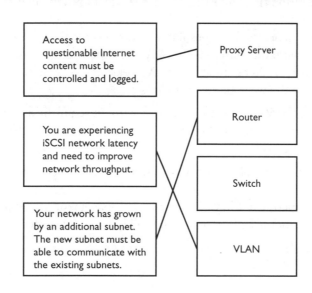

FIGURE 1-5

Network requirements and devices—the answer

20. ☑ **C** and **D.** Placing the Accounting and Research computers each into their own VLAN means Accounting and Research computers would be on different networks. If Accounting computers were on the 192.168.2.0 /24 network and Research computers were on the 192.168.3.0 /24 network, the computers would be on the same physical network but on *different* logical networks.

    ☒ **A** and **B** are incorrect. Ethernet hubs would not put Accounting and Research computers on different networks. 192.268.2.0/24 is not a valid TCP/IP network.

21. ☑ **B.** IPv6 addresses are hexadecimal (base 16) addresses with each portion separated with a colon. Double colons can be used as shorthand for :0000:.

    ☒ **A, C,** and **D** are incorrect. IPv4 addresses are decimal values separated with periods, for example, 145.76.56.87. MAC addresses are much shorter; they are only 48 bits long and might appear as something similar to 00-24-D6-9B-08-8C. DMZ is not a type of address.

22. ☑ **C** and **D.** DNS is used to resolve fully qualified domain names (FQDNs) such as www.mhprofessional.com to an IP address. The reverse is also true. An IP address such as 22.33.44.55 could be used to return an FQDN (this is called a DNS reverse lookup).

    ☒ **A** and **B** are incorrect. WINS servers resolve NetBIOS computer names to IP addresses, not DNS servers. Client requests use UDP port 53.

23. ☑ **C.** HyperText Transfer Protocol Secure (HTTPS) uses TCP port 443.

    ☒ **A, B,** and **D** are incorrect. FTPS uses TCP ports 989 and 990. HTTP uses TCP port 80. SSH uses TCP port 22.

24. ☑ **C.** The workstation IP address is currently on a different subnet from the default gateway; changing the workstation IP address to 10.17.5.8 would allow communication with the default gateway.

    ☒ **A, B,** and **D** are incorrect. The question does not specifically state name resolution as being a problem. Because this station is the only one experiencing connectivity issues, there is no reason to modify the router configuration. A workstation's default gateway (router) must be on the same subnet as the workstation IP address.

25. ☑ **C.** Trivial FTP (TFTP) allows storage of files without requiring a username or password.

    ☒ **A, B,** and **D** are incorrect. Windows file servers, FTP servers, and FTPS servers all normally require a username and password.

26. ☑ **C.** Network Time Protocol (NTP) synchronizes time between computers over UDP port 123.

    ☒ **A, B,** and **D** are incorrect. SNMP is a network management protocol using UDP port 161. Windows time sync is not a TCP/IP protocol. SMTP is a mail transfer protocol using TCP port 25.

27. ☑ **D.** Telnet gives administrators a remote command prompt to a network service.
☒ **A, B,** and **C** are incorrect. Post Office Protocol (POP) is a mail retrieval protocol that uses TCP port 110. Address Resolution Protocol (ARP) resolves IP addresses to MAC addresses. User Datagram Protocol (UDP) is a connectionless TCP/IP transport protocol.

28. ☑ **B.** Trivial File Transfer Protocol (TFTP) uses UDP port 69.
☒ **A, C,** and **D** are incorrect. FTP uses TCP ports 20 and 21. SNMP uses UDP port 161. IMAP uses TCP port 143.

29. ☑ **D.** Secure Shell (SSH), Secure CoPy (SCP), and File Transfer Protocol Secure (FTPS) encrypt data transmissions.
☒ **A, B,** and **C** are incorrect. Domain Name Service (DNS) does not encrypt data. Telnet does not encrypt data. FTP does not encrypt data.

30. ☑ **B** and **D.** Bridges and switches optimize network usage by remembering which network segments MAC addresses (network cards) are connected to.
☒ **A** and **C** are incorrect. Routers are primarily concerned with software network addresses, such as IP addresses. Hubs do not look at any type of address within a transmission.

31. ☑ **B** and **D.** Transmission Control Protocol (TCP) and User Datagram Protocol (UDP) are both considered to be transport protocols. TCP is a connection-oriented (a session is established before transmitting data) and acknowledged transport (each transmission gets an acknowledgment packet), where UDP is connection-less and unacknowledged. Because of reduced overhead, UDP is faster.
☒ **A** and **C** are incorrect. They are both application protocols, not transport protocols.

32. ☑ **A.** Trace Route (tracert) to the Seattle web server will send a reply from each router along the path so you can identify where the transmission is failing.
☒ **B, C,** and **D** are incorrect. Users can connect to other Internet web sites, so it is unlikely that ipconfig will help. Telnet does not identify network transmission problems. HTTP is the application protocol used between web browsers and web servers.

33. ☑ **D.** The command ipconfig should be used with the /renew parameter to get an IP address from the DHCP server.
☒ **A, B,** and **C** are incorrect. The ping command checks only whether a host is online. The tracert command is used to verify the path a packet takes to a destination by sending replies from each router along the path. The netstat command displays network statistics for the local computer.

34. ☑ **A.** Disabling unused switch ports prevents unwanted network connections. Assigning specific MAC addresses to specific switch ports allows you to control which stations can connect to which switch ports.

☒ **B, C**, and **D** are incorrect because half-duplex network speed is not considered a security best practice. Configuring additional VLANs is not always applicable to all networks and as such is not a security best practice. Full-duplex network speed is not considered a security best practice.

35. ☑ **C.** Remote Desktop Protocol (RDP) uses TCP port 3389.

☒ **A, B**, and **D** are incorrect. IMAP uses port 443, LDAP uses port 389, and HTTPS uses port 443.

2

Introduction to Security Terminology

QUESTIONS

This chapter outlines the meaning of terms such as *authentication*, *authorization*, *confidentiality*, and *integrity*. You will explore the concepts of authentication versus authorization, data confidentiality, and the methods through which data is considered secured. Later chapters explore these topics in detail, but a solid high-level understanding is required first.

1. Your company issues smart phones to employees for business use. Corporate policy dictates that all data stored on smart phones must be encrypted. To which fundamental security concept does this apply?

   A. Confidentiality
   B. Integrity
   C. Availability
   D. Accountability

2. You are the network administrator for your company. Your manager has asked you to evaluate cloud backup solutions for remote branch offices. To which fundamental security concept does this apply?

   A. Confidentiality
   B. Integrity
   C. Availability
   D. Accountability

3. Your company requires all desktop computers to run a malware detection program twice daily. You configure your network so that only the specific digital version of the executable program that you specify is allowed to run. To which fundamental security concept does this apply?

   A. Confidentiality
   B. Integrity
   C. Availability
   D. Accountability

4. You store personal documents and spreadsheets with a cloud provider. You would like your data to be available only to people having a special unlock key. What should you apply to your documents and spreadsheets?

   A. File permissions
   B. File hashing
   C. File backup
   D. File encryption

5. You would like to send a confidential message to a family member through e-mail, but you have no way of encrypting the message. What alternative method would allow you to achieve your goal?

    A. PKI

    B. File hashing

    C. Steganography

    D. File permissions

6. A corporate security policy emphasizes data confidentiality, and you must configure computing devices accordingly. What should you do? (Choose two.)

    A. Install smartcard readers so users can identify themselves before sending important e-mail messages.

    B. Enforce SD card encryption on smart phones issued to employees.

    C. Configure a server failover cluster to ensure sensitive documents are always available.

    D. Set file and folder permissions to control user file access.

7. Michel, an IT security expert, grants permissions to folders on a file server to allow Marketing users to modify Marketing documents. Which information security goal has been satisfied?

    A. Confidentiality

    B. Integrity

    C. Availability

    D. Safety

8. You need to implement a solution that ensures data stored on a USB removable drive has not been tampered with. What should you implement?

    A. File encryption

    B. Steganography

    C. File backup

    D. File hashing

9. Ana must send an important e-mail message to Glen, the director of Human Resources (HR). Corporate policy states that messages to HR must be digitally signed. Which of the following statements is correct?

    A. Ana's public key is used to create the digital signature.

    B. Ana's public key is used to verify the digital signature.

    C. Glen's private key is used to create the digital signature.

    D. Glen's private key is used to verify the digital signature.

10. John is issuing a digital certificate for Carolyn's computer. What can the certificate be used for? (Choose two.)

    A. Setting permissions on sensitive files

    B. Encrypting sensitive files

    C. Verifying the computer's identity to secure servers

    D. Sending encrypted e-mail messages

11. Every month, Gene downloads and tests the latest software patches before applying them to production smart phones. To which security goal does this example apply?

    A. Confidentiality

    B. Integrity

    C. Availability

    D. Safety

12. You are evaluating public cloud-based e-mail hosting solutions. All vendors state that multiple servers are always running to ensure mailboxes are available. What is this an example of?

    A. Clustering

    B. Steganography

    C. Digital mailbox signatures

    D. Mailbox duplicity

13. Your network allows only trusted scripts to run on managed devices. You write a script that must run on all managed devices. What must you do? Place the following correct steps in proper order. (Choose three.)

    A. Obtain a trusted digital certificate and install it on your computer.

    B. Export the private key from your digital certificate to all managed devices.

    C. Create the script.

    D. Digitally sign the script.

    E. On your computer, import digital certificates from all managed devices.

14. Which of the following is depicted in Figure 2-1?

    A. Authentication

    B. Authorization

    C. Nonrepudiation

    D. Identification

FIGURE 2-1

Windows Server
2012 R2 logon
screen

15. You are the server administrator for your company. You are configuring disk storage as shown in Figure 2-2. To which of the following security controls does your disk configuration apply?

    A. Nonrepudiation

    B. Clustering

    C. Fault tolerance

    D. Hashing

FIGURE 2-2   Creating a disk mirror with Windows Server 2012 R2

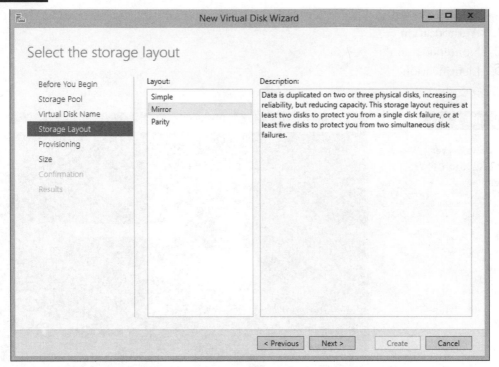

16. Match the following security controls under the appropriate headings of Confidentiality, Integrity, and Availability:

Security Controls	Confidentiality	Integrity	Availability
Nightly backups			
Disk mirroring			
File permissions			
Mailbox encryption			
Digitally signing scripts			

17. You would like to track the modification of sensitive trade secret files. What should you implement?

A. Auditing
B. Encryption
C. File hashing
D. Disk mirroring

18. Which party determines how data labels are assigned?

    A. Custodian

    B. Owner

    C. Server administrator

    D. Human Resources department

19. Which of the following organizes the appropriate identification methods from least secure to most secure?

    A. Smartcard, retinal scan, password

    B. Retinal scan, password, smartcard

    C. Username and password, smartcard, retinal scan

    D. ACL, username and password, retinal scan

20. You are explaining how the corporate file auditing policy will work to a new IT employee. Place the following items in the correct order: _C_, _B_, _A_, and _D_.

    A. A user opens a file, modifies the contents, and then saves the file.

    B. A server validates a correct username and password combination.

    C. A user provides a username and password at a logon screen.

    D. The file activity generated by the user is logged.

21. Your manager has asked you to implement a solution that will prevent users from viewing inappropriate web sites. Which solution should you employ?

    A. Router ACLs

    B. Web site permissions

    C. Proxy server

    D. Digital certificates

22. Trinity uses her building access card to enter a work facility after hours. She has access to only the second floor. What is this an example of?

    A. Authorization

    B. Authentication

    C. Accountability

    D. Confidentiality

23. Sean is capturing Wi-Fi network traffic using a packet analyzer and is able to read the contents of network transmissions. What can be done to keep network transmissions private?

   A. Install digital certificates on each transmitting device.

   B. Set a strong administrator password for the Wi-Fi router.

   C. Use smartcard authentication.

   D. Encrypt the Wi-Fi traffic.

24. Which security mechanisms can be used for the purpose of nonrepudiation? (Choose two.)

   A. Encryption

   B. Clustering

   C. Auditing

   D. Digital signatures

25. You are the network administrator for a pharmaceutical firm. Last month, the company hired a third party to conduct a security audit. From the audit findings, you learn that customers' confidential medical data is not properly secured. Which security concept has been ignored in this case?

   A. Due diligence

   B. Due care

   C. Due process

   D. Separation of duties

26. Which of the following are the best examples of the Custodian security role? (Choose three.)

   A. Human Resources department employee

   B. Server backup operator

   C. CEO

   D. Law enforcement employee responsible for signing out evidence

   E. Sales executive

27. Franco, an accountant, accesses a shared network folder containing travel expense documents to which he has read and write access. What is this an example of?

   A. Privilege escalation

   B. Due care

   C. Authorization

   D. Authentication

28. A large corporation requires new employees to present a driver's license and passport to a security officer before receiving a company-issued laptop. Which security principle does this map to?

    A. Authorization

    B. Confidentiality

    C. Identification

    D. Custodian

29. Choose the best example of authentication from the following:

    A. Each morning a network administrator visits various web sites looking for the newest Windows Server vulnerabilities.

    B. Before two systems communicate with one another across a network, they exchange PKI certificates to ensure they share a common ancestor.

    C. A file server has two power supplies in case one fails.

    D. An application has some unintended behavior that could allow a malicious user to write to the Windows registry.

30. Raylee is the new network administrator for a legal firm. She studies the existing file server folder structures and permissions and quickly realizes the previous administrator did not properly secure legal documents in these folders. She sets the appropriate file and folder permissions to ensure only the appropriate users can access the data, based on corporate policy. What security role has Raylee undertaken?

    A. Custodian

    B. Data owner

    C. User

    D. Power user

31. From the following list, which best describes authentication?

    A. Logging in to a TFTP server with a username and password

    B. Using a username, password, and token card to connect to the corporate VPN

    C. Checking corporate web mail on a secured web site at http://owa.acme.com after supplying credentials

    D. Copying files from a server to a USB flash drive

32. While experimenting with various server network configurations, you discover an unknown weakness in the server operating system that could allow a remote attacker to connect to the server with administrative privileges. What have you discovered?

   A. Exploit
   B. Bug
   C. Vulnerability
   D. Denial of service

33. Sean is a security consultant and has been hired to perform a network penetration test against his client's network. Sean's role is best described as:

   A. White-hat hacker
   B. Black-hat hacker
   C. Gray-hat hacker
   D. Purple-hat hacker

34. Which of the following are classified as availability solutions? (Choose two.)

   A. Auditing
   B. RAID
   C. File server backups
   D. Smartcard authentication

35. You are reviewing document security on your private cloud document server. You notice employees in the Sales department have been given full permissions to all project documents. Sales personnel should have only read permissions to all project documents. Which security principle has been violated?

   A. Separation of duties
   B. Least privilege
   C. Job rotation
   D. Integrity

QUICK ANSWER KEY

1.	A	13.	A, C, D	17.	A	29.	B
2.	C	14.	D	18.	B	30.	A
3.	B	15.	C	19.	C	31.	B
4.	D	16.	Nightly backups: **Availability**	20.	C, B, A, D	32.	C
5.	C			21.	C	33.	A
6.	B, D		Disk mirroring: **Availability**	22.	A	34.	B, C
7.	A		File permissions: **Confidentiality**	23.	D	35.	B
8.	D			24.	C, D		
9.	B		Mailbox encryption: **Confidentiality**	25.	B		
10.	B, C			26.	A, B, D		
11.	C		Digitally signing scripts: **Integrity**	27.	C		
12.	A			28.	C		

IN-DEPTH ANSWERS

1. ☑ **A.** Confidentiality ensures that data is accessible only to those parties who should be authorized to access the data. Encrypting data stored on smart phones protects that data if the phone is lost or stolen.

    ☒ **B, C,** and **D** are incorrect. Integrity ensures that data comes from the user or device it appears to have come from and that the data has not been altered. Making sure that data is available when needed is referred to as availability. Accountability makes people accountable for their actions, such as modifying a file. This is accomplished most often with auditing.

2. ☑ **C.** Backing up data is a safety guard in case data is corrupted or deleted, thus making that data available when required.

    ☒ **A, B,** and **D** are incorrect. Confidentiality ensures that data is accessible only to those parties that should be authorized to access the data. Integrity ensures that data comes from the user or device it appears to have come from and that the data has not been altered. Accountability makes people accountable for their actions, such as modifying a file. This is accomplished most often with auditing.

3. ☑ **B.** Integrity ensures that data comes from the user or device it appears to have come from and that the data has not been altered. File hashing can be used to validate that a specific version of a file is being used.

    ☒ **A, C,** and **D** are incorrect. Confidentiality ensures that data is accessible only to those parties who should be authorized to access the data. Availability makes data available when required. Accountability makes people accountable for their actions, such as modifying a file. This is accomplished most often with auditing.

4. ☑ **D.** File encryption can be implemented using a passphrase or unlock key such that only parties with knowledge of the unlock key can decrypt the data.

    ☒ **A, B,** and **C** are incorrect. File permissions and file backup ensure data availability. File hashing is used to verify that a specific version of a file is in use, or it can be used to verify a file has not been tampered with.

5. ☑ **C.** Steganography is the act of hiding a message within an innocent-looking medium. A common example would be storing invisible hidden messages within pictures such that the receiving party would have to extract the hidden messages. Unsuspecting parties would see only a picture.

    ☒ **A, B,** and **D** are incorrect. Public Key Infrastructure (PKI) uses digital certificates to secure data, including encrypting e-mail, but the question states that you have no way to encrypt the message (presumably because you do not have the recipient's public key). File hashing is used to verify that a file has not changed, and file permissions determine who has a specific level of access to a file; neither of these relates to sending a confidential message.

6. ☑ **B** and **D**. Encrypting data and setting file and folder permissions both keep data confidential.
    ☒ **A** and **C** are incorrect. Authenticating users after smartcard identification does not directly relate to data confidentiality. Server clustering is related to data availability, not confidentiality.

7. ☑ **A**. Confidentiality is achieved by allowing only Marketing users to modify Marketing documents.
    ☒ **B, C**, and **D** are incorrect. Integrity ensures that data comes from the user or device it appears to have come from and that the data has not been altered. Availability makes data available when required. Workplace safety protects employees and is not related to setting file permissions.

8. ☑ **D**. File hashing generates a unique value from a specific version of a file. When a file is modified and the hash value is computed once again, it will be different.
    ☒ **A, B**, and **C** are incorrect. File encryption keeps data confidential by allowing access to only authorized parties. Steganography is not related to file tampering; instead, it is the art of hiding messages within files, such as graphic images. File backup makes data available should the original files be corrupted or deleted.

9. ☑ **B**. Digital signatures are created with the sender's private key and verified with the sender's mathematically related public key.
    ☒ **A, C**, and **D** are incorrect. Public keys are not used to create signatures; rather, the sender's public key is used to verify a signature created from the sender's mathematically related private key.

10. ☑ **B** and **C**. The public and private key pair within a digital certificate can be used to encrypt and decrypt sensitive files. Digital certificates can also be used to authenticate a computer to a secure server or appliance, such as a VPN server.
    ☒ **A** and **D** are incorrect. File permissions control access to files and are not set with digital certificates. Encrypted e-mail messages are related to users, not computers. The questions states that a certificate is being generated for Carolyn's computer.

11. ☑ **C**. Patching devices helps ensure that they are available and secure.
    ☒ **A, B**, and **D** are incorrect. Confidentiality ensures that data is accessible only to those parties that should be authorized to access the data. Integrity ensures that data comes from the user or device it appears to have come from and that the data has not been altered. Workplace safety protects employees and is not related to patching computing devices.

12. ☑ **A**. Clustering makes network services, such as e-mail, always available even if a mail server goes down.
    ☒ **B, C**, and **D** are incorrect. Steganography is the act of hiding messages within files. Digitally signing mailboxes is not a common practice; digitally signing individual e-mail messages is done to assure the recipient that the message is authentic. Mailbox duplicity is a fictitious term.

13. ☑ **A, C,** and **D.** A trusted code signing digital certificate must be installed on your computer before you can sign a script. Target devices must trust the code signing certificate to allow signed scripts to run.

☒ **B** and **E** are incorrect. Private keys should never be shared. The only time you should export a private key is for backup purposes. Importing digital certificates from all managed devices is not necessary to digitally sign a script.

14. ☑ **D.** You must identify yourself, in this case with a username and password, before being authenticated and then authorized to use network resources.

☒ **A, B,** and **C** are incorrect. Authentication validates credentials after they have been provided. Logging on to a computer is considered identification. Authorization allows access to network resources for authenticated users and computers. Nonrepudiation prevents the denial of having sent a transmission or making a change to data. This might be done with auditing and smartcard authentication on patched and hardened computers.

15. ☑ **C.** Fault tolerance mechanisms ensure that the failure of one component does not render data as being inaccessible.

☒ **A, B,** and **D** are incorrect. Nonrepudiation prevents the denial of having sent a transmission or making a change to data. Clustering makes network services, such as e-mail, always available even if a mail server goes down. Hashing uses an algorithm to generate a unique value for a file or message. Changes to the file or message will result in a different hash value when the hash is recomputed.

16. ☑ Nightly backups: **Availability**. Disk mirroring: **Availability**. File permissions: **Confidentiality**. Mailbox encryption: **Confidentiality**. Digitally signing scripts: **Integrity**.

17. ☑ **A.** Auditing the modification of changes to files will identify who made changes from a specific machine at a certain date and time.

☒ **B, C,** and **D** are incorrect. Encryption scrambles data so that the data is accessible only to parties with the correct decryption key. Hashing uses an algorithm to generate a unique value for a file. Changes to the file will result in a different hash value when the hash is recomputed. Disk mirroring is a type of fault tolerance that duplicates every disk write onto a separate disk in case the first disk fails.

18. ☑ **B.** Data owners decide how data should be labeled, such as top secret or publicly available.

☒ **A, C,** and **D** are incorrect. Custodians implement security controls but do not make decisions about data labeling. Server administrators are responsible for configuring and maintaining network servers, not data labeling. The Human Resources department is responsible for managing employees.

19. ☑ **C.** Username/password is single-factor authentication (something you know). Smartcard authentication is multifactor (something you have and something you know), and retinal scans are something you are, which is difficult to forge.

☒ **A, B,** and **D** are incorrect. These do not represent the correct order of authentication methods from least secure to most. Access control lists (ACLs) are lists of parties who have access to a resource such as a file on a file server; however, this is not an identification method.

20. ☑ **C, B, A,** and **D.** After a user identifies themselves with a username and password, authentication then occurs. Upon successful authentication, a user is then authorized to access the appropriate files. If the user's current action is being audited for a given file, this information is logged.

21. ☑ **C.** Proxy servers retrieve content that users request. Because of this, proxy servers can easily prevent users from accessing inappropriate content.
☒ **A, B,** and **D** are incorrect. Router access control lists (ACLs) determine what type of network traffic the router will accept. Web site permissions control which actions are available to a user on a specific web site. Digital certificates are used to secure data and network transmissions and to verify user or computer identities.

22. ☑ **A.** Authorization means having legitimate access to specific resources such as web sites, files on a file server, or in this case access to a specific floor in a building.
☒ **B, C,** and **D** are incorrect. Authentication occurs when a user or computer correctly identifies their credentials. In this example, not only has Trinity authenticated herself, but she is also accessing a resource, in this case, a floor in her building. Accountability makes people accountable for their actions, such as modifying a file. This is accomplished most often with auditing. Confidentiality ensures that data is accessible only to those parties that should be authorized to the data.

23. ☑ **D.** The network transmissions can be kept private by encrypting all Wi-Fi traffic using Wi-Fi encryption protocols such as Wi-Fi Protected Access (WPA).
☒ **A, B,** and **C** are incorrect. Unto itself, installing digital certificates on each transmitting device does nothing. A strong administrator password for the Wi-Fi router protects the configuration of the wireless network but does nothing to protect network transmissions. Smartcard authentication is a multifactor authentication mechanism (something you have and something you know), but this is not used to keep network transmissions private.

24. ☑ **C** and **D.** Auditing can track activities from a specific user or computer. Digital signatures are unique in that they are created using a user's or computer's private key, which is accessible only to that user or computer. Both of these mechanisms invalidate any denials related to activities from the user or computer.
☒ **A** and **B** are incorrect. Encryption keeps data confidential. Clustering keeps data available. Neither of these relates to nonrepudiation.

25. ☑ **B.** Due care means taking steps to address a security problem, such as ensuring client data is kept confidential.
☒ **A, C,** and **D** are incorrect. Due diligence is the act of understanding security risks. Due process consists of the actions taken as a result of a violation of a due care policy. Separation of duties addresses internal issues resulting from one person having too much control of a business process.

26. ☑ **A, B,** and **D.** Custodians are responsible for maintaining access to and the integrity of data.
☒ **C** and **E** are incorrect. Taking care of access to and the integrity of data is not the normal direct responsibility of CEOs or sales executives.

27. ☑ **C.** Franco is accessing an item that he has legitimate access to; this is authorization.
☒ **A, B,** and **D** are not correct. Franco is not increasing his rights to the shared network folder. Due care means acting on known security issues. Authentication means proving you are who you say you are.

28. ☑ **C.** Providing a driver's license and passport means you are providing identification.
☒ **A, B,** and **D** are incorrect. In this scenario, we are not exercising our right to access corporate data (authorization), we are not preventing unauthorized access to private data (confidentiality), and we are not protecting and maintaining data (custodian).

29. ☑ **B.** Exchanging PKI certificates before allowing communication is an example of system authentication.
☒ **A, C,** and **D** are not correct. Searching for the newest vulnerabilities would be classified as due diligence. Dual power supplies is categorized as availability. Allowing malicious writing to the registry describes a vulnerability.

30. ☑ **A.** The Custodian performs data protection and maintenance duties based on established security policies, which Raylee is doing in this case.
☒ **B, C,** and **D** are incorrect. Raylee is not the data owner; the legal firm is. Raylee is a network administrator, not a user. Power user is not recognized as a standard security role in the industry.

31. ☑ **B.** Proving who you are with something you know (username/password) and something you have (token card) is authentication.
☒ **A, C,** and **D** are incorrect. TFTP servers cannot authenticate users. Secure web sites use HTTPS, not HTTP. Copying files would be an example of authorization, not authentication.

32. ☑ **C.** Vulnerabilities are unintended weaknesses in computing devices.
☒ **A, B,** and **D** are incorrect. Exploits take advantage of vulnerabilities. Bugs are problems in software that normally prevent the proper functioning or stability of software. Denial-of-service attacks render a network service unresponsive, thus denying legitimate users access to that network service.

33. ☑ **A.** White-hat hackers expose security flaws for the purposes of better protecting computers and computer networks.
☒ **B, C,** and **D** are incorrect. Black-hat hackers are malicious users who compromise systems or networks for some kind of personal gain. Gray-hat hackers discover security flaws and often make these known publicly but never for personal gain. There is no such thing as a purple-hat hacker.

34. ☑ **B** and **C.** Redundant Array of Independent Disks (RAID) groups disks together for the purpose of performance and data availability. RAID level 1 (disk mirroring), for example, ensures that all disk writes occur on two disks in case one disk fails. File server backup ensures that corrupted or deleted data is available from the backup media.
☒ **A** and **D** are incorrect. Auditing falls under the category of accountability, not availability. Smartcard authentication is not related to availability in any way.

35. ☑ **B.** The concept of least privilege is designed so that users have only the permissions they need to do their jobs.
☒ **A, C,** and **D** are incorrect. Separation of duties dictates that complex work tasks be broken down and performed by different users to avoid fraud or misuse of privileges. Job rotation places different employees in the same job role to achieve the same goals stated earlier. Making sure data is authentic and has not been altered is referred to as integrity; this is not applicable in this scenario.

3

Security Policies and Standards

QUESTIONS

Security policies provide the framework from which all types of users learn the proper procedures in using computing devices and accessing data. Management support is crucial to ensure the security policies are understood and enforced. User awareness and training provide users with this knowledge, and metrics must be gathered to determine how effective the training is, such as through testing.

1. The primary purpose of security policies is to:

   A. Establish legal grounds for prosecution

   B. Improve IT service performance

   C. Reduce the risk of security breaches

   D. Ensure users are accountable for their actions

2. You have been tasked with creating a corporate security policy regarding smart phone usage for business purposes. What should you do first?

   A. Issue smart phones to all employees.

   B. Obtain support from management.

   C. Get a legal opinion.

   D. Create the first draft of the policy.

3. Match the security policy terms with the appropriate definitions:

Security Policy Terms	Definitions
Scope _E_	A. Describes how the security policy improves security
Overview _A_	B. Consequences of policy nonadherence
Policy _D_	C. Explanation of terms used throughout the security policy
Definitions _C_	D. Collection of dos and don'ts
Enforcement _B_	E. Defines which set of users a security policy applies to

4. Christine is the server administrator for Contoso Corporation. Her manager provided step-by-step security policies outlining how servers should be configured to maximize security. Which type of security policy will Christine be implementing?

   A. Mail server acceptable use policy

   B. VPN server acceptable use policy

   C. Procedural policy

   D. File server acceptable use policy

5. Which of the following are examples of PII? (Choose two.)

   A. Private IP address on an internal network
   B. Mobile phone number
   C. Digital certificate
   D. Gender

6. After a lengthy interviewing process, your company hired a new payroll clerk named Stacey. Stacey will be using a web browser on a company computer at the office to access the payroll application on a public cloud provider web site over the Internet. Which type of document should Stacey read and sign?

   A. Internet acceptable use policy
   B. Password policy
   C. Service level agreement
   D. Remote access acceptable use policy

7. You are configuring a password policy for users in the Berlin office. Passwords must be changed every 60 days. You must ensure that user passwords cannot be changed more than once within the 60-day interval. What should you configure?

   A. Minimum password age
   B. Maximum password age
   C. Password complexity
   D. Password history

8. You have been hired as a consultant by a pharmaceutical company. The company is concerned that confidential drug research documents might be recovered from disposed hard disks. What should you recommend?

   A. Format the hard drives.
   B. Repartition the hard drives.
   C. Freeze the hard drives.
   D. Physically shred the hard drives.

9. Acme Corporation is upgrading its network routers. The old routers will be sent to the head office before they are disposed of. What must be done to the routers prior to disposal to minimize security breaches?

   A. Change the router privileged mode password.
   B. Remove DNS server entries from the router configuration.
   C. Set the router to factory default settings.
   D. Format the router hard drive.

10. Your company has decided to adopt a public cloud device management solution where all devices are centrally managed from a web site hosted on servers in a data center. Management has instructed you to ensure that the solution is reliable and always available. Which type of document should you focus on?

    A. Password policy
    B. Service level agreement
    C. Remote access acceptable use policy
    D. Mobile device acceptable use policy

11. Which of the following best embodies the concept of least privilege?

    A. Detecting inappropriate Internet use
    B. Detecting malware running without elevated privileges
    C. Assigning users full control permissions to network resources
    D. Assigning needed permissions to enable users to complete a task

12. The creation of data security policies is most affected by which two factors? (Choose two.)

    A. Industry regulations
    B. IP addressing scheme being used
    C. Operating system version being used
    D. PII

13. As the network administrator for your company, you are creating a security policy such that devices connecting to the corporate VPN must have a trusted digital certificate installed. Which type of security policy are you creating?

    A. Mobile device encryption policy
    B. Accountability policy
    C. Authentication policy
    D. Remote access policy

14. You are reviewing surveillance camera footage after items have gone missing from your company's office in the evenings. On the video you notice an unidentified person entering the building's main entrance behind an employee who unlocked the door with their swipe card. What type of security breach is this?

    A. Tailgating
    B. Mantrapping
    C. Horseback riding
    D. Door jamming

15. You receive the e-mail message shown here. What type of threat is this?

Dear valued Acme Bank customer,

Acme Bank will be updating web server banking software next week. To ensure continued access to your accounts, we ask that you go to http://www.acmebank.us./accounts and reset your password within the next 24 hours. We sincerely appreciate your business.

Acme Bank

- A. Denial of service
- B. Phishing attack
- C. Zero-day exploit
- D. Ping of death

16. You are testing your router configuration and discover a security vulnerability. After searching the Internet, you realize that this vulnerability is unknown. Which type of attack is your router vulnerable to?

- A. Denial of service
- B. Phishing attack
- C. Zero-day exploit
- D. Ping of death

17. Which of the following options best describe proper usage of PII? (Choose two.)

- A. Law enforcement tracking an Internet offender using a public IP address
- B. Distributing an e-mail contact list to marketing firms
- C. Logging into a secured laptop using a fingerprint scanner
- D. Due diligence

18. Your company restricts firewall administrators from modifying firewall logs. Only IT security personnel are allowed to do this. What is this an example of?

- A. Due care
- B. Separation of duties
- C. Principle of least privilege
- D. Acceptable use

19. You are the network administrator for a legal firm. Users in Vancouver must be able to view trade secrets for patent submission. You share a network folder called Trade Secrets and allow the following NTFS permissions:

Vancouver_Staff: Read, List Folder Contents
Executives: Write
IT_Admins: Full Control

Regarding Vancouver employees, which principle is being adhered to?

A. Job rotation

B. Least privilege

C. Mandatory vacations

D. Separation of duties

20. Your local ISP provides a PDF file stating a 99.97 percent service availability for T1 connectivity to the Internet. How would you classify this type of documentation?

A. Top secret

B. Acceptable use policy

C. Service level agreement

D. Availability

21. The Accounts Payable department notices large out-of-country purchases made using a corporate credit card. After discussing the matter with Juan, the employee whose name is on the credit card, they realize somebody has illegally obtained the credit card details. You also learn that he recently received an e-mail from what appeared to be the credit card company asking him to sign in to their web site to validate his account, which he did. How could this have been avoided?

A. Provide credit card holders with smartcards.

B. Tell users to increase the strength of online passwords.

C. Install a workstation-based firewall.

D. Provide security awareness training to employees.

22. Which of the following statements are true? (Choose two.)

A. Security labels are used for data classifications such as restricted and top secret.

B. PII is applicable only to biometric authentication devices.

C. Forcing user password changes is considered change management.

D. A person's signature on a check is considered PII.

23. Which of the following best illustrates potential security problems related to social networking sites?

    A. Other users can easily see your IP address.

    B. Talkative employees can expose a company's intellectual property.

    C. Malicious users can use your pictures for steganography.

    D. Your credit card number is easily stolen.

24. As the IT security officer, you establish a security policy requiring that users protect all paper documents so that sensitive client, vendor, or company data is not stolen. What type of policy is this?

    A. Privacy

    B. Acceptable use

    C. Clean desk

    D. Password

25. What is the primary purpose of enforcing a mandatory vacation policy?

    A. To adhere to government regulation

    B. To ensure employees are refreshed

    C. To allow other employees to experience other job roles

    D. To prevent improper activity

26. What does a privacy policy protect?

    A. Customer data

    B. Trade secrets

    C. Employee home directories

    D. Firewall configurations

27. Which of the following statements about a security policy are true? (Choose two.)

    A. Users must read and sign the security policy.

    B. It guarantees a level of uptime for IT services.

    C. It is composed of subdocuments.

    D. Management approval must be obtained.

28. You are developing a security training outline for the Accounting department that will take in the office. Which two items should not be included in the training? (Choose two.)

    A. Firewall configuration

    B. The Accounting department's support of security initiatives

    C. Physical security

    D. Social engineering

29. Choose the correct statement:

    A. Users are assigned classification labels to access sensitive data.

    B. Data is assigned clearance levels to access sensitive data.

    C. Data is assigned clearance levels to protect sensitive data.

    D. Users are assigned clearance levels to access sensitive data.

30. You are a file server administrator for a health organization. Management has asked you to configure your servers to appropriately classify files containing patient medical history data. What is an appropriate data classification for these type of files? (Choose all that apply.)

    A. High

    B. Medium

    C. Low

    D. Private

    E. Public

    F. Confidential

31. You are configuring a Wi-Fi network for a clothing retail outlet. In accordance with the Payment Card Industry (PCI) regulations for companies handling payment cards, you must ensure default passwords are changed on the wireless router. This is best described as:

    A. PCI policy

    B. Compliance with security standards

    C. User education and awareness

    D. Wi-Fi policy

32. Your company provides a paper document shredder on each floor of a building. What security issue does this address?

    A. Data handling

    B. Clean desk policy

    C. Tailgating

    D. Mantrap

33. Your company's BYOD policy pays a monthly stipend to employees who use their personal smart phones for work purposes. What type of app should the company ensure is installed and running on all BYOD smart phones?

    A. Weather app

    B. eBay app

    C. PDF reader app

    D. Antivirus app

34. What is the best defense against new viruses?

    A. Keeping antivirus definitions up to date

    B. Turning off the computer when not in use

    C. Not connecting to Wi-Fi networks

    D. Using digital certificates for authentication

35. You and your IT team have completed drafting security policies for e-mail acceptable use and remote access through the company VPN. Users currently use both e-mail and the VPN. What must be done next? (Choose two.)

    A. Update VPN appliance firmware.

    B. Provide security user awareness training.

    C. Encrypt all user mail messages.

    D. Mandate security awareness testing for users.

QUICK ANSWER KEY

1. C

2. B

3. Scope: **E**
   Overview: **A**
   Policy: **D**
   Definitions: **C**
   Enforcement: **B**

4. C

5. B, C

6. A

7. A

8. D

9. C

10. B

11. D

12. A, D

13. D

14. A

15. B

16. C

17. A, C

18. B

19. B

20. C

21. D

22. A, D

23. B

24. C

25. D

26. A

27. C, D

28. A, B

29. D

30. A, D, F

31. B

32. A

33. D

34. A

35. B, D

IN-DEPTH ANSWERS

I. ☑ **C.** Security policies are an organized manner through which the corporate security strategy is realized in order to reduce the risk of security breaches.

☒ **A, B,** and **D** are incorrect. Legal consequences might arise as a result of security policy violations, but they are not the primary purpose of security policies. IT service performance is improved through the implementation of Information Technology Infrastructure Library (ITIL) processes, not security policies. User accountability is one of many desired results of security policy implementation but not the primary reason.

2. ☑ **B.** Management support is crucial in the successful implementation of corporate security policies.

☒ **A, C,** and **D** are incorrect. The issuing of smart phones should be done only after having obtained management approval and having created the appropriate policies. Legal counsel can be an important part of the policy creation process, but management approval must be obtained first, even before the first draft of the policy.

3. ☑ Scope: **E**, Overview: **A**, Policy: **D**, Definitions: **C**, Enforcement: **B**

4. ☑ **C.** Procedural policies provide step-by-step instructions for configuring servers.

☒ **A, B,** and **D** are incorrect. Acceptable use policies are usually user-centric documents outlining rules and regulations for appropriate computing use, and they do not provide step-by-step instructions.

5. ☑ **B** and **C.** Personally identifiable information (PII) is data that uniquely identifies a person, such as a mobile phone number or digital certificate.

☒ **A** and **D** are incorrect. Private IP addresses are nonroutable addresses used on private networks. The same private IP address could be used on separate private networks. Gender is a generic categorization that unto itself does not uniquely identify a person.

6. ☑ **A.** Because Stacey will be using company equipment to access the Internet, she should read and sign an Internet use acceptable use policy.

☒ **B, C,** and **D** are incorrect. Password policies are rules stating how often passwords change and so on. Service level agreements are contractual documents guaranteeing a specific availability of network services. Remote access acceptable use policies define how remote access to a network, such as through a VPN, is to be done securely.

7. ☑ **A.** The minimum password age is a period of time that must elapse before a password can be changed.

☒ **B, C,** and **D** are incorrect. The maximum password age defines the interval by which the password must be changed, in this case, 60 days. Password complexity prevents users from using simple passwords, for example, a variation of the username. Password history prevents the reuse of passwords.

8. ☑ **D.** Physically shredding the hard disk is the most effective way of ensuring confidential data cannot be retrieved.

   ☒ **A, B,** and **C** are incorrect. Formatting a hard disk simply wipes the File Allocation Table (FAT); the file data blocks are left intact on disk. Data retrieval is possible even after repartitioning a hard disk, sometimes even if new partitions are created and populated with files. Properly wrapping and freezing a failing hard drive is an alleged urban myth for saving hard disk data.

9. ☑ **C.** Network equipment such as routers should be reset to factory default settings before disposal to remove company-specific configurations.

   ☒ **A, B,** and **D** are incorrect. The router privileged mode password is required to configure all aspects of the router, but this does not wipe the router configuration. DNS server entries as well as all other router configuration data must be removed; DNS entries alone are not enough. Routers do not have hard drives.

10. ☑ **B.** A service level agreement is a contract stipulating what level of service and availability can be expected.

    ☒ **A, C,** and **D** are incorrect. Password policies specify how user password behavior will be implemented. Remote access acceptable use policies dictate how users will securely access corporate networks remotely, for example, from home or from hotels when traveling. Mobile device acceptable use policies dictate how mobile devices are to be used to conduct business.

11. ☑ **D.** The least privilege principle specifies that only the needed permissions to perform a task should be assigned to users.

    ☒ **A, B,** and **C** are incorrect. None of these options is related to the concept of least privilege. Inappropriate Internet use might be detected by a proxy server or by analyzing firewall logs. Malware detection is performed by anti-malware software. Users should never be granted full control to network resources; IT staff is a different consideration.

12. ☑ **A** and **D.** Industry regulations as well as the protection of personally identifiable information (PII) will have a large impact on the details contained within data security policies.

    ☒ **B** and **C** are incorrect. The IP addressing scheme or operating system in use could influence security policies, but not as much as industry regulations and PII.

13. ☑ **D.** VPNs are remote access solutions, so in this case you would be creating a remote access policy.

    ☒ **A, B,** and **C** are incorrect. The mobile device encryption policy details how data stored on mobile devices is protected with encryption. There is no such thing as an accountability or authentication policy.

14.   ☑   **A.** Tailgating occurs when an unauthorized person follows an authorized person closely to gain access to a restricted resource such as a building or room.

☒   **B, C,** and **D** are incorrect. Mantraps are small rooms with two doors, one for entry and one for exit; their purpose is to separate secured areas from nonsecured areas. Horseback riding is not related to computer security. Door jamming is a fictitious term.

15.   ☑   **B.** Phishing attacks attempt to fool people to connect to seemingly authentic web sites in order for the unsuspecting user to disclose personal information such as bank account numbers and passwords.

☒   **A, C,** and **D** are incorrect. Denial-of-service attacks render a network service unusable to legitimate users. Zero-day exploits are recently discovered vulnerabilities for which there is no current solution. The ping-of-death attack is an old attack that sends a malformed or oversized ping packet to a device with the intent of causing the device to hang or malfunction in some way.

16.   ☑   **C.** Zero-day exploits are recently discovered vulnerabilities for which there is no fix, usually because it is unknown to the manufacturer.

☒   **A, B,** and **D** are incorrect. Denial-of-service attacks render a network service unusable to legitimate users. Phishing attacks attempt to fool people to connect to seemingly authentic web sites in order for the unsuspecting user to disclose personal information such as bank account numbers and passwords. The ping-of-death attack is an old attack that sends a malformed or oversized ping packet to a device with the intent of causing the device to hang or malfunction in some way.

17.   ☑   **A** and **C.** Proper use of PII means not divulging a person or entity's personal information to other parties. Tracking criminals using IP addresses and logging in with a fingerprint scanner are proper uses of PII.

☒   **B** and **D** are incorrect. Distributing e-mail contact lists is an improper use of PII. Due diligence does not imply PII.

18.   ☑   **B.** Separation of duties requires more than one person to complete a process such as controlling a firewall and its logs.

☒   **A, C,** and **D** are not correct. Due care means implementing policies to correct security problems. The principle of least privilege requires users to have only the rights they need to do their jobs. Although this does apply in this case, **B** is a much stronger fit. Acceptable use refers to proper conduct when using company assets.

19.   ☑   **B.** The principle of least privilege states you should allow people access only to do what their job requires, such as Vancouver staff members having only read access to trade secrets.

☒   **A, C,** and **D** are not correct. Job rotation refers to periodically having different people occupy job roles for a variety of reasons, such as employee skill enhancement or exposure to a wider range of business processes. Mandatory vacations are used to ensure employees are not involved in improper activity. Separation of duties is not related to file system security; it prevents a single person from having end-to-end control of a single business process.

20. ☑ **C.** Service level agreements (SLAs) formally define an expected level of service, such as 99.97 percent availability.

    ☒ **A, B,** and **D** are not correct. Service availability information is not considered confidential. Acceptable use policies are defined for and within an organization, not by external businesses. Availability is not a type of documentation.

21. ☑ **D** is correct. If Juan had been aware of phishing scams, he would have ignored the e-mail message.

    ☒ **A, B,** and **C** are incorrect. Smartcards allow users to authenticate to a resource but would not have prevented this problem. Even the strongest password means nothing if the user willingly types it in. Although very important, a workstation-based firewall will not prevent phishing scams.

22. ☑ **A** and **D.** Restricted and top secret are examples of security data labeling. A signature on a check is considered PII, since it is a personal characteristic.

    ☒ **B** and **C** are incorrect. PII applies also to other personal traits such as speech, handwriting, tattoos, and so on. Change management ensures standardized procedures are applied to the entire life cycle of IT configuration changes.

23. ☑ **B.** People tend to speak more freely on social networking sites than anywhere else. Exposing important company information could pose a problem.

    ☒ **A, C,** and **D** are incorrect. Knowing a computer's IP address has nothing to do with social networking risks. Secretly embedding messages in pictures is not a threat tied specifically to social networks. Credit card numbers are not normally stolen through social networks.

24. ☑ **C.** A clean desk policy requires paper documents to be safely stored (and not left on desks) to prevent malicious users from acquiring them.

    ☒ **A, B,** and **D** are not correct. Privacy policies are designed to protect personal data. Acceptable use policies govern the proper use of corporate assets. Password policies control all aspects of passwords for authentication, not securing paper documents.

25. ☑ **D.** Knowledge that vacation time is mandatory means employees are less likely to engage in improper business practices. A different employee filling that job role is more likely to notice irregularities.

    ☒ **A, B,** and **C** are incorrect. Adhering to regulations is not the primary purpose of mandatory vacations as they pertain to security policies. Refreshed employees tend to be more productive, but this is not the reason for mandatory vacations. One definition for a job rotation policy is to allow other employees to gain experience in additional job roles.

26. ☑ **A.** Privacy policies are designed to protect customer, guest, or patient confidential information.

    ☒ **B, C,** and **D** are incorrect. Privacy policies are not intended to protect trade secrets, employee home directories, or firewall configurations.

27. ☑ **C** and **D.** Security policies are composed of subdocuments such as an Internet use policy and remote access policy. Management approval is required for security policies to make an impact.

☒ **A** and **B** are incorrect. Users may be required to read and sign one or more subdocuments, or specific policies, but not necessarily the entire security policy. Service level agreements (SLAs) guarantee a level of uptime for IT services.

28. ☑ **A** and **B.** The IT technical team will be interested in firewall configurations; this is not relevant to the Accounting department. Management must support security initiatives as a first step, even before creating security policies; this is not the job of the Accounting department.

☒ **C** and **D** are incorrect. Physical security and social engineering are important security topics for all users including business users such as people in the Accounting department.

29. ☑ **D.** Data is assigned a specific classification label such as top secret, and only users with the appropriate clearance levels can access that data.

☒ **A**, **B**, and **C** are incorrect. Data, not users, is assigned a classification label such as top secret. Users, not data, are assigned clearance levels such as top secret.

30. ☑ **A**, **D**, and **F.** Organizations will differ in how they specifically label sensitive data. Patient medical history is considered sensitive; therefore, classifying the data as a high security risk if exposed to the public, as private, or as confidential are all valid labels.

☒ **B**, **C**, and **E** are incorrect. A patient's medical history is considered highly confidential data.

31. ☑ **B.** Securing a wireless network to meet industry regulations is best described as complying with security standards.

☒ **A**, **C**, and **D** are incorrect. PCI policy is not a standard type of security policy within an organization; it is an industry standard some organizations must adhere to. Ensuring user awareness to security issues is relevant, but this is not related the scenario, nor is the Wi-Fi policy.

32. ☑ **A.** Part of data handling includes the physical shredding of physical documents to prevent unauthorized persons from viewing printed sensitive information.

☒ **B**, **C**, and **D** are incorrect. Clean desk policies dictate that documents are not to be left out in the open; instead, they should be stored in locked file cabinets behind locked doors. Tailgating and mantraps deal with unauthorized entry to a facility and the prevention of this happening.

33. ☑ **D.** Companies with BYOD policies should ensure some type of anti-malware is running on smart phones, whereas other companies might strictly prohibit personally owned devices being used for business purposes.

☒ **A**, **B**, and **C** are incorrect. Depending on the type of business, the listed apps could prove useful but, generally speaking, not as useful as an antivirus app that detects malware and could help prevent unauthorized access to sensitive data.

34. ☑ **A.** New viruses come into existence every day. Antivirus software must be updated on a regular basis to counter these new threats.

☒ **B, C,** and **D** are incorrect. While all of the listed practices are good ones, the best defense against new viruses is updated virus definitions.

35. ☑ **B** and **D.** The best defense against security breaches of any kind is user awareness. This is provided through training. To ensure the training is effective, users should be tested.

☒ **A** and **C** are incorrect. Updating VPN appliance firmware and encrypting user mail messages can be effective steps to mitigate security threats, but this should have already been done.

4

Types of Attacks

QUESTIONS

Understanding different types of attacks is an important topic for any security professional in the workforce, but it is also important for the Security+ certification exam because you are sure to receive questions related to different types of attacks on the exam.

Social engineering attacks involve the hacker contacting a person through e-mail, via a phone call, or in person, and trying to trick the person into compromising security. You also need to be familiar with the different types of network attacks, such as buffer overflow attacks, which are popular today, and SQL injection attacks, which are typically performed against web sites that have been developed without considering programming best practices. You also should be familiar with the different password attacks for the exam, such as dictionary attacks, hybrid attacks, and brute-force attacks. This chapter is designed to help review these critical points.

1. You are inspecting a user's system after she has complained about slow Internet usage. After analyzing the system, you notice that the MAC address of the default gateway in the ARP cache is referencing the wrong MAC address. What type of attack has occurred?

   A. Brute force
   B. DNS poisoning
   C. Buffer overflow
   D. ARP poisoning

2. You want to implement a security control that limits the amount of tailgating in a high-security environment. Which of the following protective controls would you use?

   A. Swipe cards
   B. Mantrap
   C. Locked door
   D. CMOS settings

3. Which of the following descriptions best describes a buffer overflow attack?

   A. Injecting database code into a web page
   B. Using a dictionary file to crack passwords
   C. Sending too much data to an application that allows the hacker to run arbitrary code
   D. Altering the source address of a packet

4. You are analyzing web traffic in transit to your web server and you notice someone logging on with a username of Bob with a password of *"pass'* or *1=1--"*. Which of the following describes what is happening?

    A. XML injection

    B. A SQL injection attack

    C. LDAP injection

    D. Denial of service

5. A user on your network receives an e-mail from the bank stating that there has been a security incident at the bank. The e-mail continues by asking the user to log on to her bank account by following the link provided and verify that her account has not been tampered with. What type of attack is this?

    A. Phishing

    B. Spam

    C. Dictionary attack

    D. Spim

6. What type of attack involves the hacker modifying the source IP address of the packet?

    A. Xmas attack

    B. Spear phishing

    C. Spoofing

    D. Pharming

7. Which of the following files might a hacker modify after gaining access to your system in order to achieve DNS redirection?

    A. /etc/passwd

    B. Hosts

    C. SAM

    D. Services

8. What type of attack involves the hacker sending too much data to a service or application that typically results in the hacker gaining administrative access to the system?

    A. Birthday attack

    B. Typo squatting/URL hijacking

    C. Eavesdrop

    D. Buffer overflow

9. Which of the following methods could be used to prevent ARP poisoning on the network? (Choose two.)
   A. Static ARP entries
   B. Patching
   C. Antivirus software
   D. Physical security
   E. Firewall

10. As a network administrator, what should you do to help prevent buffer overflow attacks from occurring on your systems?
    A. Static ARP entries
    B. Antivirus software
    C. Physical security
    D. Patching

11. Which of the following is the term for a domain name that is registered and deleted repeatedly as to avoid paying for the domain name?
    A. DNS redirection
    B. Domain poisoning
    C. Domain kiting
    D. Transitive access

12. You receive many calls from customers stating that your web site seems to be slow in responding. You analyze the traffic and notice that you are receiving a number of malformed requests on that web server at a high rate. What type of attack is occurring?
    A. Eavesdrop
    B. Denial of service
    C. Man in the middle
    D. Social engineer

13. What type of attack is a smurf attack?
    A. Distributed denial of service (DDoS)
    B. Denial of service (DoS)
    C. Privilege escalation
    D. Malicious insider threat

14. Your manager has ensured that a policy is implemented that requires all employees to shred sensitive documents. What type of attack is your manager hoping to prevent?

   A. Tailgating

   B. Denial of service

   C. Social engineering

   D. Dumpster diving

15. What type of attack involves the hacker inserting a client-side script into the web page?

   A. XSS   *CROSS SITE SCRIPTING*

   B. Watering hole attack

   C. ARP poisoning

   D. SQL injection

16. Your manager has read about SQL injection attacks and is wondering what can be done to protect against them for your applications that were developed in-house. What would you recommend?

   A. Patching

   B. Antivirus

   C. Input validation

   D. Firewall

17. A hacker is sitting in an Internet cafe and ARP poisons everyone connected to the wireless network so that all traffic passes through the hacker's laptop before she routes the traffic to the Internet. What type of attack is this?

   A. Rainbow tables

   B. Man in the middle

   C. DNS poison

   D. Spoofing

18. Which of the following best describes a zero-day attack?

   A. An attack that modifies the source address of the packet

   B. An attack that changes the computer's system date to 00/00/00

   C. An attack that never happens

   D. An attack that uses an exploit that the product vendor is not aware of yet

19. What type of file on your hard drive stores preferences from web sites?

   A. Cookie

   B. Hosts

   C. LMHOSTS

   D. Attachments

20. What type of attack involves the hacker disconnecting one of the parties from the communication and continues the communication while impersonating that system?

    A. Man in the middle
    B. Denial of service
    C. SQL injection
    D. Session hijacking

21. What type of password attack involves the use of a dictionary file and modifications of the words in the dictionary file?

    A. Dictionary attack
    B. Brute-force attack
    C. Hybrid attack
    D. Modification attack

22. Which of the following countermeasures is designed to protect against a brute-force password attack?

    A. Patching
    B. Account lockout
    C. Password complexity
    D. Strong passwords

23. Three employees within the company have received phone calls from an individual asking about personal finance information. What type of attack is occurring?

    A. Phishing
    B. Whaling
    C. Tailgating
    D. Vishing

24. Tom was told to download a free tax program to complete his taxes this year. After downloading and installing the software, Tom notices that his system is running slowly and he is receiving notification from his antivirus software. What type of malware has he installed?

    A. Keylogger
    B. Trojan
    C. Worm
    D. Logic bomb

25. Jeff recently reports that he is receiving a large number of unsolicited text messages to his phone. What type of attack is occurring?

A. Bluesnarfing

B. Whaling

C. Bluejacking

D. Packet sniffing

26. An employee is suspected of sharing company secrets with a competitor. After seizing the employee laptop, the forensics analyst notices that there are a number of personal photos on the laptop that have been e-mailed to a third party on the Internet. When the analyst compares the hashes of the personal images on the hard drive to what is found in the employee's mailbox, the hashes do not match. How was the employee sharing company secrets?

A. Digital signatures

B. Steganography

C. MP3Stego

D. Whaling

27. You arrive at work today to find someone outside the building digging through their purse. As you approach the door, the person says, "I forgot my pass at home. Can I go in with you?" What type of attack could be occurring?

A. Tailgating

B. Dumpster diving

C. Brute force

D. Whaling

28. Your manager has requested that the combo pad locks used to secure different areas of the company facility be replaced with electronic swipe cards. What type of social engineering attack is your manager hoping to avoid with this change?

A. Hoaxes

B. Tailgating

C. Dumpster diving

D. Shoulder surfing

29. Your manager has been hearing a lot about social engineering attacks and wonders why such attacks are so effective. Which of the following identifies reasons why the attacks are so successful? (Choose three.)

A. Authority

B. DNS poisoning

C. Urgency

D. Brute force

E. Trust

30. Jane is the lead security officer for your company and is monitoring network traffic. Jane notices suspicious activity and asks for your help in identifying the attack. Looking at Figure 4-1, what type of attack was performed?

A. Integer overflow

B. Directory traversal/command injection   *AKA. COMMAND INTERJECTION*

C. Malicious add-on

D. Header manipulation

FIGURE 4-1   Identify the attack type.

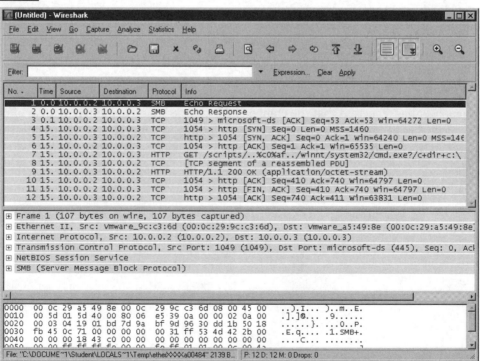

QUICK ANSWER KEY

1.	D	9.	A, D	17.	B	25.	C
2.	B	10.	D	18.	D	26.	B
3.	C	11.	C	19.	A	27.	A
4.	B	12.	B	20.	D	28.	D
5.	A	13.	A	21.	C	29.	A, C, E
6.	C	14.	D	22.	B	30.	B
7.	B	15.	A	23.	D		
8.	D	16.	C	24.	B		

IN-DEPTH ANSWERS

1. ☑ **D.** ARP poisoning is when the hacker alters the ARP cache in order to redirect communication to a particular IP address to the wrong MAC address. This is a popular attack with wireless networks.

   ☒ **A, B,** and **C** are incorrect. A brute-force attack is a type of password attack that involves the hacker calculating all potential passwords. DNS poisoning is when the attacker poisons the DNS cache so that the DNS server gives out the wrong IP address. Buffer overflow happens when too much data is sent to an application or service, causing the data to go beyond the buffer area (memory). The result of a buffer overflow is that the hacker typically gets administrative access to the system.

2. ☑ **B.** Tailgating is the concept that someone tries to slip through a secured door after you open it. A mantrap is a way to help prevent tailgating by having an area between two locked doors— the second door does not open until the first door closes. This allows you to watch who enters the building with you.

   ☒ **A, C,** and **D** are incorrect. Swipe cards are a mechanism to unlock doors, but they do not prevent someone from tailgating. A locked door does not prevent someone from tailgating through the door after you open it. CMOS settings are a way to implement a level of security to prevent someone from booting from a CD and bypassing the security of the local system.

3. ☑ **C.** A buffer overflow attack is when a hacker sends more data to an application or service than what it is expecting. The extra data that is sent flows out of the area of memory (the buffer) assigned to the application. It has been found that if the hacker can write information beyond the buffer, he can run whatever code he wants. Hackers typically write code that gives them remote shell access to the system with administrative capabilities.

   ☒ **A, B,** and **D** are incorrect. Injecting database code into a web page is an example of a SQL injection attack. Using a dictionary file to crack passwords is known as a dictionary attack—a form of password attack. Altering the source address of a packet is known as spoofing.

4. ☑ **B.** A SQL injection attack is when the hacker inserts database (SQL) statements into an application, such as a web site, that manipulates the way the application executes. In this example, the hacker is trying to bypass the logon by typing **"pass'** or **1=1--"** into the password box.

   ☒ **A, C,** and **D** are incorrect. XML injection is when the hacker manipulates the execution of the application by inserting XML statements in the application. An LDAP injection is when the hacker inserts an LDAP call into an application to control the flow of the application. Denial of service is when the hacker tries to overload your system so that it cannot service valid request from clients.

5. ☑ **A.** Phishing is when the hacker e-mails a victim and hopes she clicks the link that leads her to a fake site (typically a bank). At this point the hacker hopes the user types information into the fake site (such as bank account information) that he can use to gain access to her real account.

☒ **B, C,** and **D** are incorrect. Spam is unsolicited e-mails you receive that try to encourage you to buy a product or a service. A dictionary attack is a type of password attack that reads a text file and uses all words in the text file as password attempts. Spim is spam-type messages sent via instant messaging instead of e-mail.

6. ☑ **C.** A spoof attack is when the hacker modifies the source address of the packet. IP spoofing is when the source IP address is modified, MAC spoofing is when the source MAC address is modified, and e-mail spoofing is when the hacker alters the source e-mail address of the message.

☒ **A, B,** and **D** are incorrect. An Xmas attack is a type of port scan that has the Fin, Urg, and Psh flags set in the TCP header. Spear phishing is a phishing e-mail that is spoofed so that it looks like it is coming from a trusted employee. Pharming is when the hacker modifies the hosts file or poisons DNS to lead a victim to a bogus server when surfing a particular web site.

7. ☑ **B.** The hosts file on the local hard drive of the computer is used to resolve fully qualified domain names (FQDNs) to IP addresses and could be used to redirect an unsuspecting person to the wrong site.

☒ **A, C,** and **D** are incorrect. The /etc/passwd file is where passwords are stored in Linux. The SAM file is where the user accounts in Windows are stored. The services file is a file that maps ports to actual friendly names of services.

8. ☑ **D.** A buffer overflow attack involves the hacker sending too much data to an application to gain administrative access to the system.

☒ **A, B,** and **C** are incorrect. A birthday attack is an attack type on hashing functions to generate the same hash value from different data input. Typo squatting/URL hijacking is when the hacker foresees common typos of common URLs and runs a bogus site at those URLs in hopes the user will think they are at the real site, but they are on the hacker's site. An eavesdrop attack is when the hacker listens in on a conversation or captures traffic off the network with a packet analyzer such as Wireshark.

9. ☑ **A** and **D.** ARP poisoning can be countered by adding static ARP entries to your ARP cache and by implementing physical security so that unauthorized persons cannot gain access to the network and poison everyone's ARP cache.

☒ **B, C,** and **E** are incorrect. Patching a system will not prevent ARP poisoning because patching a system is used to remove vulnerabilities in software. Antivirus software will not prevent ARP poisoning because there is no virus involved. A firewall is not the solution either, because you will need to ensure that ARP messages can reach all the stations, which will allow ARP poisoning messages.

10. ☑ **D.** The best countermeasure to buffer overflow attacks is to ensure that you keep up to date with system and application patches. As the vendor finds the vulnerabilities, that vendor will fix the issues through a patch.

    ☒ **A, B,** and **C** are incorrect. Static ARP entries will help protect against ARP poisoning, antivirus software will protect against viruses and other malicious software as long as you keep the virus definitions up to date, and physical security will help control who gets physical access to an asset such as a server—but buffer overflow attacks are typically network-based attacks where physical access to the asset is not required by the hacker.

11. ☑ **C.** Domain kiting is a vulnerability in the domain name system where the hacker registers a DNS name but does not have to pay for the five-day grace period. After a few days, he deletes the name and re-creates it to get the five-day grace period again.

    ☒ **A, B,** and **D** are incorrect. DNS redirection is the concept of the hacker ensuring your system is given an incorrect IP address for a DNS name. Domain poisoning is a method of ensuring your system is given the wrong IP address for a specific domain name, and transitive access is a type of attack that is based on trust models. If machine A trusts machine B and machine B trusts machine C, then in some environments machine C would trust machine B by default, granting potential access to unwanted sources.

12. ☑ **B.** The fact that you are receiving a high number of requests at a high rate is a great indication that someone is trying to perform a denial-of-service (DoS) attack on your system. The results of a DoS could be to keep your system so busy servicing bogus requests that it cannot service valid requests from customers, or the hacker may try to crash your system.

    ☒ **A, C,** and **D** are incorrect. Eavesdropping is a passive-type attack, which involves the hacker capturing traffic—not sending traffic to your system. A man-in-the-middle attack involves the hacker inserting himself or herself into a conversation so that all traffic passes through the hacker. A social engineering attack is when someone tries to trick you into compromising security through social contact (e-mail or phone call).

13. ☑ **A.** A smurf attack is a distributed denial-of-service (DDoS) attack, which is a DoS attack involving multiple systems. The smurf attack involves the hacker pinging a number of systems but spoofing the address of the ping packet so that all those systems reply to an intended victim. The victim would be so overburdened with the ping replies that it would cause a denial of service.

    ☒ **B, C,** and **D** are incorrect. A denial-of-service (DoS) attack involves only one system doing the attack, but the smurf attack has many systems doing the attack. Privilege escalation is when someone with user-level access is able to exploit a vulnerability with the system and gain administrative-level access. A malicious insider threat is when someone inside the company purposely destroys or intentionally discloses sensitive company data.

14. ☑ **D.** Dumpster diving is when the hacker goes through a company's garbage trying to locate information that can help the hacker perform an attack or gain access to the company assets.
☒ **A, B,** and **C** are incorrect. Tailgating is when someone tries to sneak past a locked door after you have opened it for yourself. Denial of service is when a hacker overloads a system causing it to become unresponsive or crash, and social engineering is when the hacker tries to trick someone into compromising security through social contact—such as phone call or e-mail.

15. ☑ **A.** Cross-site scripting (XSS) is an attack that involves the hacker inserting script code into a web page so that it is then processed and executed by a client system.
☒ **B, C,** and **D** are incorrect. A watering hole attack is when a hacker plants malicious code on a site you may visit so that when you navigate to the site, the code attacks your system from a site you trust. ARP poisoning is when the hacker inserts incorrect MAC addresses into the ARP cache, thus leading systems to the hacker's system. SQL injection is inserting SQL code into an application in order to manipulate the underlying database or system.

16. ☑ **C.** A SQL injection attack involves the hacker inserting database code into an application (such as a web site) where it is not expected. The best countermeasure to this is to have your programmers validate any information (check its accuracy) passed into an application.
☒ **A, B,** and **D** are incorrect. Although patching a system solves a lot of problems, it will not solve a SQL injection attack for applications that you build. Antivirus software is not going to help you in this instance either, because this is not a virus problem—it is a problem based on your own coding habits. Firewalls are not going to help you because you need to allow people access to the application and the problem is not about the type of traffic reaching the system— the problem is about the data that is being inserted into the application.

17. ☑ **B.** When a hacker poisons everyone's ARP cache in order to have them send any data destined for the Internet through the hacker's system, this is known as a man-in-the-middle attack because the hacker is receiving all traffic before it is sent to the Internet. The hacker will do this in order to see what you are doing on the Internet and ideally capture sensitive information.
☒ **A, C,** and **D** are incorrect. A rainbow table is a file that contains all mathematically calculated passwords so that a brute-force attack can be performed quickly. DNS poisoning involves the hacker modifying the DNS cache in order to lead you to the wrong web sites, and spoofing is the altering of a source address to make a packet look as if it is coming from somewhere different.

18. ☑ **D.** A zero-day attack is considered a new exploit that the vendor is not aware of yet but the hacking community is.
☒ **A, B,** and **C** are incorrect. An attack that involves the source address being modified is known as a spoof attack. There is no such attack as one that modifies the system date to 00/00/00, and an attack that never happens is not really an attack.

19. ☑ **A.** A cookie is a text file on the hard drive of your system that stores preferences for specific web sites.

    ☒ **B, C,** and **D** are incorrect. The hosts file stores the FQDNs and matching IP addresses, the LMHOSTS file in Windows stores the computer names and matching IP addresses, and attachments are files included in e-mail messages. Note that attachments could contain malicious code and are a potential avenue of attack.

20. ☑ **D.** Session hijacking involves the hacker taking over a conversation by impersonating one of the parties involved in the conversation after the hacker kicks that party off. The hacker typically does a DoS attack in order to kick one of the parties out of the communication.

    ☒ **A, B,** and **C** are incorrect. A man-in-the-middle attack involves the hacker inserting himself or herself into a conversation so that all traffic passes through the hacker. A denial of service is when a hacker overloads a system causing it to become unresponsive or crash. SQL injection is inserting SQL code into an application in order to manipulate the underlining database or system.

21. ☑ **C.** A hybrid password attack is when the hacker uses a dictionary file, and then the software uses modifications of the dictionary words by placing numbers at the end of each word.

    ☒ **A, B,** and **D** are incorrect. Although a dictionary attack does use a dictionary file, it uses only the entries found in the file and does not try modifications of the words in the file. A brute-force attack mathematically calculates each possible password and does not use a file at all. There is no such thing as a modification attack.

22. ☑ **B.** Because brute-force attacks mathematically calculate all possible passwords, if you give the hacker enough time, the hacker will crack passwords, including complex passwords. The key point here is you need to take the time away from the hacker, and how you do that is to enable account lockout—after a certain number of bad logon attempts, the account is locked.

    ☒ **A, C,** and **D** are incorrect. Patching will not protect against any type of password attack, while strong passwords and password complexity (which are the same thing) constitute a countermeasure to dictionary attacks—not brute-force attacks.

23. ☑ **D.** Vishing is a form of social engineering attack where the hacker calls a user trying to trick the person into divulging secure information over the phone. Vishing as a term comes from the fact that it is similar to phishing, but instead of the attack coming through e-mail, it is using the phone (voice).

    ☒ **A, B,** and **C** are incorrect. Phishing is when the user receives an e-mail typically asking the user to click a link to visit a site. Whaling is a form of phishing attack, but it is designed to target the head of a company (the big fish!). Tailgating is when someone follows you into a locked area by slipping in the door after you unlock it.

24. ☑ **B.** Tom has installed a Trojan virus that is a program disguised to do one thing but does something else or something additional.

☒ **A, C,** and **D** are incorrect. A keylogger is a program that records keystrokes and sends them to the hacker. A worm is a self-replicating virus, and a logic bomb is malicious code that is triggered by an event such as a specific date.

25. ☑ **C.** Bluejacking is when the hacker sends unsolicited text messages to a Bluetooth device such as a phone.

☒ **A, B,** and **D** are incorrect. Bluesnarfing is the exploiting of a Bluetooth device such as a phone. Whaling is a form of phishing attack but is targeted toward the head of the company. Packet sniffing is capturing traffic off the network and trying to find sensitive information.

26. ☑ **B.** Steganography is the hiding of text file data in an image file and is a common technique used by hackers to share information.

☒ **A, C,** and **D** are incorrect. Digital signatures are used to verify the sender of a message. MP3Stego is a program used to hide text information in MP3 files (not image files), and whaling is a type of phishing attack that is targeted toward the head of the company.

27. ☑ **A.** Tailgating is when someone slips in behind you and is able to bypass the security control used at the door.

☒ **B, C,** and **D** are incorrect. Dumpster diving is when the hacker goes through the garbage looking for sensitive information. Brute force is a type of password attack that mathematically calculates all possible passwords. Whaling is a form of phishing attack that targets the head of the company.

28. ☑ **D.** Shoulder surfing is a form of social engineering attack that involves someone looking over your shoulder to spy your passcode or other sensitive information.

☒ **A, B,** and **C** are incorrect. Hoaxes are e-mail messages received giving a false story and asking the user to take some form of action such as forward the message on to others. Tailgating is when someone slips in behind you and is able to bypass the security control used at the door. Dumpster diving is when the hacker goes through the garbage looking for sensitive information.

29. ☑ **A, C,** and **E.** There are a number of reasons why social engineering attacks are successful. Three reasons are because the victim feels they are receiving communications from a person of authority. Also, the attacker speaks with a sense of urgency, which makes the victim want to help out as quickly as possible. Trust is correct because social engineering works based on the fact we trust people, especially people in need or people of authority. There are a number of other reasons why social engineering is effective such as intimidation, consensus or social proof, scarcity of the event, and familiarity or liking of a person. Most social engineering experts have mastered being likeable, which transforms into trust.

☒ **B** and **D** are incorrect. DNS poisoning is when the hacker alters the DNS data to redirect victims to a malicious web site. Brute force is a type of password attack that mathematically calculates all potential passwords.

30. ☑ **B.** Directory traversal, also known as command injection, is when the hacker navigates the folder structure of the web server in the URL to call upon commands found in the operating system of the web server.

☒ **A, C, and D** are incorrect. Integer overflow is a form of attack that presents security risks because of the unexpected response of a program when a mathematical function is performed, and the result is larger than the space in memory allocated by the programmer. A malicious add-on is when your system downloads a piece of software used by the browser and slows the system down or exploits a vulnerability in the system. Header manipulation is when the hacker modifies the header data in the packet in order to manipulate how the application processes the information.

5
System Security Threats

QUESTIONS

IT security threats can apply to software or hardware. Software threats include the exploitation of vulnerabilities and the wide array of malware such as worms and spyware. Hardware threats apply when a malicious entity gains physical access, for example, to a handheld device or a server hard disk. Physical security threats could include employees being tricked to allow unauthorized persons into a secured area such as a server room. Identifying these threats is an important step in properly applying security policies.

1. Which type of threat is mitigated by shredding paper documents?

    A. Rootkit

    B. Spyware

    C. Shoulder surfing

    D. Physical

2. Which of the following statements are true? (Choose two.)

    A. Worms log all typed characters to a text file.

    B. Worms propagate themselves to other systems.

    C. Worms can carry viruses.

    D. Worms infect the hard disk MBR.

3. One of your users, Christine, reports that when she visits web sites, pop-up advertisements appear incessantly. After further investigation, you learn one of the web sites she had visited had infected Flash code. Christine asks what the problem was. What do you tell her caused the problem?

    A. Cross-site scripting attack

    B. Worm

    C. Adware

    D. Spyware

4. Which description *best* defines a computer virus?

    A. A computer program that replicates itself

    B. A file with a .vbs file extension

    C. A computer program that gathers user information

    D. A computer program that runs malicious actions

5. An exploit connects to a specific TCP port and presents the invoker with an administrative command prompt. What type of attack is this?

    A. Botnet

    B. Trojan

    C. Privilege escalation

    D. Logic bomb

6. Ahmid is a software developer for a high-tech company. He creates a program that connects to a chat room and waits to receive commands that will gather personal user information. Ahmid embeds this program into an AVI file for a current popular movie and shares this file on a P2P file-sharing network. Once Ahmid's program is activated as people download and watch the movie, what will be created?

  A. Botnet
  B. DDoS
  C. Logic bomb
  D. Worm

7. A user reports USB keyboard problems. You check the back of the computer to ensure the keyboard is properly connected and notice a small connector between the keyboard and the computer USB port. After investigation you learn this piece of hardware captures everything a user types in. What type of hardware is this?

  A. Smartcard
  B. Trojan
  C. Keylogger
  D. PS/2 converter

8. What is the difference between a rootkit and privilege escalation?

  A. Rootkits propagate themselves.
  B. Privilege escalation is the result of a rootkit.
  C. Rootkits are the result of privilege escalation.
  D. Each uses a different TCP port.

9. Which of the following are true regarding backdoors? (Choose two.)

  A. They are malicious code.
  B. They allow remote users access to TCP port 25.
  C. They are made accessible through rootkits.
  D. They provide access to the Windows root account.

10. You are hosting an IT security meeting regarding physical server room security. A colleague, Syl, suggests adding CMOS hardening to existing server security policies. What kind of security threat is Syl referring to?

  A. Changing the amount of installed RAM
  B. Changing CPU throttling settings
  C. Changing the boot order
  D. Changing power management settings

11. You are the IT security officer for a government department. You are amending the USB security policy. Which items apply to USB security? (Choose two.)

   A. Disallow external USB drives larger than 1TB.

   B. Disable USB ports.

   C. Prevent corporate data from being copied to USB devices unless USB device encryption is enabled.

   D. Prevent corporate data from being copied to USB devices unless USB port encryption is enabled.

12. Which of the following are *not* considered serious cell phone threats? (Choose two.)

   A. Hackers with the right equipment posing as cell towers

   B. Having Bluetooth enabled

   C. Changing the boot order

   D. Spyware

13. What is defined as the transmission of unwelcome bulk messages?

   A. Worm

   B. Ping of death

   C. Spam

   D. DOS

14. Which technology separates storage from the server?

   A. Router

   B. Switch

   C. NAS NETWORK ATTATCHED STORAGE

   D. Wireless router

15. You are responsible for determining what technologies will be needed in a new office space. Employees will need a single network to share data, traditional voice calls, VoIP calls, voice mailboxes, and other services such as call waiting and call transfer. What type of service provides this functionality?

   A. Ethernet switch

   B. PBX

   C. NAS

   D. Router

16. Botnets can be used to set what type of coordinated attack in motion?

    A. DDoS

    B. Cross-site scripting

    C. Privilege escalation

    D. Rootkit

17. As a Windows administrator, you configure a Windows networking service to run with a specially created account with limited rights. Why would you do this?

    A. To prevent computer worms from entering the network.

    B. To prevent a hacker from receiving elevated privileges because of a compromised network service.

    C. Windows networking services will not run with administrative rights.

    D. Windows networking services must run with limited access.

18. Discovered in 1991, the Michelangelo virus was said to be triggered to overwrite the first 100 hard disk sectors with null data each year on March 6, the date of the Italian artist's birthday. What type of virus is Michelangelo?

    A. Zero day

    B. Worm

    C. Trojan

    D. Logic bomb

19. The Stuxnet attack was discovered in June 2010. Its primary function is to hide its presence while reprogramming industrial computer systems. The attack is believed to be spread through USB flash drives, where it transmits copies of itself to other hosts. To which of the following does Stuxnet apply? (Choose two.)

    A. Rootkit

    B. Spam

    C. Worm

    D. Adware

20. A piece of malicious code uses dictionary attacks against computers to gain access to administrative accounts. The code then links compromised computers together for the purpose of receiving remote commands. What term *best* applies to this malicious code?

    A. Exploit

    B. Botnet

    C. Logic bomb

    D. Backdoor

21. Windows 8 User Account Control (UAC) allows users to change Windows settings but displays prompts when applications attempt to configure the operating system. Which of the following is addressed by UAC?

   A. Privilege escalation

   B. Adware

   C. Spyware

   D. Worms

22. Which of the following items are affected by spyware? (Choose two.)

   A. Memory

   B. IP address

   C. Computer name

   D. Network bandwidth

23. Juanita uses the Firefox web browser on her Linux workstation. She reports that her browser home page keeps changing to web sites offering savings on consumer electronic products. Her virus scanner is running and is up to date. What is causing this problem?

   A. Firefox on Linux automatically changes the home page every two days.

   B. Juanita is experiencing a denial-of-service attack.

   C. Juanita's user account has been compromised.

   D. Juanita's browser configuration is being changed by adware.

24. Which of the following is true regarding Trojan software?

   A. It secretly gathers user information.

   B. It is self-replicating.

   C. It can be propagated through peer-to-peer file sharing networks.

   D. It automatically spreads through Windows file and print sharing networks.

25. While attempting to access documents in a folder on your computer, you notice all of your files have been replaced with what appear to be random filenames. In addition, you notice a single text document containing payment instructions that will result in the decryption of your files. What type of malicious software is described in this scenario?

   A. Cryptoware

   B. Malware

   C. Criminalware

   D. Ransomware

26. Refer to Figure 5-1. Which two items should be configured? (Choose two.)

A. Real-time protection should be enabled.

B. A custom scan should be configured.

C. Virus and spyware definitions should be updated.

D. The last scan should have been in the evening.

FIGURE 5-1   Windows Defender settings

27. What type of malware dynamically alters itself to avoid detection?

A. Chameleon malware

B. Polymorphic malware

C. Changeling malware

D. Armored virus

28. Which of the following actions would not reduce the likelihood of malware infection? (Choose all that apply.)

    A. Keeping virus definitions up to date
    B. Scanning removable media
    C. Encrypting hard disk contents
    D. Using NAT-capable routers

29. A user complains that their system has all of a sudden become unresponsive and ads for various products and services are popping up on the screen and cannot be closed. Which user actions could have led to this undesirable behavior? (Choose all that apply.)

    A. Clicking a web search result
    B. Viewing a web page
    C. Watching a move in AVI file format
    D. Inserting a USB flash drive

QUICK ANSWER KEY

1.	D	9.	A, C	17.	B	25.	D
2.	B, C	10.	C	18.	D	26.	A, C
3.	C	11.	B, C	19.	A, C	27.	B
4.	D	12.	B, C	20.	B	28.	C, D
5.	C	13.	C	21.	A	29.	A, B, C, D
6.	A	14.	C	22.	A, D		
7.	C	15.	B	23.	D		
8.	B	16.	A	24.	C		

IN-DEPTH ANSWERS

1. ☑ **D.** Shredding document prevents physical threats such as theft of those documents or acquiring information from them.
   ☒ **A, B,** and **C** are incorrect. Rootkits hide themselves from the OS while allowing privileged access to a malicious user. Spyware gathers user computing habits without user knowledge. This can be valuable to marketing firms. The direct observation of somebody using sensitive information is an example of shoulder surfing.

2. ☑ **B** and **C.** Worms are programs that multiply and spread, and they sometimes carry viruses (the worm is the delivery mechanism).
   ☒ **A** and **D** are incorrect. Keyloggers capture data as it is typed. Boot sector viruses infect the MBR, not worms.

3. ☑ **C.** Adware is responsible for displaying pop-up advertisements pertaining to a user's interest, usually as a result of spyware.
   ☒ **A, B,** and **D** are incorrect. Cross-site scripting attacks are malicious scripts that appear to be from a trusted source. The script runs locally on a user station, usually in the form of a malicious URL that a user is tricked into executing. Worms are self-replicating programs that propagate themselves. Although spyware tracks personal user data, the component that results in pop-up advertisements is referred to as *adware*.

4. ☑ **D.** Viruses are applications that run malicious actions without user consent.
   ☒ **A, B,** and **C** are incorrect. Worms replicate themselves. A .vbs file extension does not always mean the file is malicious. Spyware is defined as a computer program that gathers user information.

5. ☑ **C.** Privilege escalation occurs when a user gains higher rights than they should have, either because they were given too many rights or because of a security flaw.
   ☒ **A, B,** and **D** are incorrect. A botnet refers to a group of computers under the control of a malicious user. A Trojan is malware that appears to be benign. Logic bombs are malware triggered by specific conditions or dates.

6. ☑ **A.** Botnets consist of computers infected with malware that are under hacker control.
   ☒ **B, C,** and **D** are incorrect. DDoS attacks can be facilitated with botnets, but they do not gather personal user information; they render network services unusable by legitimate users. Logic bombs are malware triggered by specific conditions. Worms replicate and proliferate.

7. ☑ **C.** Hardware keyloggers capture every keystroke and store them in a chip.
   ☒ **A, B,** and **D** are incorrect. Smartcards are the size of a credit card, contain a microchip, and are used to authenticate a user. A Trojan is malware posing as legitimate software; the question is referring to hardware. The question refers to a USB keyboard and port, not a PS/2 keyboard.

8. ☑ **B.** Rootkits conceal themselves from operating systems and allow remote access with escalated privileges.

☒ **A, C**, and **D** are incorrect. Worms propagate themselves, not rootkits. Privilege escalation is the result of a rootkit. Privilege escalation does not refer to network software that uses a TCP port.

9. ☑ **A** and **C.** Malicious code produces undesired results, such as a rootkit providing access to a backdoor.

☒ **B** and **D** are incorrect. SMTP uses TCP port 25. Windows has an administrator account, while Unix and Linux have a root account.

10. ☑ **C.** Changing the boot order means having the ability to boot through alternative means, thus bypassing any operating system controls.

☒ **A, B**, and **D** are incorrect. Changing the amount of RAM, CPU throttling, or power management settings would not compromise server security like changing the boot order would.

11. ☑ **B** and **C.** Disabling USB ports on a system blocks malicious code on infected USB devices. Forcing USB device encryption ensures data confidentiality of departmental data.

☒ **A** and **D** are incorrect. Larger USB drives do not pose more of a threat than smaller USB drives. Encryption is not enabled on USB ports; it is enabled on USB devices.

12. ☑ **B** and **C.** Enabling Bluetooth itself is not a threat any more than surfing the Web is. Most Bluetooth devices have security options such as passwords and device trust lists. You cannot change the "boot order" on a cell phone like you could on a computer system.

☒ **A** and **D** are incorrect. Posing as a cell tower means cell phone information and conversations could be compromised. Most modern cell phones have the ability to download apps. As a result, spyware on cell phones has become a serious problem.

13. ☑ **C.** Spam affects business productivity by consuming enormous amounts of bandwidth and storage space for unsolicited messages.

☒ **A, B**, and **D** are incorrect. Worms don't send unwelcome messages with the intent of being read (although they do send themselves). Ping of death is an older denial-of-service attack executed by sending many large or malformed ping packets to a host, thus rendering it unusable. Denial-of-service (DoS) attacks render systems unusable; spammers want our systems to work so we can read their junk mail.

14. ☑ **C.** Network attached storage (NAS) devices are network appliances that contain disks. Client and server operating systems can access this NAS using various protocols such as TCP/IP or Network File System (NFS).

☒ **A, B**, and **D** are incorrect. Routers do not have disks. Routers route packets between networks. Switches do not have disks; their primary concern is increasing network efficiency by making each port its own collision domain. Wireless routers have nothing to do with disk storage.

15. ☑ **B.** A private branch exchange (PBX) offers telecommunication and data networking services in the form of hardware or software. PBXs may exist at the customer or provider premise.

☒ **A, C,** and **D** are incorrect. Ethernet switches do not offer a full range of telecommunications options such as voice mailboxes and call waiting; instead, they increase the efficiency of a data network. Network attached storage (NAS) is concerned with disk storage. Routers transmit data between networks.

16. ☑ **A.** Botnets (groups of computers under singular control) can be used to dispatch distributed denial-of-service (DDoS) attacks against hosts or other networks.

☒ **B, C,** and **D** are incorrect. Cross-site scripting attacks trick users into running malicious scripts, often in the form of a URL. Privilege escalation means a user having more rights than they normally would have, usually by means of malware. Rootkits are malware that grant elevated rights while remaining undetected by the OS.

17. ☑ **B.** In the event that the Windows networking service is compromised, it is important that the service not have full rights to the system.

☒ **A, B,** and **D** are incorrect. Worms can enter networks in many ways including through privilege escalation, but it is not a better reason to run services with limited access. Depending on the service, sometimes administrative permissions might be required; other times limited access is sufficient.

18. ☑ **D.** Logic bombs trigger malicious code when specific conditions are satisfied, such as a date.

☒ **A, B,** and **C** are incorrect. Zero-day exploits are not triggered by certain conditions; they are exploits that are unknown to most others and therefore have no remedy. Worms are self-replicating and self-propagating. Trojans are malicious code posing as legitimate code.

19. ☑ **A** and **C.** Stuxnet replicates itself, like worms do, and masks itself while running, like rootkits do.

☒ **B** and **D** are incorrect. Spam refers to the bulk sending of unsolicited email. Stuxnet is not triggered by any specific conditions.

20. ☑ **B.** Botnets are collections of computers under the sole control of the attacker.

☒ **A, C,** and **D** are incorrect. The term *exploit* does not best describe the scenario, although an exploit can lead to the creation of a botnet. An exploit takes advantage of a vulnerability. A specific condition is not triggering the code to run. Backdoors are typically open doors in computer code that bypass normal authentication mechanisms.

21. ☑ **A.** UAC limits software to having only standard user rights and requires authorization for code needing elevated rights.

☒ **B, C,** and **D** are incorrect. Adware displays advertising messages to users without their permission. Spyware is malicious code that monitors computer usage patterns and personal information. Self-replicating worms should be detected by antivirus software.

22. ☑ **A** and **D.** Spyware is software that gets installed covertly and gathers user information without the user's knowledge. In some cases, users may know it is being installed, such as when free software is being installed. Spyware consumes memory resources because it is normally running all the time. Network bandwidth is utilized when the spyware sends data to an external source.

☒ **B** and **C** are incorrect. Neither the IP address nor the computer name gets changed by spyware.

23. ☑ **D.** Adware attempts to expose users to advertisements in various ways including by displaying pop-ups or by changing the web browser home page. Spyware often analyzes user habits so that adware displays relevant advertisements. Some antivirus software also scans for spyware, but not in this case.

☒ **A**, **B**, and **C** are incorrect. Firefox on Linux does not change the home page every two days. Denial-of-service attacks prevent legitimate access to a network resource; Juanita is not being denied access. The presence of spyware or adware does not imply the user account has been compromised. Often these types of malware are silently installed when visiting web sites or installing freeware.

24. ☑ **C.** Trojans are malicious code that appears to be useful software. For example, a user might use a peer-to-peer file-sharing network on the Internet to illegally download pirated software. The software may install and function correctly, but a Trojan may also get installed. This Trojan could create a backdoor method for attackers to gain access to the system.

☒ **A**, **B**, and **D** are incorrect. Trojans don't secretly gather user information; spyware does. Trojans are not self-replicating on Windows file and print sharing or any other network like worms are; they are spread manually.

25. ☑ **D.** Ransomware makes data or an entire system inaccessible until a ransom is paid.

☒ **A**, **B**, and **C** are incorrect. There are no such things as cryptoware and criminalware. Malware refers to malicious software.

26. ☑ **A** and **C.** Real-time protection must always be enabled for normal use of a computing device. Some software installations require that real-time protection be disabled but only temporarily. The virus definitions in this case are four days old and need to be updated immediately.

☒ **B** and **D** are incorrect. Custom scans are not required to keep machines protected from malware. Scans performed in the evening are no more effective than scans performed in the morning.

27. ☑ **B.** Polymorphic malware dynamically adjusts itself to avoid detection while maintaining its original functionality.

☒ **A**, **B**, and **D** are incorrect. There are no such things as chameleon malware and changeling malware. Armored viruses prevent software engineers from decompiling the program to reveal the programming code that makes it run.

28. ☑ **C** and **D.** Encrypting hard disk contents maintains data confidentiality but does not prevent malware infections. Network Address Translation (NAT) routers send all internal network traffic to a public network after translating the source IP address to match that of the NAT router's public interface address. This does not prevent malware infections.

    ☒ **A** and **D** are incorrect. Keeping virus definitions up to date and scanning removable media will certainly reduce the likelihood of malware infection.

29. ☑ **A, B, C** and **D.** All listed items have the potential of infecting a computer. Certain controls might be in place, such as which web sites can be viewed or which files can execute, but this type of preventative measure must have been in place first.

6
Mitigating Security Threats

QUESTIONS

The ability to identify security threats is important. Understanding how to minimize or prevent threats is critical and often motivated by the potential for loss of revenue, the potential of diminishing shareholder confidence, or even the possibility of litigation. *Hardening*, or minimizing security risk, of computing equipment and software is an important step in the right direction. Applying security settings from a central point such as Group Policy through Active Directory achieves maximum effect. Application developers must adhere to secure coding guidelines so that their code does not afford malicious users an entry point.

1. The web developers at your company are testing their latest web site code before going live to ensure that it is robust and secure. During their testing they provide malformed URLs with additional abnormal parameters as well as an abundance of random data. What term describes their actions?

   A. Cross-site scripting

   B. Fuzzing

   C. Patching

   D. Debugging

2. The process of disabling unneeded network services on a computer is referred to as what?

   A. Patching

   B. Fuzzing

   C. Hardening

   D. Debugging

3. You are on a conference call with your developers, Serena and Thomas, discussing the security of your new travel site. You express concern over a recent article describing how user submissions to web sites may contain malicious code that runs locally when others simply read the post. Serena suggests validating user input before allowing the user submissions. Which problem might validation solve?

   A. Cross-site scripting

   B. Fuzzing

   C. Hardening

   D. Patching

4. Which of the following lessens the success of dictionary password attacks?

   A. Password complexity requirements

   B. Account lockout threshold

   C. Password hints

   D. Enforce password history

5. A RADIUS server is used to authenticate your wireless network users. While creating a new user account, you notice there are many more user accounts than actual users. What should be done?

   A. Delete all accounts not linked to a user.

   B. Disable all accounts not linked to a user.

   C. Verify how accounts are used and then delete unnecessary accounts.

   D. Verify how accounts are used and then disable unnecessary accounts.

6. The 802.11n wireless network in your department must be layer 2 secured. You would like to control which specific wireless devices are allowed to connect. How can you do this?

   A. SIM card

   B. NetBIOS computer name

   C. MAC address

   D. IP address

7. What is the best definition of the IEEE 802.1x standard?

   A. It defines a group of wireless standards.

   B. It defines the Ethernet standard.

   C. It defines network access control only for wireless networks.

   D. It defines network access control for wired and wireless networks.

8. You are hardening a Linux computer and have disabled SSH in favor of Telnet. You ensure passwords are required for Telnet access. Identify your error.

   A. Secure Telnet should have public key authentication enabled.

   B. Only strong passwords should be used with Telnet.

   C. SSH should have been used instead of Telnet.

   D. The Telnet port should have been changed from 23 to 8080.

9. As the IT director of a high school using Group Policy and Active Directory, you plan the appropriate standard security settings for newly deployed Windows 7 workstations. Some teachers require modifications to these settings because of the specialized software they use. Which term refers to the standardized security parameters?

   A. Initial baseline configuration

   B. Principle of least privilege

   C. Sysprepped image

   D. Local security policy

10. The periodic assessment of security policy compliance is referred to as what?

    A. Remediation

    B. Hardening

    C. Continuous security monitoring

    D. Trend analysis

11. You are a Windows Server 2012 administrator. You install and configure the Network Policy Server (NPS) role and configure health policies that require all connecting clients to have firewall and spyware software enabled. Clients violating these health policies will receive an IP address placing them on a restricted subnet containing servers with client firewall and spyware software to install. What term accurately refers to the role the servers on this restricted subnet play?

    A. Isolation

    B. Remediation

    C. Validation

    D. Authentication

12. IT security personnel respond to the repeated misuse of an authenticated user's session cookie on an e-commerce web site. The affected user reports that they occasionally use the site but not for the transactions in question. The security personnel decide to reduce the amount of time an authentication cookie is valid. What type of attack have they responded to?

    A. DoS

    B. Dictionary

    C. Privilege escalation

    D. Cross-site request forgery

13. A network administrator places a network appliance on the DMZ network and configures it with various security thresholds, each of which will notify the IT group via e-mail. The IT group will then adhere to the incident response policy and take action. What will be triggered when any of these thresholds is violated?

    A. Alarm

    B. Alert

    C. Remediation

    D. Input validation

14. A user reports repeated instances of Windows 7 slowing down to the point where they can no longer be productive. You view the Windows Event Viewer logs for the past month and notice an exorbitant amount of SMTP traffic leaving the local machine each morning between 10 A.M. and 11 A.M. What type of analysis was performed to learn of this anomaly?

    A. Forensic

    B. Trend

    C. Network statistical

    D. Vulnerability

15. Roman is developing an application that controls the lighting system in a large industrial complex. A piece of code calls a function that controls a custom-built circuit board. While running his application, Roman's application fails repeatedly because of unforeseen circumstances. Which secure coding guideline did Roman not adhere to?

    A. Packet encryption

    B. Digital signatures

    C. Error handling

    D. Hardening

16. What can be done to harden the Windows operating system? (Choose three.)

    A. Disable system restore points.

    B. Disable unnecessary services.

    C. Patch the operating system.

    D. Configure EFS.

    E. Disable Group Policy.

17. You are configuring a fleet of Windows 7 laptops for traveling employees, some of whom prefer using USB mice. It is critical that the machines are as secure as possible. What should you configure? (Choose three.)

    A. Disable USB ports.

    B. Require USB device encryption.

    C. Enable and configure the Windows firewall.

    D. Install and configure antivirus software.

    E. Enable a power management scheme.

18. A shipment of new Windows computers has arrived for Accounting department employees. The computers have the operating system preinstalled but will require additional financial software. In which order should you perform all of the following?

   3 **A.** Join the Active Directory domain.

   2 **B.** Apply all operating system patches.

   1 **C.** Ensure the virus scanner is up to date.

   4 **D.** Log in to the Active Directory domain to receive Group Policy security settings.

   5 **E.** Install the additional financial software.

19. Which of the following items can help prevent ARP cache poisoning? (Choose three.)

   A. Use 802.1x security.

   B. Disable ARP.

   C. Patch the operating system.

   D. Configure the use of digital signatures for all network traffic.

   E. Disable unused switch ports.

20. Your intranet provides employees with the ability to search through an SQL database for their past travel expenses once they have logged in. One employee from the IT department discovers that if they enter an SQL string such as SELECT * FROM EXPENSES WHERE EMPID = 'x'='x';, it returns all employee travel expense records. What secure coding guideline was ignored?

   A. SQL injection prevention

   B. Input validation

   C. Disabling of SQL indexes

   D. User authentication

21. You capture and examine network traffic weekly to ensure the network is being used properly. In doing so, you notice traffic to TCP port 53 on your server from an unknown IP address. After reviewing your server logs, you notice repeated failed attempts to execute a zone transfer to your server. What type of attack was attempted?

   A. ARP poisoning

   B. Cross-site scripting

   C. DNS poisoning

   D. MAC flooding

22. A network security audit exposes three insecure wireless routers using default configurations. Which security principle has been ignored?

    A. Application patch management

    B. Device hardening

    C. Input validation

    D. Principle of least privilege

23. Which of the following standards must authenticate computing devices before allowing network access?

    A. Router

    B. Hub

    C. IEEE 802.1x

    D. IEEE 802.11n

24. What will prevent frequent repeated malicious attacks against user account passwords?

    A. Minimum password age

    B. Password hints

    C. Password history

    D. Account lockout

25. Which item would *best* apply a standard security baseline to many computers?

    A. A disk image of the operating system

    B. Security templates distributed through Group Policy

    C. Password settings distributed through Group Policy

    D. Security templates distributed through a local security policy

26. After patching and hardening your computers, how would you determine whether your computers are secure?

    A. Performance baseline

    B. Security templates

    C. Penetration testing

    D. Password cracking

27. While hardening a Windows server, you decide to disable a number of services. How can you ensure that the services you are disabling will not adversely affect other services?

    A. Run the net start 'service name' / dep command.

    B. Disable the services, let the system run for a few days, and then check the Event Viewer logs.

    C. Right-click the service and choose Show Dependency Chain.

    D. Double-click the service and view the Dependencies tab.

28. Your company uses Microsoft IIS to host multiple intranet web sites on a two-node cluster. All sites store their configuration and content on drive C: and log files are stored on D:. All sites share a common application pool. The IT director has asked that you ensure a single hacked web site will not adversely affect other running web sites. What should you do?

    A. Move each web site configuration to a separate hard disk.

    B. Move each web site content to a separate hard disk.

    C. Configure each web site to use its own application pool.

    D. Add a third node to the two-node cluster.

29. You are developing your Windows 8.1 enterprise rollout strategy. IT security policies have been updated to reflect the company's stricter security standards. Which of the following will harden Windows 8.1? (Choose two.)

    A. Use a Class C IP address.

    B. Configure log archiving.

    C. Configure USB device restrictions.

    D. Disable unused services.

30. How can you prevent rogue machines from connecting to your network?

    A. Deploy an IEEE 802.1x configuration.

    B. Use strong passwords for user accounts.

    C. Use IPv6.

    D. Deploy an IEEE 802.11 configuration.

31. What can be done to secure the network traffic that is generated when administering your wireless router?

    A. Use HTTPS with IPv6.

    B. Use HTTP with PKI.

    C. Use HTTP with IPv6.

    D. Use HTTPS with PKI.

32. Your company is upgrading to a new office suite. The spreadsheet application must only trust macros digitally signed by the company certificate authority. You have servers installed in a single Windows Active Directory domain. What should you configure to ensure macro security on all stations is configured properly?

    A. Configure the spreadsheet application on each computer to trust company macros.

    B. Create an EFS PKI certificate for signing the macros.

    C. Use Group Policy to enforce the described application configuration baseline.

    D. Use Group Policy to distribute macros to all stations.

33. Match the security descriptions on the left of Figure 6-1 with the correct technology listed on the right.

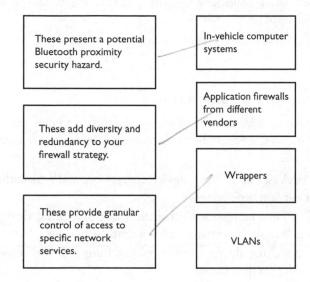

FIGURE 6-1

Security descriptions and technologies

34. Aidan is creating a Linux operating system image that will be used to deploy Linux virtual machines from a template. After patching the operating system, he installs the required application software, installs and updates the anti-malware software, creates the image, and stores it on the imaging server. What did Aidan forget to do?

    A. He forgot to Sysprep the installation before capturing the image.

    B. He forgot to patch the application software.

    C. He forgot to turn on anti-malware real-time monitoring.

    D. He forgot to encrypt the hard drive.

35. You are the founder of Acme Data Mining. The business focuses on retrieving relevant consumer habits from various sources, and that data is then sold to retailers. Because of the amount of data that must be processed, you must implement the fastest possible solution. Which type of technology should you implement?

    A. SQL

    B. NoSQL

    C. SATA

    D. NoSATA

36. You have been asked to develop secure web application for a wine home brewing retailer. The app will read and write to a back-end database for customer transactions. The database has rules in place to check that data is valid. The web site uses HTTPS. What else should be done to further secure the web app?

   A. Use JavaScript for server-side data validation.

   B. Use PKI.

   C. Use a VPN.

   D. Use JavaScript for client-side data validation.

37. Your company has issued Android-based smart phones to select employees. Your manager asks you to ensure that data on the smart phones is protected. How do you address your manager's concerns?

   A. Implement SCADA, screen locking, device encryption, and anti-malware, and disable unnecessary software on the phones.

   B. Implement PKI VPN authentication certificates, screen locking, device encryption, and anti-malware, and disable unnecessary software on the phones.

   C. Implement screen locking, device encryption, patching, and anti-malware, and disable unnecessary software on the phones.

   D. Implement HTTPS, screen locking, device encryption, and anti-malware, and disable unnecessary software on the phones.

38. While hardening your home office network, you decide to check that the firmware in all your network devices is updated. To which of the following devices would this apply?

   A. Smart TV, gaming console, printer, HVAC, wireless router

   B. Refrigerator, printer, wireless router, electrical outlets, printer

   C. HVAC, fire extinguisher, gaming console, printer, wireless router

   D. Gaming console, Android devices, Apple iOS devices, printers, fire extinguisher

39. Which enterprise-class items within your organization should be patched regularly? (Choose all that apply.)

   A. Mainframes

   B. Thin clients

   C. Public cloud virtualization hosts

   D. IP addresses

QUICK ANSWER KEY

1. B	**11.** B	**21.** C	**31.** D
2. C	**12.** D	**22.** B	**32.** C
3. A	**13.** A	**23.** C	**33.** See Figure 6-2.
4. A	**14.** B	**24.** D	**34.** B
5. D	**15.** C	**25.** B	**35.** B
6. C	**16.** B, C, D	**26.** C	**36.** D
7. D	**17.** B, C, D	**27.** D	**37.** C
8. C	**18.** C, B, A, D, E	**28.** C	**38.** A
9. A	**19.** A, D, E	**29.** C, D	**39.** A, B
10. C	**20.** B	**30.** A	

FIGURE 6-2

Security descriptions and technologies—the answer

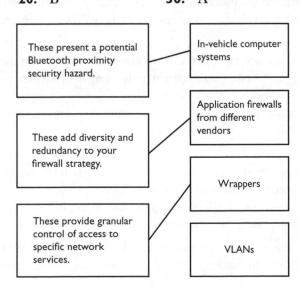

IN-DEPTH ANSWERS

1. ☑ **B.** Fuzzing is a means of injecting data into an application that it does not expect in order to ensure there are no weaknesses.
   ☒ **A, C,** and **D** are incorrect. Cross-site scripts do not ensure applications are secure; they are a type of attack. Patching would occur after flaws were discovered. Debugging implies software flaws are already known.

2. ☑ **C.** Hardening includes actions such as disabling unneeded services to make a system more secure.
   ☒ **A, B,** and **D** are incorrect. Patches fix problems with software. Fuzzing refers to testing your own software for vulnerabilities. Debugging is the methodical testing of software to identify the cause of a flaw.

3. ☑ **A.** Cross-site scripting attacks take advantage of dynamically generated web pages on sites that allow unvalidated user input. User submissions can be validated to ensure malicious scripts do not exist on the site.
   ☒ **B, C,** and **D** are incorrect. Fuzzing is essentially in-house software penetration testing. Hardening and patching serve to protect computing equipment and are not considered problems.

4. ☑ **A.** Complex password enforcement means dictionary words or username variations, to name just a few, cannot be used as passwords.
   ☒ **B, C,** and **D** are incorrect. Account lockout thresholds best mitigate brute-force password attacks. Password hints aid the user in remembering their password. Although an important password security consideration, password history alone will not minimize dictionary attack risks.

5. ☑ **D.** Disable only those accounts that are not required; the account may be needed later. Further investigation is needed to determine whether any accounts are used by network services and not users.
   ☒ **A, B,** and **C** are incorrect. Accounts are sometimes used for network devices and services. Accounts not in current use may be needed later.

6. ☑ **C.** The MAC address is an OSI layer 2 (Data Link layer) 48-bit unique hexadecimal address assigned to all network cards and is often used to restrict connecting wireless clients.
   ☒ **A, B,** and **D** are incorrect. Subscriber Identity Module (SIM) cards are used in cell phones and not for 802.11n networks. NetBIOS computer names apply to OSI layers 4 (Transport layer) and 5 (the Session layer). IP addresses are OSI layer 3 (Network layer) addresses.

7. ☑ **D.** 802.1x applies to wired and wireless networks. 802.1x connectivity devices forward authentication requests to an authentication server before allowing access to a network.

☒ **A, B,** and **C** are incorrect. IEEE 802.11 defines a group of wireless standards. IEEE 802.3 is the Ethernet standard. 802.1x is a security authentication standard; it is not exclusive to wireless networks.

8. ☑ **C.** Secure Shell (SSH) encrypts all packet payloads unlike Telnet and therefore should be used when hardening.
☒ **A, B,** and **D** are incorrect. Telnet does not support public key authentication. Strong passwords should be used at all times, not only if you must use Telnet. Changing the Telnet port does not constitute a configuration error.

9. ☑ **A.** The initial baseline configuration implies blanket security settings that are the minimum standard.
☒ **B, C,** and **D** are incorrect. The principle of least privilege ensures users have only the rights they require to do their jobs. Sysprepping a disk image ensures the installation is unique when it is deployed, but it does not specifically refer to security. Local security policy would not be the best way to implement standardized security to more than one computer.

10. ☑ **C.** Continuous security monitoring ensures security policies are adhered to and enforced.
☒ **A, B,** and **D** are incorrect. Remediation implies taking action to correct flaws. Hardening eliminates security risks but has nothing to do with security assessments. Trend analysis refers to collecting data and noticing patterns.

11. ☑ **B.** Remediation servers provide a method of correcting security deficiencies.
☒ **A, C,** and **D** are incorrect. The servers on the restricted subnet do not isolate, validate, or authenticate the clients on the restricted subnet; the NPS server does.

12. ☑ **D.** Cross-site request forgeries involve the malicious use of a trusted party's cookie against a web site.
☒ **A, B,** and **C** are incorrect. Denial-of-service (DoS) attacks render a network service unusable, which is not the case here. Dictionary attacks are applied to user accounts to guess passwords. Privilege escalation raises the rights a user would normally have. In this example, the violated user has the same rights they would normally have during a legitimate transaction.

13. ☑ **A.** An alarm is a warning of danger that requires action (adherence to an incident response policy), such as a security threshold that might warn of excessive types of network traffic (which could imply a denial-of-service attack).
☒ **B, C,** and **D** are incorrect. Alerts notify of changes in state that may not always warrant a response, such as the fact that a workstation has come online. Remediation actively corrects a problem; notifying the IT group of a situation in itself does not correct a problem. Input validation verifies the integrity of submitted data; this would not be triggered if some activity met a preconfigured threshold.

14. ☑ **B.** A trend analysis seeks patterns within data sets, such as events happening around the same time each day.

    ☒ **A, C,** and **D** are incorrect. Forensic analysis seeks legal evidence of wrongdoing that can be used in a court of law, but this scenario does not imply collection of evidence for legal proceedings. Network statistic gathering is proactive, but in this case you are reacting to previously gathered data. A vulnerability analysis is proactive and tests for weaknesses; in this case, you are reacting to an anomaly.

15. ☑ **C.** Error handling is a secure coding guideline that requires developers to write code that will capture any unforeseen situations instead of allowing applications to fail.

    ☒ **A, B,** and **D** are incorrect. The lack of packet encryption would not cause an application to fail; it would simply be insecure. Digital signatures verify the identity of the sender of a transmission. There is no mention of transmitting data in this case. Hardening would minimize security risks in Roman's application, but it would not increase its stability.

16. ☑ **B, C,** and **D.** Hardening is defined as making hardware or software less vulnerable to security breaches. Disabling unnecessary services reduces the potential attack surface of an operating system. Patching applies solutions for known flaws and weaknesses. Encrypting File System (EFS) protects files and folders by encrypting them in such a way that parties without the decryption keys cannot decrypt the data.

    ☒ **A** and **E** are incorrect. System restore points take snapshots of the Windows configuration periodically for the purpose of reverting to those snapshots. This could be used to revert a compromised or infected system to a stable point in time, so it should not be disabled when hardening. Group Policy contains many security settings that can be distributed centrally to many computers to harden them.

17. ☑ **B, C,** and **D.** USB device encryption can be enforced, which disallows copying of data to USB drives unless the USB device is encrypted. This ensures copied data remains confidential even if the USB drive is lost. The Windows firewall is critical in controlling inbound and outbound network traffic. For example, when connected to public networks, the firewall might block all incoming traffic, but when connected to the Active Directory domain network, the firewall might allow inbound remote control. Antivirus software is always essential to protecting operating systems from the enormous amount of known malware.

    ☒ **A** and **E** are incorrect. Some users will need USB ports enabled for their USB mice. Power management options serve to conserve power, not secure laptops.

18. ☑ **C, B, A, D,** and **E.** The virus scanner must first be updated either manually or automatically to protect against malicious code while the system is updating. Applying operating system patches is the second thing to do to ensure any software and security flaws are addressed. Next you would join the computer to the domain, but only after patching and ensuring that there are no viruses. Once the computer is joined to the domain, you would log in

to ensure Group Policy security settings are applied. Finally, the financial software required by Accounting department employees should be installed and tested.

19. ☑ **A**, **D**, and **E**. ARP cache poisoning is a process by which a malicious device sends unsolicited broadcasts including its MAC address and another node's IP address, thus redirecting traffic through itself instead of to that other node. This can happen only if network access is granted. Unused switch ports should be disabled to prevent unauthorized access to the network. 802.1x security requires device authentication before allowing network access. Unauthorized computers should not be able to authenticate to the network. ARP cache poisoning requires having network access to transmit forged ARP broadcast packets. Digital signatures assure the recipient of a transmission that the sender is valid. This can be done in many ways such as by using Internet Protocol Security (IPSec), which can require that computers first authenticate to Active Directory before they can participate in secure transmissions.

☒ **B** and **C** are incorrect. Disabling ARP is not an option; ARP is required in TCP/IP networks to resolve IP addresses to MAC addresses. There are not patches addressing this issue because ARP, by design, is stateless and is required for TCP/IP to function.

20. ☑ **B**. Had the SQL query string been properly validated, returning all records would have been prevented.

☒ **A**, **C**, and **D** are incorrect. SQL injection prevention is not a secure coding guideline. The lack of indexes may make searching slower, but it will not prevent the flaw in this example, and it is not considered a secure coding guideline. User authentication is not correct because the question clearly states that users are logging in.

21. ☑ **C**. Domain Name Service (DNS) poisoning means including incorrect name resolution data with the intent of secretly redirecting users to malicious hosts. TCP port 53 is used by DNS servers to synchronize DNS records and, in this case, to, and not from, your server.

☒ **A**, **B**, and **D** are incorrect. Address Resolution Protocol (ARP) poisoning links IP addresses to incorrect MAC addresses, the result of which is to redirect traffic to a malicious device. The question involves port 53 and zone transfers, which are DNS attributes, not ARP attributes. Cross-site scripting injects malicious scripts in normally trustworthy web sites. Web sites use ports 80 and 443, so clearly the question relates to DNS, not HyperText Transfer Protocol (HTTP). MAC flooding does not relate in any way to port 53 or zone transfers; MAC flooding attempts to overwhelm a network switch to the point where the switch forwards all traffic to all switch ports.

22. ☑ **B**. Had the wireless routers been properly hardened, the default configurations would have been changed such as lack of MAC filtering, encryption, and default admin passwords.

☒ **A**, **C**, and **D** are incorrect. Patching may correct security flaws, but it will not normally change default configurations. There is no input being applied to the wireless routers. Input validation is best suited to areas where users can supply data that is sent to a server. Granting users only the rights they need is inapplicable to wireless routers but is applicable to network resources.

23. ☑ **C.** IEEE 802.1x is a standard that authenticates computers against a server before allowing access to wired or wireless networks.

    ☒ **A, B,** and **D** are incorrect. Routers and hubs are network devices, not standards. IEEE 802.11n is a wireless networking standard with theoretical rates of up to 600 Mbps, but the 802.11n standard does not authenticate computers prior to allowing network access.

24. ☑ **D.** Account lockout locks an account after a predetermined number of incorrect password attempts renders the account unusable for a period of time, thus preventing further password attempts.

    ☒ **A, B,** and **C** are incorrect. Minimum password age ensures users do not reset their current password to an old easy-to-remember one. This setting would still allow incessant password attempts. Password hints simply help the user remember a complex password, not restrict repeated password attempts. Password history prevents users from reusing the same passwords, but it does not restrict the number of times hackers can attempt to compromise user accounts.

25. ☑ **B.** Security templates can contain many security settings that are best distributed to groups of computers through Group Policy.

    ☒ **A, C,** and **D** are incorrect. Despite that an image could already be configured with standard security settings, it is tied to the image and is therefore not as flexible as security templates and Group Policy. There are many more security items to consider than just password settings. Local security policy applies to a single machine only; in this case, you must deploy settings to many computers.

26. ☑ **C.** Penetration testing exploits hardware and software vulnerabilities to determine how secure computing devices or networks really are.

    ☒ **A, B,** and **D** are incorrect. Performance baselines determine what type of performance can be expected under normal conditions, but they do not directly relate to how secure a system is. Security templates are used to apply settings to harden a system, but not to test that security. Although password cracking does test computer security, there are many more aspects of computer security that would be covered in a penetration test.

27. ☑ **D.** The Dependencies tab in a service's properties lists other services that depend on the one you are considering disabling.

    ☒ **A, B,** and **C** are incorrect. There is no /dep switch for net start, nor is there a dependency chain option when viewing services. Checking logs after a few days is too time-consuming.

28. ☑ **C.** Web sites running in separate application pools prevent one pool from affecting other pools, as in the event of a compromised web site.

    ☒ **A, B,** and **D** are incorrect. The question clearly states all sites share the same application pool. Each site should have its own application pool for security and stability reasons.

29. ☑ **C** and **D.** Disabling or restricting the use of USB ports and services and their listening ports helps make operating systems more secure.

☒ **A** and **B** and incorrect. Class C IP addresses are no more secure than Class A or B addresses. Log archiving keeps copies of older log files. This is useful for auditing and troubleshooting, but it is not considered hardening.

30. ☑ **A.** The IEEE 802.1x standard requires that devices be authenticated before being given network access. For example, this might be configured for VPN appliances, network switches, and wireless access points that adhere to the IEEE 802.1x standard.

☒ **B, C,** and **D** are incorrect. Strong passwords might prevent the compromising of user accounts, but it will not prevent rogue machines from connecting to the network. IPv6 does not prevent rogue machine network connections. IEEE 802.11 defines the Wi-Fi standard; this does not prevent rogue machine network connections.

31. ☑ **D.** HyperText Transfer Protocol Secure (HTTPS) uses at least one Public Key Infrastructure (PKI) security certificate to encrypt transmissions between the client web browser and the wireless router. This protects the router's management interface.

☒ **A, B,** and **C** are incorrect. IPv6 with HTTPS is no more secure than IPv4 with HTTPS. PKI means the connection will use HTTPS, not HTTP.

32. ☑ **C.** Group Policy can be used to centrally configure these options.

☒ **A, B,** and **D** are incorrect. Configuring each computer is not necessary. Creating a PKI certificate for signing macros is required, but this is not configured on all stations. The macros themselves do not need to be distributed, only the fact that macros are to be trusted.

33. See Figure 6-3.

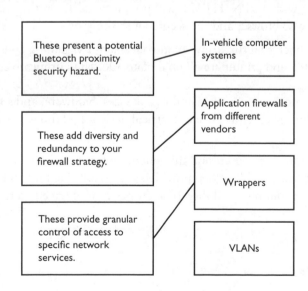

FIGURE 6-3

Security descriptions and technologies—the answer

These present a potential Bluetooth proximity security hazard. — In-vehicle computer systems

These add diversity and redundancy to your firewall strategy. — Application firewalls from different vendors

Wrappers

These provide granular control of access to specific network services.

VLANs

34. ☑ **B.** Application software patches must be applied regularly.
☒ **A, C,** and **D** are incorrect. Sysprep applies only to Windows computers, not Linux. Most anti-malware software enables real-time monitoring by default. Encrypting the hard disk is an enhanced security measure but, generally speaking, is not as important as patching application software.

35. ☑ **B.** NoSQL is a simplified database standard (nonrelational) designed for quick retrieval when processing large volumes of data.
☒ **A, C,** and **D** are incorrect. SQL databases are relational databases that do not scale well when processing enormous amounts of data. The SATA standard relates to data storage and not directly to data mining.

36. ☑ **D.** JavaScript code executes in the client web browser. Even though server-side database validation is in place, it is wise to also configure client-side validation to ensure invalid data does not even reach the server.
☒ **A, B,** and **C** are incorrect. PKI certificates are already in use; this is implied by HTTPS. VPNs are not feasible for the potentially large number of customers. JavaScript is not used for server-side validation.

37. ☑ **C.** Hardening a smart phone includes configuring automatic screen locking, encrypting data on the device, patching the OS and required apps, installing and updating anti-malware, and disabling unnecessary features and software.
☒ **A, B,** and **D** are incorrect. Supervisory Control And Data Acquisition (SCADA) is a special system used in industrial environments to monitor operations and to provide alarms if any systems are tampered with. The questions asks about securing data on the phone, not through the network with a VPN. HTTPS will not protect data on the phone; only data in transit between the web browser and the secured web site is protected.

38. ☑ **A.** You should check that the firmware in your smart TV, gaming console, printer, HVAC system, wireless router, and printer are all up to date. Outdated firmware could expose device vulnerabilities.
☒ **B, C,** and **D** are incorrect. Android and iOS devices, hardware, and software should always be kept up to date, but most refrigerators, electrical outlets, and fire extinguishers do not contain firmware.

39. ☑ **A** and **B.** Mainframe computers and thin clients computers should be patched regularly.
☒ **C** and **D** are incorrect. Public cloud providers are responsible for patching their computing environment; it is not your responsibility. IP addresses cannot have patches applied to them.

7

Implementing System Security

QUESTIONS

Various forms of malware are created every day. Preventing and removing this malware is more important now than ever, especially as mobile, handheld devices become increasingly popular. Even on firewall-protected networks, host-based firewalls offer protection from network attacks. Because they are desirable and easy to steal, mobile devices should encrypt data and have a tracking mechanism such as GPS enabled. Continuing with modern technology trends, cloud computing allows us to quickly provision and deprovision IT services as business needs dictate. Virtualization provides the advantage of maximizing computing hardware resource usage among multiple virtual machines. All of these technologies offer advantages that you must weigh against the security risks.

1. Which security measure would protect hard disk contents even if server hard disks were physically stolen?

   A. NTFS permissions

   B. Power-on password

   C. Complex administrative passwords

   D. Encryption

2. Trinity's user account is mistakenly deleted when she goes on a three-month maternity leave. When she returns, a new account with appropriate NTFS permissions is created for her. When she tries to open her old files, she keeps getting "Access Denied" messages. What is the problem?

   A. Trinity does not have proper NTFS permissions.

   B. Trinity's new user account has a different SID than her old one.

   C. Trinity's files are encrypted with her old account.

   D. Trinity's account should be made a member of the Power Users group.

3. Nate has been using his work e-mail address when surfing the Web and filling in forms on various web sites. To which potential problem has Nate exposed himself?

   A. Spam

   B. Phishing

   C. SQL injection

   D. DNS poisoning

4. You are a server virtualization consultant for Not Really There, Inc. During a planning meeting with a client, the issue of virtual machine point-in-time snapshots comes up. You recommend careful use of snapshots because of the security ramifications. What is your concern?

   A. Snapshots can consume a large amount of disk space.

   B. The use of snapshots could trigger a MAC flood.

   C. Invoked snapshots will mean that the virtual machine is temporarily unavailable.

   D. Invoked snapshots will be patched less often than the currently running virtual machine.

5. What can be done to harden a mobile, handheld device? (Choose two.)

   A. Disable Wi-Fi.

   B. Ensure it is used only in physically secured areas.

   C. Set Bluetooth discovery to disabled.

   D. Enable screen lock.

6. A private medical practice hires you to determine the feasibility of cloud computing whereby e-mail and medical applications, as well as patient information, would be hosted by an Internet provider. You are asked to identify possible security issues. (Choose two.)

   A. Data storage is not local but instead on the provider's premises, where other businesses also have access to cloud computing services.

   B. HTTPS will be used to access remote services.

   C. Should the provider be served a subpoena, the possibility of full data disclosure exists.

   D. Data will be encrypted in transit as well as when stored.

7. Which option will protect employee laptops when they travel and connect to wireless networks?

   A. Personal firewall software

   B. MAC address filtering

   C. Virtualization

   D. 802.11n-compliant wireless card

8. What can be done to ensure the confidentiality of sensitive data copied to USB flash drives?

   A. File hash

   B. Encryption

   C. NTFS permissions

   D. Share permissions

9. Which standard is a firmware solution for drive encryption?

   A. TPM

   B. DLP

   C. EFS

   D. NTFS

10. What can be done to protect data after a handheld device is lost or stolen?

   A. Enable encryption.

   B. Execute a remote wipe.

   C. Enable screen lock.

   D. Disable Bluetooth discovery.

11. How can the specific location of a mobile device be tracked?

    A. IP address

    B. MAC address

    C. SIM card code

    D. GPS

12. What type of software filters unsolicited junk e-mail?

    A. Antispam

    B. Antivirus

    C. Antispyware

    D. Antiadware

13. What type of software works against the collection of personal information?

    A. Antispam

    B. Antivirus

    C. Antispyware

    D. Antiadware

14. Which of the following best protects against operating system defects?

    A. Antivirus software

    B. Firewall software

    C. Encryption

    D. Patching

15. What is the best way to prevent laptop theft?

    A. GPS

    B. Cable lock

    C. Host-based firewall

    D. Antivirus software

16. A server administrator must adhere to legislation that states financial data must be kept secure in the event of a physical security breach. What practices will ensure the administrator complies with the law? (Choose two.)

    A. Applying NTFS permissions

    B. Storing backup tapes in a safe

    C. Encrypting server hard disks

    D. Storing backup tapes in a locked cabinet

17. What type of software examines application behavior, logs, and events for suspicious activity?

    A. NIDS

    B. Host-based firewall

    C. HIDS

    D. Spyware

18. A database administrator requests a method by which malicious activity against a Microsoft SQL database server can be detected. All network traffic to the database server is encrypted. What solution should you recommend?

    A. HIDS

    B. NIDS

    C. IPSec

    D. SSL

19. Which of the following are true regarding virtualization? (Choose two.)

    A. Each virtual machine has one or more unique MAC addresses.

    B. Virtual machine operating systems do not need to be patched.

    C. Virtual machines running on the same physical host can belong to different VLANs.

    D. A security compromise in one virtual machine means all virtual machines on the physical host are compromised.

20. Cloud computing offers which benefits? (Choose two.)

    A. Simple scalability

    B. Fewer hardware purchases

    C. Better encryption

    D. Local data storage

    E. No requirement for antivirus software

21. Mitch is responsible for three payroll servers that store data on a SAN. The chief financial officer (CFO) requests observation of access to a group of budget files by a particular user. What should Mitch do?

    A. Create file hashes for each budget file.

    B. Encrypt the budget files.

    C. Configure a HIDS to monitor the budget files.

    D. Configure file system auditing.

22. Your company has acquired security software that will monitor application usage on all workstations. Before the software can function properly, you must have users run their applications as they normally would for a short period. Why does the security software require this to be done?

    A. To update antivirus definitions for application files

    B. To establish a normal usage baseline

    C. To verify the security software has the required permissions to run

    D. To verify licensed software is being used

23. Kevin is a trial lawyer in southern California. He requires secure, high-quality voice communication with clients. What can he do?

    A. Use VoIP with packet encryption over the Internet.

    B. Use cell phone voice encryption.

    C. Use only landline telephones.

    D. Use his cell phone on a special voice network for legal professionals.

24. Your IT manager asks you to ensure e-mail messages and attachments do not contain sensitive data that could be leaked to competitors. What type of solution should you propose?

    A. Antivirus software

    B. NIDS

    C. DLP *DATA LOSS PREVENTION*

    D. HIDS

25. Your server performance has decreased since the introduction of digitally signing and encrypting all network traffic. You would like to release the servers from this function. Which device should you use?

    A. Smartcard

    B. TPM

    C. HSM *HARDWARE SECURITY MODULE*

    D. EFS

26. Your company has decided that all new server hardware will have TPM support. You receive a new server, and you enable TPM through the CMOS utility and enable drive encryption using TPM in your operating system. What should you do next?

    A. Reboot the server.

    B. Enable EFS on the server.

    C. Enable IPSec.

    D. Back up the TPM keys.

27. You attempt to encrypt a folder on drive D: using EFS, but the encryption option is unavailable. What should you do?

    A. Issue the *convert d: /fs:ntfs* command.

    B. Add your account to the Administrators group.

    C. Enable EFS through Group Policy.

    D. Enable TPM in the CMOS utility.

28. Which capabilities are present in an all-in-one security appliance? (Choose three.)

    A. URL filter

    B. Content inspection

    C. Malware inspection

    D. EFS

29. As the database administrator for your company, you are evaluating various public cloud offerings to test customer database programming changes. Which category of cloud service should you research?

    A. Software as a Service

    B. Platform as a Service

    C. Infrastructure as a Service

    D. Security as a Service

30. Your company hosts an on-premises Active Directory server to authenticate network users. Mailboxes and productivity applications for users are hosted in a public cloud. You have configured identity federation to allow locally authenticated users to seamlessly connect to their mailboxes and productivity applications. What type of cloud do you have?

    A. Public

    B. Private

    C. Hybrid

    D. Community

31. You are deploying Android-based smart phones to employees in your Toronto office. Because of the sensitive nature of your business, you want to employ mechanisms that will protect sensitive data that may exist on phones. Which set of mechanisms should you employ?

    A. Full device encryption, run virtual machines, separation of duties

    B. Remote wiping, lockout, FTP app

    C. Screen locks, GPS, larger-capacity mini SD card

    D. Limiting which apps can be installed, segmenting OS storage location from app storage location, and disabling unused features

32. You are installing a mail app on your smart phone that requires the trusted root PKI certificate of the server. The mail server must authenticate the smart phone using a PKI certificate. Which of the following lists applies to this scenario?

    A. Key management, credential management, authentication

    B. Geotagging, transitive trust/authentication, data ownership

    C. Support ownership, patch management, antivirus management

    D. Mobile forensic data recovery, privacy, onboarding/offboarding

33. Management has decided to support a BYOD corporate policy. You have been asked to recommend points of consideration before BYOD is put into effect. Which of the following points should be considered regarding BYOD? (Choose three.)

    A. More storage capacity for servers

    B. Legal ramifications

    C. Network infrastructure changes

    D. Disabling on-board camera/video

34. Which of the following correctly identifies an operating system that meets specific government or regulatory security standards?

    A. Hardened OS

    B. Trusted OS

    C. Security OS

    D. Patched OS

35. Use Figure 7-1 to match all the individual steps on the left under the correct heading on the right.

36. A comprehensive data policy encompasses which of the following?

    A. Wiping, disposing, retention, storage

    B. Disposing, patching, retention storage

    C. Retention, storage, virtualization

    D. Storage, virtualization, elasticity

37. Which of the following is a valid way of handling Big Data?

    A. Data at rest

    B. NoSQL

    C. EFS

    D. Cloud storage

| FIGURE 7-1 | Baselining and virtualization exercise |

Host Software Baselining

Create sandbox environments to ensure operating systems are kept isolated from production systems.

Test security mechanisms to ensure operating system segregation.

Install user productivity applications.

Configure failover clustering to ensure host availability.

Rapidly provision and deprovision IT services.

Install anti-malware applications.

Create a snapshot before applying patches.

Run multiple operating systems concurrently on a single set of hardware.

Test patches to ensure compatibility with hypervisor guests.

Disable unecessary operating system services.

Virtualization

QUICK ANSWER KEY

1. D	11. D	20. A, B	29. B
2. C	12. A	21. D	30. C
3. A	13. C	22. B	31. D
4. D	14. D	23. B	32. A
5. C, D	15. B	24. C	33. B, C, D
6. A, C	16. B, C	25. C	34. B
7. A	17. C	26. D	35. See Figure 7-2.
8. B	18. A	27. A	36. A
9. A	19. A, C	28. A, B, C	37. B
10. B			

FIGURE 7-2

Baselining and
virtualization—
the answer

Host Software Baselining

> Disable unnecessary operating
> system services.
>
> Install anti-malware applications.
>
> Install user productivity applications.

Virtualization

> Create a snapshot before applying
> patches.
>
> Run multiple operating systems
> concurrently on a single set of hardware.
>
> Test patches to ensure compatibility
> with hypervisor guests.
>
> Rapidly provision and deprovision
> IT services.
>
> Configure failover clustering to
> ensure host availability.
>
> Test security mechanisms to ensure
> operating system segregation.
>
> Create sandbox environments to
> ensure operating systems are kept
> isolated from production systems.

IN-DEPTH ANSWERS

1. ☑ **D.** Encryption is the best answer because NTFS permissions, power-on password, and complex passwords are all meaningless when someone gains physical access to hard disks.
   ☒ **A, B,** and **C** are incorrect. NTFS permissions are easily circumvented by taking ownership of the disk contents after plugging the disk into another machine. The power-on password is tied to the specific machine, not the hard disk. Passwords can be reset if somebody gets local physical access to a hard disk.

2. ☑ **C.** Encrypting File System (EFS) encrypts files and folders using keys that are unique to the user. Newly created user accounts, even with the same name, will not use the same keys, which means decryption will not occur. A recovery agent is required to decrypt Trinity's files.
   ☒ **A, B,** and **D** are incorrect. The question states the appropriate NTFS permissions are put into place. Although Trinity does have a different SID, the SID does not get used to encrypt files; the user's public key does. Members of the Power Users group have no special access to EFS-encrypted files.

3. ☑ **A.** Despite perhaps being illegal (this is currently a legal gray area), there is money to be made in providing valid e-mail addresses to spammers and also in spammers sending unsolicited advertisements to those e-mail addresses. Spam filters can reduce the amount of spam showing up in mailboxes.
   ☒ **B, C,** and **D** are incorrect. Phishing directs unsuspecting users via what appears to be a legitimate e-mail to false web sites in an attempt to gather private user information. In this case, Nate is surfing the Web, not clicking links in e-mail messages. SQL injections are intentionally crafted by malicious users to retrieve more records from databases than they normally should. DNS poisoning has nothing to do with e-mail addresses; instead, it has to do with fully qualified domain names (FQDNs) being directed to malicious sites.

4. ☑ **D.** Reverting a running virtual machine to an older snapshot could mean going back to a point in time before critical patches or virus scanning updates were applied, thus rendering your virtual machine vulnerable.
   ☒ **A, B,** and **C** are incorrect. Snapshot disk space usage and snapshot invocation are not directly applicable to security. MAC address floods are not invoked when reverting to a virtual machine snapshot.

5. ☑ **C** and **D.** Bluetooth discovery mode makes it possible for anybody within range (10 meters) to see and potentially connect to the mobile device. Screen lock is essential to secure mobile devices; a password or fingerprint scan is used to unlock the screen and make the device usable.
   ☒ **A** and **B** are incorrect. Completely disabling Wi-Fi is not a recommended hardening solution. Wi-Fi hardening is more often configured on the wireless access point. Disabling

Bluetooth discovery and configuring screen lock are much better hardening options. Requiring handheld devices be used in physically secured areas is inconvenient, and convenience is the primary reason for the success of handheld devices.

6. ☑ **A and C.** Because there are many customers sharing the same cloud computing services, it is reasonable to approach the issue of data storage cautiously. Third-party audit findings may dispel or confirm these fears. Depending on the provider's geographic location, different laws may apply to whether data hosted by the provider can legally be disclosed.

   ☒ **B and D** are incorrect. HyperText Transfer Protocol Secure (HTTPS) is considered a secure transmission protocol (data in transit); HTTP is not. Data encryption does not warrant security concerns; it addresses them.

7. ☑ **A.** Personal firewall software could be configured to prevent all inbound network traffic, which also prevents its discovery on a wired or wireless network.

   ☒ **B, C, and D** are incorrect. MAC address filtering is configured on the wireless routers, which would not all be under your control. Even virtualized operating systems need firewall protection. An 802.11n-compliant wireless card offers no more protection than an 802.11g-compliant wireless card.

8. ☑ **B.** Encrypting USB flash drives prevents unauthorized parties from viewing the data. Stored data (data at rest) encryption protects data while it is not in use.

   ☒ **A, C, and D** are incorrect. Although file hashing is important for file integrity (any changes in the file invalidate the file hash), it does not apply to confidentiality. NTFS permissions can be circumvented by taking ownership of files and folders. Share permissions apply only across a network.

9. ☑ **A.** Trusted Platform Module (TPM) chips can store cryptographic keys or certificates used to encrypt and decrypt drive contents. If the drive were moved to another computer (even one with TPM), the drive would remain encrypted and inaccessible.

   ☒ **B, C, and D** are incorrect. Data loss prevention (DLP) refers to fault tolerance and related mechanisms for ensuring data is safe, such as preventing sensitive data from being copied while it is being viewed (data in use). Encrypting File System (EFS) is purely software, not a firmware chip. NTFS uses ACLs to control access to data, but the data is not encrypted.

10. ☑ **B.** Remote wipe is an option administrators can exercise to remotely wipe the contents of a handheld device.

    ☒ **A, C, and D** are incorrect. These settings would have to be either set before the device was lost or stolen or pushed out the next time the device was connected.

11. ☑ **D.** GPS is a common feature in mobile devices that provides coordinates (longitude and latitude) for geographic tracking.

☒ **A, B,** and **C** are incorrect. Network Address Translation (NAT) and proxy servers both mask the originating IP address, thus making it unreliable for tracking devices. The originating device MAC address is used only on a LAN. Once packets leave a LAN, the source MAC address changes as the packet travels through routers. Although subscriber identification module (SIM) cards in mobile devices do register with the nearest cell tower, the location is not as specific as GPS.

12. ☑ **A.** Spam is unsolicited junk e-mail. Antispam software attempts to filter out these messages, but it sometimes flags legitimate messages as spam.
☒ **B, C,** and **D** are incorrect. They do not offer protection against unsolicited junk e-mail.

13. ☑ **C.** Spyware gathers personal information and computer usage habits without user knowledge.
☒ **A, B,** and **D** are incorrect. Antispam software reduces the amount of junk e-mail in a mail user's inbox. Antivirus software prevents the propagation of malware such as worms and Trojans. Adware does not collect personal information, but it does display advertisements selected on the basis of personal information. Pop-up blocker software can help mitigate adware intrusions.

14. ☑ **D.** Patching addresses specific operating system defects.
☒ **A, B,** and **C** are incorrect. These are all important and are critical security components, but the question asks for the best protection against bugs in the operating system.

15. ☑ **B.** A cable lock is a steel cable designed to secure a laptop to a secure object, such as a desk.
☒ **A, C,** and **D** are incorrect. GPS allows tracking of the laptop but does not prevent its theft. Firewalls and antivirus software do nothing to physically protect equipment.

16. ☑ **B and C.** In the event of a physical security breach, data will be kept secure in a safe. If server hard disks are stolen, encryption will ensure the data cannot be decrypted by unauthorized parties.
☒ **A and D** are incorrect. NTFS permissions are easily defeated locally (not across the network). Locked cabinets are not as secure as storing backup tapes in a safe and encrypting server hard disks.

17. ☑ **C.** Host-based intrusion detection system (HIDS) software monitors applications, logs, and events for suspicious activity.
☒ **A, B,** and **D** are incorrect. A network intrusion detection system (NIDS) examines network packets to identify suspicious network activity, not application-specific anomalies. Host-based firewalls either allow or deny inbound and outbound packets. Spyware gathers personal user information. Spyware is not designed to look at logs and application events.

18. ☑ **A.** Host-based intrusion detection systems are application specific (such as to a SQL database). Databases can also benefit from encryption. Encryption presents no problems, since HIDS runs on the target computer.
☒ **B, C,** and **D** are incorrect. Network intrusion detection systems do not single out suspicious application activity; instead, they attempt to single out suspect network activity. IPSec encrypts

and digitally signs packets; it does not apply to specific applications. Secure Sockets Layer (SSL) is used to secure HTTP network traffic.

19. ☑ **A** and **C.** Each virtual machine does have a unique MAC address that is configurable by the virtual machine administrator. Virtual machines running on the same host can connect to different VLANs (physical or internal); this is simply a virtual network configuration setting.
    ☒ **B** and **D** are incorrect. Virtualized operating systems must be patched. A compromised machine does not imply full access to all other machines.

20. ☑ **A** and **B.** Scalability with cloud computing is simple because a third party takes care of hardware, software, software licensing, and so on. Because a third party is hosting some (or all) of your IT services, you will require fewer hardware resources.
    ☒ **C** and **D** are incorrect. The question does not specify what (if any) type of encryption either party is using. Cloud computing normally implies data storage is hosted by the provider, not locally. Even for firms relying exclusively on cloud computing, their employees will still use a computing device to connect to cloud services and therefore will still need antivirus software.

21. ☑ **D.** File system auditing should be configured for budget file access by the employee in question.
    ☒ **A**, **B**, and **C** are incorrect. File hashing is useful only in determining whether a file has changed, not if anybody in particular accessed the file. Encryption is used for data confidentiality. HIDS looks for abnormal activity; Mitch was asked only to observe file access.

22. ☑ **B.** To detect abnormal behavior, the security software must know what is normal in this environment.
    ☒ **A**, **C**, and **D** are incorrect. Antivirus software will update its own virus definitions. Verifying run permissions is normally done by the installation routine. Checking software license compliance would not require users to use the software for a short period.

23. ☑ **B.** Cell phone voice encryption software ensures that your voice calls are confidential after establishing a secure session with the other cell phone. The encrypted voice is transmitted through the cell phone's data channel as opposed to the normal voice channel.
    ☒ **A**, **C**, and **D** are incorrect. VoIP is time sensitive such that encrypting and decrypting each packet over the Internet means VoIP will suffer from delay. Landline phones are not considered secure. There is no such voice network for legal professionals.

24. ☑ **C.** Data loss prevention (DLP) hardware and software solutions perform deep content inspection of data (such as e-mail bodies and attachments) to prevent information leakage.
    ☒ **A**, **B**, and **D** are incorrect. Antivirus software scans for viruses, not company secrets. NIDS and HIDS both look for abnormalities (NIDS on the network, HIDS on a host).

25. ☑ **C.** Hardware security module (HSM) devices are designed to handle cryptographic duties, thus allowing servers to focus on other tasks.

☒ **A**, **B**, and **D** are incorrect. Smartcards are an authentication mechanism used to identify users and do not remove server cryptographic responsibilities. Trusted Platform Module (TPM) chips are used to encrypt and decrypt disk contents, not network traffic. Encrypting File System (EFS) is not a device; it is software.

26. ☑ **D.** Trusted Platform Module (TPM) stores keys, certificates, and passwords used for disk encryption in a chip. In the event the chip or motherboard fails, it is important to have a copy of keys so that disk contents can be decrypted. TPM can also store data related to the boot environment on that machine such that the TPM will know whether the boot environment has been tampered with and can lock the device.
    ☒ **A**, **B**, and **C** are incorrect. Rebooting the server is not required by all operating systems using TPM. Although Encrypting File System (EFS) can be used in conjunction with TPM, enabling it is not the next thing you should do. The question refers to TPM disk encryption, not Internet Protocol (IP) encryption.

27. ☑ **A.** Encrypting File System (EFS) requires NTFS file systems.
    ☒ **B**, **C**, and **D** are incorrect. You do not need to be in the Administrators group to encrypt a folder. EFS does not need to be enabled through Group Policy. Trusted Platform Module (TPM) is not required for EFS to function.

28. ☑ **A**, **B**, and **C.** All-in-one security appliances can control access to web content based on the URL and data in the payload of the packet. Data transmitted through this type of security appliance can also be subject to malware scanning.
    ☒ **D.** EFS is a Windows file and folder encryption feature.

29. ☑ **B.** Platform as a Service (PaaS) provides IT services over a network such as virtual servers, databases, and programming APIs.
    ☒ **A**, **C**, and **D** are incorrect. Software as a Service (SaaS) allows productivity software to be rapidly provisioned over a network. Infrastructure as a Service refers to network, storage, and backup services offered in the cloud. Security as a Service (also sometimes referred to as SaaS) provides hosted and managed security solutions through a third party, such as malware scanning.

30. ☑ **C.** Hybrid cloud solutions combine on-premises IT services with IT services hosted in the cloud.
    ☒ **A**, **B**, and **D** are incorrect. Public cloud services are hosted on computing resources owned and managed by the public cloud provider. Private cloud services are hosted on computing resources owned and managed by a private organization. Community clouds pool computing resources to offer IT services to organizations with similar needs.

31. ☑ **D.** Only apps that have been thoroughly tested and are required should be allowed on smart phones. Enforcing a list of only what is allowed to run is referred to as application white listing. Application black listing specifies restricted apps. App data can be segmented from OS storage to increase security. Encrypting data, especially on removable storage, is critical.

    ☒ **A, B,** and **C** are incorrect. Virtual machines should not be run on smart phones because of lack of hardware resources. Separation of duties requires more than one person to complete a sensitive task—this does not apply to securing smart phones. FTP apps should not be used on a smart phone containing sensitive data. Device access control, including screen locks and software controls, can secure smart phones, as can GPS for asset tracking and inventory control, but larger storage capacities are not related to securing smart phones.

32. ☑ **A.** Valid PKI certificates (containing public and private keys) are used by the smart phone and mail server to mutually authenticate in this example; the keys should be backed up. PKI certificates, as well as usernames and passwords, are considered credentials.

    ☒ **B, C,** and **D** are incorrect. Geotagging includes geographic coordinates with data such as pictures or video for documentation or tracking purposes. Transitive trust/authentication refers to end-point devices trusting third-party servers indirectly through a trusted proxy device. Data ownership relates to the owner of the data, where support ownership describes entities responsible for supporting a device. Even smart phones require patching and antimalware scanners. Mobile data recovery is performed by forensic IT specialists. Data privacy is normally achieved with encryption. Onboarding is a term used to describe adding or extending user identity capabilities to an organization's identity management system. Offboarding is a term describing the removal of a user from an identity management system.

33. ☑ **B, C,** and **D.** Bring your own device (BYOD) policies allow users to bring their own computing devices (laptops, tablets, smart phones) to an organization's network. As a result, infected user devices could threaten an organization's network or assets, which could result in litigation. The network infrastructure should be configured with a separate network for BYOD devices. To protect the confidentiality of sensitive data, consider disabling onboard cameras on mobile devices.

    ☒ **A** is incorrect. Implementing a BYOD policy does not translate into requiring more storage capacity.

34. ☑ **B.** A trusted OS is a secured operating system that meets or exceeds stringent security standards.

    ☒ **A, C,** and **D** are incorrect. These terms do not apply in the context of the question. A security OS provides security tools. There are many Linux distributions built for this purpose. A hardened OS is the process of securing an OS by disabling or removing unnecessary services and software. A patched OS is one that has had OS and application patches applied.

35. ☑ See Figure 7-3. Host software baselining involves installing and configuring an operating system, security software, and only required productivity applications. Virtualization allows multiple concurrent operating systems to share the same hardware. Snapshots are point-in-time images of virtual machines and can be reverted to if something goes wrong with a virtual machine. Cloud computing implies the use of virtualization, which allows rapid elasticity of IT services.

FIGURE 7-3

Baselining and
virtualization—
the answer

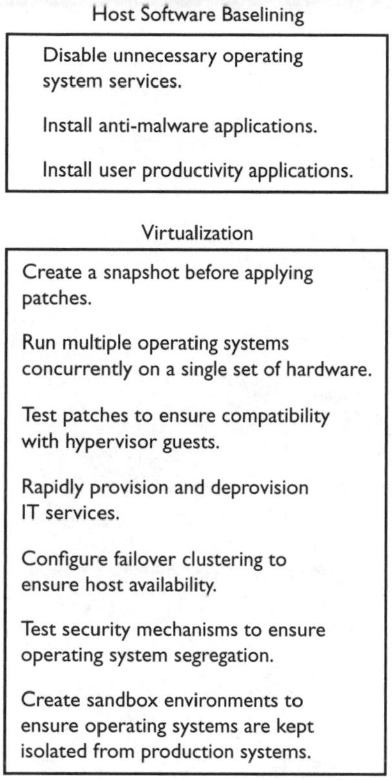

Host Software Baselining

Disable unnecessary operating
system services.

Install anti-malware applications.

Install user productivity applications.

Virtualization

Create a snapshot before applying
patches.

Run multiple operating systems
concurrently on a single set of hardware.

Test patches to ensure compatibility
with hypervisor guests.

Rapidly provision and deprovision
IT services.

Configure failover clustering to
ensure host availability.

Test security mechanisms to ensure
operating system segregation.

Create sandbox environments to
ensure operating systems are kept
isolated from production systems.

36. ☑ **A.** Wiping a drive or device can remove sensitive data. Disposal of used computing
equipment, such as hard disks, can be accomplished with physical shredding. Data retention
might be required for regulatory compliance. A data policy might specify types of storage
devices and specific configurations where data safety is maintained.
☒ **B, C,** and **D** are incorrect. Items such as patching, virtualization and elasticity do not apply
to data policies.

37. ☑ **B.** NoSQL is a type of database designed to process enormous amounts of data in a
columnar format. Most SQL database technologies work with data in rows.
☒ **A, C,** and **D** are incorrect. Data at rest refers to stored data. EFS is a Microsoft file and
folder encryption feature. Cloud storage allows saving data on a cloud provider's equipment that
is accessible from anywhere using any type of device.

8

Securing the Network Infrastructure

QUESTIONS

Firewalls are an integral part of computer networks and come in various forms such as NAT firewalls, packet filtering firewalls, and proxy servers. Some firewalls perform deep packet inspection where others examine only packet headers. Intrusion detection analyzes and identifies suspicious activity. Intrusion prevention extends this detection by attempting to block the suspicious activity. Both can be performed for a network or for a specific host. Besides firewalling, it's also important to remember basic network security options including switch port security, placement of network devices, and changing default configurations.

1. You are a guest at a hotel offering free Wi-Fi Internet access to guests. You connect to the wireless network at full signal strength and obtain a valid TCP/IP configuration. When you try to access Internet web sites, a web page displays instead asking for a code before allowing access to the Internet. What type of network component is involved in providing this functionality?

    A. DHCP server
    B. NAT
    C. Proxy server
    D. Switch

2. You are configuring a wireless router at a car repair shop so that waiting customers can connect to the Internet. You want to ensure wireless clients can connect to the Internet but cannot connect to internal computers owned by the car repair shop. Where should you plug in the wireless router?

    A. LAN
    B. Port 24 on the switch
    C. Port 1 on the switch
    D. DMZ

3. What will detect network or host intrusions and take actions to prevent the intrusion from succeeding?

    A. IPS
    B. IDS
    C. IPSec
    D. DMZ

4. What technology uses a single external IP address to represent many computers on an internal network?

    A. IPSec
    B. DHCP
    C. NAT
    D. NIDS

5. You must purchase a network device that supports content filtering and virus defense for your LAN. What should you choose?

   A. NAT router

   B. HIPS

   C. Web security gateway

   D. Packet filtering firewall

6. You have been asked to somehow separate Engineering departmental network traffic from Accounting departmental traffic because of a decrease in network throughput. What should you use?

   A. VLAN

   B. DMZ

   C. NAT

   D. VPN

7. Based on the following LAN firewall rule set, choose the best description:

   Allow inbound TCP 3389
   Allow outbound TCP 80
   Allow outbound TCP 443

   A. LAN users can connect to external FTP sites. External users can use RDP to connect to LAN computers.

   B. LAN users can connect to external SMTP servers. External users can use LDAP to connect to LAN computers.

   C. LAN users can connect to external web servers. External users can use RDP to connect to LAN computers.

   D. LAN users can connect to external proxy servers. External users can use IPSec to connect to LAN computers.

8. Which tool would allow you to capture and view network traffic?

   A. Vulnerability scanner

   B. Port scanner

   C. Protocol analyzer

   D. NAT

9. You are reviewing router configurations to ensure they comply with corporate security policies. You notice the routers are configured to load their configurations using TFTP and also that TCP port 22 is enabled. What security problem exists with these routers?

   A. Telnet should be disabled.

   B. Telnet should have a password configured.

   C. TFTP is an insecure protocol.

   D. Telnet should limit concurrent logins to 1.

10. A router must be configured to allow traffic only from certain hosts. How can this be accomplished?

   A. ACL

   B. Subnet

   C. Proxy server

   D. NAT

11. Which technologies allow analysis of network traffic? (Choose two.)

   A. Port scanner

   B. Sniffer

   C. DMZ

   D. NIDS

12. What term describes the network between the two firewalls, shown here?

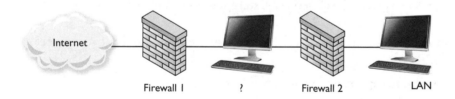

Firewall 1   ?   Firewall 2   LAN

   A. Proxy server

   B. NAT

   C. DMZ

   D. NIDS

13. You have received a new VPN concentrator to allow traveling users access to LAN B. Where should you place the VPN concentrator?

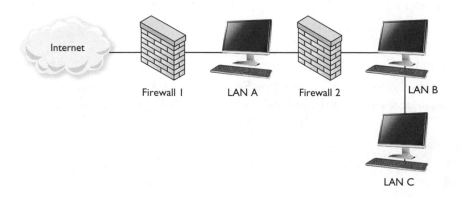

- **A.** Internet
- **B.** LAN A
- **C.** LAN B
- **D.** LAN C

14. Sylvia's workstation has been moved to a new cubicle. On Monday morning, Sylvia reports that even though the network card is plugged into the network jack, there is no link light on the network card. What is the problem?

- **A.** The workstation has an APIPA address. Issue the ipconfig / renew command.
- **B.** The default gateway has not been set.
- **C.** Sylvia must first log on to the domain.
- **D.** Since the MAC address has changed, switch port security has disabled the port.

15. You need a method of authenticating Windows 7 workstations before allowing local LAN access. What should you use?

- **A.** VPN concentrator
- **B.** Router
- **C.** 802.1x-compliant switch
- **D.** Proxy server

16. An attacker sends thousands of TCP SYN packets with unreachable source IP addresses to a server. After consuming server resources with this traffic, legitimate traffic can no longer reach the server. What can prevent this type of attack?

    A. Packet filtering firewall

    B. Proxy server

    C. Antivirus software

    D. SYN flood protection

17. A junior IT employee links three network switches together such that each switch connects to the two others. As a result, the network is flooded with useless traffic. What can prevent this situation?

    A. Web application firewall

    B. Loop protection

    C. SYN flood guard

    D. Router ACL

18. Your boss asks that specific HTTP traffic be monitored and blocked. What should you use?

    A. Web application firewall

    B. Protocol analyzer

    C. Packet filtering firewall

    D. Layered security/defense in depth

19. A high school principal insists on preventing student access to known malware web sites. How can this be done?

    A. DMZ

    B. URL filtering

    C. DNS forwarding

    D. 802.1x-compliant switch

20. Which of the following scenarios best describes implicit deny?

    A. Allow network access if it is 802.1x authenticated.

    B. Block outbound network traffic destined for TCP port 25.

    C. Block network traffic unless specifically permitted.

    D. Allow network traffic unless specifically forbidden.

21. A university student has a wired network connection to a restrictive university network. At the same time, the student is connected to a Wi-Fi hotspot for a nearby coffee shop that allows unrestricted Internet access. What potential problem exists in this case?

    A. The student computer could link coffee shop patrons to the university network.

    B. The student computer could override the university default gateway setting.

    C. Encrypted university transmissions could find their way onto the Wi-Fi network.

    D. Encrypted coffee shop transmissions could find their way onto the university network.

22. Which network device encrypts and decrypts network traffic over an unsafe network to allow access to private LANs?

    A. Proxy server

    B. IPSec

    C. VPN concentrator

    D. TPM

23. You suspect malicious activity on your DMZ. In an effort to identify the offender, you have intentionally configured an unpatched server to attract further attention. What term describes what you have configured?

    A. Honeynet

    B. Logging server

    C. Exploit

    D. Honeypot

24. Your NIDS incorrectly reports legitimate network traffic as being suspicious. What is this known as?

    A. False positive

    B. Explicit false

    C. False negative

    D. Implicit false

25. Your corporate network access policy states that all connecting devices require a host-based firewall, an antivirus scanner, and the latest operating system updates. You would like to prevent noncompliant devices from connecting to your network. What solution should you consider?

    A. NIDS

    B. NAC

    C. VLAN

    D. HIDS

26. Which of the following are true regarding NAT? (Choose two.)

    A. The NAT client is unaware of address translation.

    B. The NAT client is aware of address translation.

    C. Internet hosts are unaware of address translation.

    D. NAT provides a layer.

27. You are a sales executive for a real estate firm. One of your clients calls you wondering why you have not e-mailed them critical documentation regarding a sale. You check your mail program to verify the message was sent two days ago. You also verify the message was not sent back to you as undeliverable. You tell your client that you did in fact send the message. What should you next tell your client?

    A. Clean your mailbox; there is no room for new incoming mail.

    B. Wait a few hours; Internet e-mail is slow.

    C. NAT might have prevented the message from being delivered.

    D. Check your junk mail; antispam software sometimes incorrectly identifies legitimate mail as spam.

28. You are an IT network consultant. You install a new wireless network for a hotel. What must you do to prevent wireless network users from gaining administrative access to wireless routers?

    A. Apply MAC filtering.

    B. Disable SSID broadcasting.

    C. Change the admin password.

    D. Enable WPA.

29. You are an IT specialist with a law enforcement agency. You have tracked illegal Internet activity down to an IP address. Detectives would like to link a person to the IP address in order to secure an arrest warrant. Which of the following are true regarding this situation? (Choose two.)

    A. The IP address might be that of a NAT router or a proxy server.

    B. The IP address could not have been spoofed; otherwise, it would not have reached its destination.

    C. IP addresses can be traced to a regional ISP.

    D. IP addresses are unique for every individual device connecting to the Internet.

30. Your IT security director asks you to configure packet encryption for your internal network. She expresses concerns about how existing packet filtering firewall rules might affect this encrypted traffic. How would you respond to her concerns?

    A. Encrypted packets will not be affected by existing packet filtering firewall rules.

    B. Encrypted packet headers could prevent outbound traffic from leaving the internal network.

    C. Encrypted packet payloads will prevent outbound traffic from leaving the internal network.

    D. Inbound encrypted traffic will be blocked by the firewall.

31. Draw a line in Figure 8-1 linking the desired outcome listed on the left with the correct solution listed on the right.

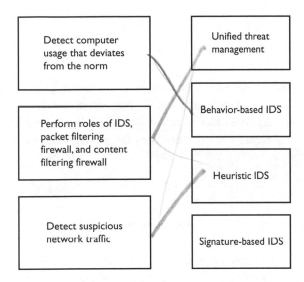

FIGURE 8-1

Desired outcomes and potential solutions

32. You are configuring inbound firewall rules on a Linux host. Which command-line tool would you use?

iptables

33. You are configuring inbound firewall rules on a Windows host. Which command-line tool would you use?

netsh

34. Acme Inc. has hired you to implement security solutions as recommended by the findings of a network security audit. Stations connecting to the network must have a host-based firewall enabled and must have an up-to-date antivirus solution installed. What should you implement?

A. ACL
B. NAC
C. 802.1x
D. VLAN

35. Acme Inc. has hired you to implement security solutions as recommended by the findings of a network security audit. Stations used by Accounting staff should not be able to communicate with other stations on the network. What should you implement?

    A. ACL

    B. NAC

    C. 802.1x

    D. VLAN

36. Acme Inc. has hired you to implement security solutions as recommended by the findings of a network security audit. Currently, any station plugged into a switch can communicate on the network without any type of authentication. Acme Inc. would like to limit network communications by connecting stations until they have been authenticated. What should you implement?

    A. ACL

    B. NAC

    C. 802.1x

    D. VLAN

37. Acme Inc. has hired you to implement security solutions as recommended by the findings of a network security audit. Currently, all users have read access to project files on the main file server. Your configuration must ensure that only members of the Project Managers group have access to project files. What should you implement?

    A. ACL

    B. NAC

    C. 802.1x

    D. VLAN

QUICK ANSWER KEY

1. C	11. B, D	21. A	31. See Figure 8-2.
2. D	12. C	22. C	32. iptables
3. A	13. B	23. D	33. netsh
4. C	14. D	24. A	34. B
5. C	15. C	25. B	35. D
6. A	16. D	26. A, C	36. C
7. C	17. B	27. D	37. A
8. C	18. A	28. C	
9. C	19. B	29. A, C	
10. A	20. C	30. B	

FIGURE 8-2

Desired
outcomes
and potential
solutions—the
answer

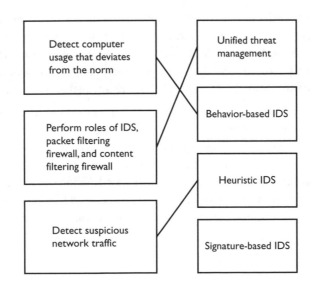

IN-DEPTH ANSWERS

1. ☑ **C.** Proxy servers retrieve content for connected clients and can also require authentication before doing so.

   ☒ **A, B,** and **D** are incorrect. Dynamic Host Configuration Protocol (DHCP) provides to clients a valid IP address, subnet mask, default gateway, Domain Name System (DNS) server, and so on; there is no mechanism for authentication. Network Address Translation (NAT) uses a single public IP address to represent all internal computers. Like DHCP, NAT does not authenticate connections. Switches isolate network conversations between hosts and track which computers are plugged into which switch port using the machine's MAC address.

2. ☑ **D.** A demilitarized zone (DMZ) is a network allowing external unsecure access to resources while preventing direct access to internal resources. If the wireless router is plugged into the DMZ, this will provide Internet access to customers while disallowing them access to internal business computers. Plugging the wireless router into the internal LAN would also allow Internet access but would place customers on a business LAN.

   ☒ **A, B,** and **C** are incorrect. A LAN would allow customer access to internal computers and is therefore incorrect. Ports 24 and 1 on a switch generally have no special DMZ meaning any more than any other port does, although some network devices do have special designated DMZ ports.

3. ☑ **A.** An intrusion prevention system (IPS) actively monitors network or system activity for abnormal activity and also takes steps to stop it. Abnormal activity can be detected by checking for known attack patterns (signature-based) or variations beyond normal activity (anomaly-based).

   ☒ **B, C,** and **D** are incorrect. Like an IPS, an intrusion detection system (IDS) monitors network or system activity for irregular activity but does not attempt to stop this activity. IP Security (IPSec) provides data confidentially and integrity to network transmissions and does not detect or prevent intrusions. A DMZ does not detect or prevent attacks; it is a network segment hosting services (and ideally an IPS) that are accessible to an untrusted network.

4. ☑ **C.** NAT runs on a router and allows computers on an internal network to access an external network using only a single external IP address. NAT routers track outbound connections in order to deliver inbound traffic to the originating internal host.

   ☒ **A, B,** and **D** are not correct. IPSec provides a means of encrypting and digitally signing network packets and has nothing to do with translating IP addresses. DHCP and NIDS do not use a single IP address on behalf of internal computers. DHCP provides a valid TCP/IP configuration for network nodes. NIDS analyzes network traffic to identify and report network attacks.

5. ☑ C is correct. Web security gateways can perform deep packet inspection (content) to filter network traffic. They also include the ability to detect and deal with malware.
   ☒ A, B, and D are not correct. NAT does not support content filtering or virus protection; it merely analyzes and modifies packet headers. Host Intrusion Prevention System (HIPS) detects and stops attacks on a computer system and does not monitor the content of LAN network traffic. Packet filtering firewalls look only at packet headers to allow or deny traffic; they do not analyze packet payloads.

6. ☑ A. Virtual local area networks (VLANs) create separate broadcast domains in the same way a router physically separates two network segments. Both the Engineering and Accounting departments should be configured on their own VLANs thus separating their network traffic.
   ☒ B, C, and D are incorrect. A DMZ does not isolate departmental traffic; it is a network between a private LAN and an unsafe external network such as the Internet. Network services such as e-mail or web servers that must be reachable from the external network reside in the DMZ. Network services on the private LAN are kept unreachable from the external network. NAT devices are not designed to separate busy networks; they are designed to allow many internal computers access to an external network using only one IP address. VPNs allow external connectivity to a private LAN over an untrusted network such as the Internet via an encrypted data stream, but they are not used to separate networks to increase throughput.

7. ☑ C is correct. Connecting to external web servers means connecting to HTTP (port 80) for unencrypted sites and HTTPS (port 443) for encrypted sites. Remote Desktop Protocol (RDP) uses port 3389.
   ☒ A, B, and D are not correct. FTP uses TCP ports 20 and 21. SMTP uses TCP port 25. IPSec uses UDP port 500 in addition to specific protocol IDs, which would have to be allowed through the firewall.

8. ☑ C. Protocol analyzers capture and view network traffic by placing the network card into promiscuous mode. In a switched environment you will only capture network traffic involving your machine in addition to multicast and broadcast packets. Enable port monitoring or mirroring on your switch to view all network activity on the switch.
   ☒ A, B, and D are incorrect. The question refers to capturing and viewing traffic, not scanning the network for vulnerable hosts. Port scanning identifies services running on a host, but it does not capture network traffic. NAT connects internal computers to an external network using a single IP address.

9. ☑ C. Trivial File Transfer Protocol (TFTP) transmits data (such as router configurations) in clear text. TFTP does not have an authentication mechanism; therefore, anybody with network access could have access to all router configurations. It would be more secure to store router configurations locally on the router and to secure the router with the appropriate passwords.
   ☒ A, B, and D are incorrect. Telnet was not implied in the question. Secure Shell (SSH) uses TCP port 22.

10. ☑ **A.** Access control lists (ACLs) are router settings that allow or deny various types of network traffic from or to specific hosts.

☒ **B, C,** and **D** are incorrect. A subnet cannot restrict network traffic. Routers can be used to divide larger networks into smaller subnets. The question specifically states configuring a router, and proxy hosts should have routing disabled. Proxy servers do have the ability to limit network access from certain hosts, though. NAT routers do not restrict network traffic from certain hosts; instead, they use a single external IP address to allow many internal computers access to an external network.

11. ☑ **B** and **D.** Sniffers use network card promiscuous mode to capture all network traffic instead of only traffic addresses to the host running the sniffer. Switches isolate each port from one another, so sniffers will not see all switch network traffic unless a switch port is configured to do so. NIDSs are placed on the network strategically so they can analyze all network traffic to identify and report on suspicious activity.

☒ **A** and **C** are incorrect. Port scanners identify running services on network hosts. Port scanners do not analyze all network traffic; they are directed to scan one or more hosts. A DMZ does not analyze network traffic, although sniffers and NIDS are important to use in a DMZ. A DMZ is a network containing hosts that are accessible to external users. Firewalls limit access from the DMZ to internal resources.

12. ☑ **C.** A DMZ hosts services that are externally accessible while preventing access to internal LANs. Firewall 1 could ensure that only appropriate traffic enters the DMZ. Firewall 2 could be enabled with NAT to allow LAN users access to the Internet while blocking any traffic initiated from outside of the LAN.

☒ **A, B,** and **D** are incorrect. The question refers to a network, not a single device on a network.

13. ☑ **B** is correct. To allow traveling users to connect to LAN B, the VPN concentrator should be placed in the DMZ (LAN A). Placing the VPN concentrator on LAN B is not recommended because it would allow direct access to an internal LAN from the Internet. Firewall 1 should be configured to allow inbound VPN traffic to the VPN concentrator. Firewall 2 should be configured to allow only authenticated VPN users into LAN B.

☒ **A, C,** and **D** are incorrect. You want the VPN concentrator behind firewall 1 so that firewall 1 can control which packets get sent to the VPN device. Placing the VPN device on LANs B or C would open a direct line from the Internet to LAN B.

14. ☑ **D** is correct since it is the only choice that would result in an unlit link light on a network card.

☒ **A, B,** and **C** are incorrect. An automatic IP address (APIPA) or lack of a default gateway entry would result only in limited network connectivity; the network card link light would still be lit. Domain connectivity is not possible without a network link.

15. ☑ **C.** The 802.1x protocol defines how devices must first be authenticated before getting LAN access.

☒ **A, B,** and **D** are not correct. A VPN device allows remote access to a LAN, not local access. Routers do not authenticate devices. LAN access is needed before connecting to a proxy server.

16. ☑ **D.** SYN flood protection prevents the described DoS attack by limiting the number of half-open TCP connections. A normal TCP conversation follows a three-way handshake whereby a SYN packet is sent to the target, which responds with a SYN-ACK packet. The originator then sends an ACK packet to complete the handshake. A large number of SYN packets consume server resources.

☒ **A, B,** and **C** are incorrect. Packet filtering firewalls can allow or deny packets based on IP addresses, ports, protocol IDs, and so on, but they cannot prevent SYN floods. Proxy servers do not check for half-open TCP handshakes; they retrieve external content for internal clients. Antivirus software scans for malware, not DoS attacks.

17. ☑ **B.** Loop protection is a switch feature that prevents uplink switch ports from switching to "forwarding" mode, thus preventing bridging loops.

☒ **A, C,** and **D** are incorrect. Web application firewalls have nothing to do with switches; they monitor HTTP conversations to prevent inappropriate activity. SYN floods are not a result of improperly wired switches; they are specific to TCP. Router ACLs do not correct problems stemming from incorrectly linked switches.

18. ☑ **A.** Web application firewalls can stop inappropriate HTTP activity based on a configured policy.

☒ **B, C,** and **D** are incorrect. Protocol analyzers can capture network traffic and generate reports, but they do not block any type of traffic. Packet filtering firewalls do not perform deep packet inspection; that is, they only examine packet headers and not packet payloads, which is where HTTP content exists. Layered security, also known as defense in depth, uses network firewalls, IDSs, host-based firewalls, and so on, to provide multiple layers of security.

19. ☑ **B.** URL filtering examines where traffic is going and compares that against a list of allowed and forbidden sites to allow or prevent access. This can be done on a dedicated network appliance, or it could simply be server software.

☒ **A, C,** and **D** are incorrect. A DMZ does not control access to web sites; it is a network hosting services to external users, and it exists between a private and public network. If a DNS server receives a specific DNS query that it cannot answer and DNS forwarding is configured, it will direct the query to DNS servers that can resolve the specific request. This will not prevent students from visiting malware web sites. 802.1x-compliant switches do not perform detailed packet analysis; they simply authenticate devices against an authentication server before granting network access.

20. ☑ **C.** Implicit denial applies when there is no setting explicitly stating network traffic is allowed.

☒ **A, B,** and **D** are incorrect. Specifically allowing network traffic is an example of an explicit allowance. Specifically, blocking outbound traffic is an example of explicit deny. Allowing traffic to pass unless specifically forbidden is an implicit allowance.

21. ☑ **A.** Many operating systems automatically create a network connection between networks when two network interfaces are detected. This would link network segments together in a single broadcast domain but create multiple collision domains. This means, for example, that a coffee shop patron could get a valid TCP/IP configuration from a university DHCP server.

☒ **B, C,** and **D** are incorrect. Being connected to two networks simultaneously will not override a network's default gateway settings. There is no problem with encrypted data finding its way onto either network; only authorized parties can decrypt the transmissions.

22. ☑ **C.** VPNs are encrypted tunnels established over an unsafe network with the goal of safely connecting to a private LAN.

☒ **A, B,** and **D** are incorrect. Proxy servers do not encrypt or decrypt network traffic; they retrieve content based on client requests. IPSec is not a network device; it is a software method of encrypting and digitally signing packets. Trusted Platform Module (TPM) is a chip storing keys or passphrases used to encrypt and decrypt disk contents, not network traffic.

23. ☑ **D.** A honeypot is designed to attract the attention of hackers or malware in an effort to learn how to mitigate the risk or to identify the offender. This is done by analyzing log files on the honeypot host.

☒ **A, B,** and **C** are incorrect. The question states a single computer was configured, not an entire network. A logging server would never be left intentionally unpatched. An exploit takes advantage of a vulnerability. An intentional vulnerability has been created, but not an exploit.

24. ☑ **A.** Reporting there is a problem when in truth there is not is known as a false positive.

☒ **B, C,** and **D** are incorrect. Explicit false and implicit false are not terms commonly used in IT security. False negatives mean no problem is stated as existing when in fact one does. The question states the exact opposite.

25. ☑ **B.** Network Access Control (NAC) ensures connecting devices are compliant with configured health requirements before allowing network access. This can be done with 802.1x network equipment such as a switch, or it can be done with software such as a VPN server checking connecting clients.

☒ **A, C,** and **D** are incorrect. NIDS analyzes network packets looking for abnormal activity; it does not check whether connecting devices meet health requirements. VLANs do not verify client health compliance; they segment larger broadcast domains into smaller ones to maximize network throughput. HIDS seek problems by analyzing data received by a host as well as its logs and local activity.

26. ☑ **A** and **C**. The NAT client simply sees the NAT router as its default gateway. Beyond that, it has no idea that for outbound packets its source IP address is being changed to that of the NAT router's public interface. To Internet hosts, the traffic appears to come from the NAT router's public interface (which it really does); there is no indication of IP address translation.

   ☒ **B** and **D** are incorrect. NAT is transparent to clients and Internet hosts.

27. ☑ **D**. Assuming the message was sent according to the sender's system two days ago and the sender did not receive an undeliverable message, the most likely answer is that it was flagged as junk mail by the receiver's mail system.

   ☒ **A**, **B**, and **C** are incorrect. Although mail servers can hold e-mail until a user cleans out their mailbox, this is not as likely as the message having been flagged by antispam software. Internet e-mail is generally not that slow. NAT simply changes IP addresses in packet headers. This would not prevent e-mail from getting to its destination.

28. ☑ **C**. Wireless routers ship with a standard admin username and password. It is critical that the wireless router admin password be changed to prevent unauthorized admin access.

   ☒ **A**, **B**, and **D** are incorrect. MAC address filtering controls which wireless devices can connect to a wireless network, but it would not prevent admin access to a wireless router using a default admin password. Disabling SSID broadcasting prevents wireless clients from seeing the wireless network name when they are within range, but it does not prevent admin access to an unsecured wireless router. Encrypting wireless network traffic with WPA might secure wireless traffic, but it does not secure the wireless router itself.

29. ☑ **A** and **C**. NAT routers and proxy servers change the source IP address of packets going to the Internet to be that of their public interface, so on the Internet the packets appear to have originated from those hosts; the internal IP address of a client behind the NAT router or proxy server is not known. Law enforcement could obtain a warrant to examine the logs on a NAT router or proxy server to identify internal clients, but privacy laws in some countries prevent Internet service providers from disclosing this information.

   ☒ **B** and **D** are incorrect. IP addresses can be spoofed easily with freely available software. Packets with spoofed source IP addresses will reach their destination, but responses will not reach the originator; instead, they will go to the spoofed IP address. Most networks around the planet have a NAT router (or multiple layers of NAT routers) to allow internal clients using a nonunique IP address access to the Internet. The NAT router modifies the source IP address in outbound packets to be that of its public interface, and it tracks this change so that any responses to the sent packet can be delivered to the internal client.

30. ☑ **B**. Packet headers include addressing information such as IP and port addresses. These are used to get a packet to its destination. Packet filtering firewalls allow or deny traffic based on IP or port addresses, to name just a few criteria. If, for example, packets headers containing port addresses are encrypted, packet filtering firewalls may block traffic when perhaps it should be allowed.

☒ **A, C,** and **D** are incorrect. Packet filtering firewalls do not examine the payload of each packet, and assuming only the payload is encrypted, the traffic will not be affected. Packet filtering firewalls do not examine packet payload, only the headers. The question discusses encrypting internal traffic; there is no mention of allowing inbound encrypted traffic.

31. See Figure 8-3.

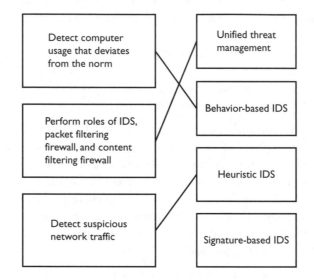

FIGURE 8-3

Desired outcomes and potential solutions—the answer

32. ☑ iptables

33. ☑ netsh

34. ☑ **B.** Network Access Control (NAC) checks connecting stations (VPN, switch, Wi-Fi, and so on) to ensure they meet configured policies, such as having a firewall and antivirus solution running.

☒ **A, C,** and **D** are incorrect. Access control lists (ACLs) are used to determine what actions a user can issue against a network resource such as a shared folder. 802.1x is a security standard that requires devices connecting to a network to be authenticated before allowing full network communication. Virtual local area networks (VLANs) create communication boundaries between network devices without the use of multiple routers.

35. ☑ **D.** Virtual local area networks (VLANs) create communication boundaries between network devices without the use of multiple routers.

☒ **A, C,** and **D** are incorrect. Access control lists (ACLs) are used to determine what actions a user can issue against a network resource such as a shared folder. Network Access Control

(NAC) checks connecting stations (VPN, switch, Wi-Fi, and so on) to ensure they meet configured policies, such as having a firewall and antivirus solution running. 802.1x is a security standard that requires devices connecting to a network to be authenticated before allowing full network communication.

36. ☑ **C.** 802.1x is a security standard that requires devices connecting to a network to be authenticated before allowing full network communication.
☒ **A, B,** and **D** are incorrect. Access control lists (ACLs) are used to determine what actions a user can issue against a network resource such as a shared folder. Network Access Control (NAC) checks connecting stations (VPN, switch, Wi-Fi, and so on) to ensure they meet configured policies, such as having a firewall and antivirus solution running. Virtual local area networks (VLANs) create communication boundaries between network devices without the use of multiple routers.

37. ☑ **A.** Access control lists (ACLs) are used to determine what actions a user can issue against a network resource such as a shared folder.
☒ **B, C,** and **D** are incorrect. Network Access Control (NAC) checks connecting stations (VPN, switch, Wi-Fi, and so on) to ensure they meet configured policies, such as having a firewall and antivirus solution running. 802.1x is a security standard that requires devices connecting to a network to be authenticated before allowing full network communication. Virtual local area networks (VLANs) create communication boundaries between network devices without the use of multiple routers.

9

Wireless Networking and Security

QUESTIONS

The popularity of wireless network connectivity has introduced a wide array of security concerns. Bluetooth wireless networks are personal networks designed for short ranges and are useful for transferring data among handheld devices. Wi-Fi networks have a greater range than Bluetooth and are used by computers. Knowing when to apply various wireless standards can help insulate your wireless network from unauthorized access.

1. While reviewing wireless router logs, you notice wireless network usage by unfamiliar systems. How can you control which systems connect to your wireless network?

    A. Change the SSID.

    B. Disable DHCP.

    C. Change the wireless router admin password.

    D. Enable MAC address filtering.

2. Enabling WPA on a WLAN provides what? (Choose two.)

    A. Confidentiality

    B. Integrity

    C. Availability

    D. Authorization

3. In addition to encrypting wireless traffic, you configure your wireless router to require connecting users to authenticate against a RADIUS server. What type of security have you configured?

    A. WEP

    B. TKIP

    C. WPA2 Personal

    D. WPA2 Enterprise

4. You decide to capture network traffic with a sniffer while connected to a busy public Wi-Fi hotspot. After several minutes you realize you can see only your own network traffic in addition to broadcasts and multicasts. Why can you not see anybody else's wireless network traffic?

    A. WPA encryption is in use.

    B. The SSID is not broadcasting.

    C. MAC filtering is enabled.

    D. Isolation mode is enabled.

5. A curious IT professional drives through an industrial park late at night while scanning for unsecured wireless networks with a PDA. What is this called?

- **A.** Network scanning
- **B.** War driving
- **C.** War dialing
- **D.** War chalking

6. To which of the following security concerns does EAP apply?

- **A.** Virus scanning
- **B.** Hard disk encryption
- **C.** Network authentication
- **D.** Firewall rules

7. Which mechanism requires only a server-side PKI certificate to encrypt user authentication traffic?

- **A.** EAP
- **B.** PEAP
- **C.** LEAP
- **D.** EAP-TLS

8. You are configuring access to a wireless LAN on a Windows 8.1 laptop. When you list available wireless networks, you notice multiple listings of Hidden Network. What wireless router option is in use for these hidden networks?

- **A.** Disable SSID broadcast
- **B.** MAC address filtering
- **C.** WEP
- **D.** WPA

9. Which wireless encryption protocol uses counter mode to make pattern detection difficult?

- **A.** CCMP
- **B.** CHAP
- **C.** WEP
- **D.** RSA

10. You are conducting a wireless site survey at a client site. The client expresses a desire to keep wireless transmissions secure. There is a single 802.11n wireless router with omnidirectional antennae in the server room at one end of the building. WPA2 enterprise and MAC filtering have been configured. What additional security issue should you address?

    A. WPA2 Personal should be used.

    B. MAC filtering is useless; MAC addresses are easily spoofed.

    C. Move the wireless router to the center of the building.

    D. Upgrade the wireless router to 802.11m.

11. What can be done to secure a wireless network?

    A. Decrease power transmission level to cover only the intended area.

    B. Use a wireless encryption standard such as 802.3.

    C. Change the DHCP-supplied default gateway address.

    D. Configure wireless router admin access to use HTTP.

12. A Windows user in your company issues the following command on their company wireless laptop: netsh wlan set hosted network mode=allow ssid=AcmeWLAN key=password. What best describes the security problem created by this user?

    A. The user has administrative rights in Windows 7.

    B. The key is not complex enough.

    C. The user has created a rogue access point.

    D. The SSID name is invalid.

13. You are the wireless network administrator. Users report unstable wireless 802.11g network connectivity. After careful examination, you realize 2.4GHz wireless phones and Bluetooth devices are interfering with the Wi-Fi signal. Which choice offers the best solution?

    A. Replace the 802.11g network with 802.11n.

    B. Cease using all 2.4GHz wireless phones and Bluetooth devices.

    C. Purchase a high-gain antenna for your wireless router.

    D. Change the Wi-Fi channel used by your wireless router.

14. A hacker configures a rogue access point to appear as a legitimate Wi-Fi hotspot. Which term best describes this configuration?

    A. Evil twin

    B. Bad rogue

    C. War driving

    D. War chalking

15. Which of the following refers to unsolicited messages sent to nearby Bluetooth devices?

    A. Bluespamming

    B. Bluejacking

    C. Bluehacking

    D. Bluedriving

16. Which of the following refers to unauthorized data access of a Bluetooth device over a Bluetooth wireless network?

    A. Bluejacking

    B. Bluesnarfing

    C. Packet sniffing

    D. Port scanning

17. You are working at a client site to solve wireless performance issues. In doing so, you notice WEP is configured on the client's wireless routers. What type of attack might this network be susceptible to?

    A. DDoS

    B. IV attack

    C. ARP poisoning

    D. Dictionary attack

18. How can you control whether all wireless devices will see your WLAN name?

    A. Disable SSID broadcasting.

    B. Block packet sniffing.

    C. Reduce transmission power level.

    D. Change antenna placement.

19. Which of the following items could interfere with an 802.11g wireless network?

    A. Remote garage door opener

    B. Microwave oven

    C. Television infrared remote

    D. Cell phone

20. In securing a wireless network, you decide to enable EAP-TLS to authorize wireless client access to the wireless LAN. What should you do next?

    A. Install a public key certificate on the client and a smartcard on the server.

    B. Install a smartcard on the client and a public key certificate on the server.

    C. Install MS-CHAP on the client and a public key certificate on the server.

    D. Install a smartcard on the client and MS-CHAP on the server.

21. TKIP is used primarily by which wireless standard?

  A. 802.11n

  B. WEP

  C. WPA

  D. 802.1x

22. You are a Wi-Fi IT specialist. Users report that the new 802.11g network is not running at the advertised 54Mbps. What should you tell your wireless users?

  A. 802.11g runs at 11Mbps.

  B. Wireless encryption will be disabled to increase bandwidth.

  C. Wi-Fi bandwidth is shared by all users connected to the same wireless network.

  D. SSID broadcasting will be disabled to increase bandwidth.

23. Which standard requires stations to authenticate prior to gaining network access?

  A. 802.11a

  B. 802.11b

  C. 802.1x

  D. 802.3   WIRED

24. You are securing your Wi-Fi network infrastructure. You configure network monitoring software with a list of valid wireless access point MACs allowed on the network. What type of threat will this enable you to detect?

  A. Rogue access points

  B. War driving

  C. Bluesnarfing

  D. Bluejacking

25. You are configuring a wireless network for your home office. Which options are applicable to a home network? (Choose two.)

  A. WPA2 PSK

  B. WPA2 Enterprise

  C. EAP-TLS

  D. WPA PSK

26. A traveling user calls the help desk regarding her wireless connectivity problem. When she attempts to connect to a visible wireless network at full strength, it eventually times out with no further messages. What is the problem?

    A. The user does not have the WPA2 PSK configured on her station.

    B. MAC address filtering is blocking her wireless network card.

    C. The user needs an external antenna for her wireless card.

    D. She must enter the SSID.

27. You are enjoying a cup of coffee at the local coffee shop when all of a sudden your cell phone displays an anonymous message complimenting you on your Hawaiian shirt. What are you a victim of?

    A. Bluetoothing

    B. Bluesnarfing

    C. Bluejacking

    D. Bluedriving

28. Match the security policy terms with the correct scenario:

Security Policy Terms	Scenarios
Captive portal _B C_	A. You are upgrading wireless access points in your company. Your manager has asked that you purchase equipment that will increase wireless transmission speeds.
MIMO _A_	B. To adhere to corporate security policies, you must ensure that Wi-Fi devices cannot access corporate network resources without additional authentication.
Directional antenna _D_	C. To adhere to corporate security policies, you must ensure that Wi-Fi devices cannot access the Internet without first authenticating.
VPN _e B_	D. You are a network infrastructure technician for a university. Your colleague, Franco, is tweaking wireless connectivity between two buildings on campus using a specialized antenna on each wireless router. Franco is carefully adjusting the positioning of the antennae to cover the long distance between the two buildings.

29. You are the owner of Stacey's Coffee Spot, a coffee shop providing customers with international coffee flavors in a relaxing environment. To collect payment, you would like to implement a technology whereby your clients can simply wave their smart phone a few centimeters from a payment terminal. Which of the following should you employ?

    A. MIMO

    B. NFC _NEAR FIELD COMM_

    C. Channel bonding

    D. Captive portal

30. Which of the following statements regarding replay attacks is true?

    A. They are applicable only to WEP-configured wireless networks.

    B. They can be prevented by configuring the use of captive portal.

    C. They can be prevented by disabling SSID broadcasting.

    D. They are conducted by capturing and resending wireless network traffic.

31. You are configuring a new wireless router and notice a PIN on the back of the wireless router. What is the purpose of the PIN?

    A. It allows home users to easily secure a wireless network.

    B. It is a Bluetooth pairing code.

    C. It is the WEP key.

    D. It is the WPA key.

32. Patchy-Adams is a unique medical research facility specializing in the use of laugher and vitamin C to cure illness. You have been hired by Patchy-Adams to propose a wireless network implementation strategy adhering to the following requirements:

- The fastest possible throughput is needed.
- Wireless users must be authenticated against their network user accounts.
- Administrative access to wireless networks must be secure.
- Only company-issued wireless devices are allowed to connect to the wireless network.

Which of the following lists meets the requirements listed above?

    A. Directional antenna, WEP, SSH, MAC filtering

    B. MIMO, WPA2 Enterprise, SSH, MAC filtering

    C. MIMO, WEP, SSL, MAC filtering

    D. MIMO, WPA2 Enterprise, SSL, MAC filtering

33. You are configuring a home wireless router for use with your home medical practice. The network consists of two Windows 7 desktops, an iPhone, and an Android-based tablet. Privacy laws state that all wireless network communication must be as secure as possible. Which security mode in Figure 9-1 should you configure?

FIGURE 9-1

Configuring
wireless security
modes on a Linksys
wireless router

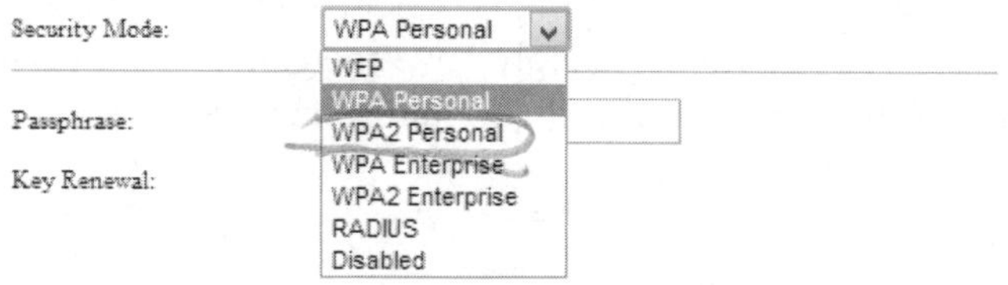

Security Mode: WPA Personal

Passphrase:

Key Renewal:

WEP
WPA Personal
WPA2 Personal
WPA Enterprise
WPA2 Enterprise
RADIUS
Disabled

QUICK ANSWER KEY

1. D	10. C	19. B	28. Captive portal: **C**, MIMO: **A**, Directional antenna: **D**, VPN: **B**
2. A, B	11. A	20. B	
3. D	12. C	21. C	
4. D	13. D	22. C	
5. B	14. A	23. C	29. B
6. C	15. B	24. A	30. D
7. B	16. B	25. A, D	31. A
8. A	17. B	26. B	32. D
9. A	18. A	27. C	33. WPA2 Personal

IN-DEPTH ANSWERS

1. ☑ **D.** MAC addresses are unique 48-bit hexadecimal identifiers for network cards. You can configure a list of allowed and blocked MAC addresses on your wireless router to limit which devices can connect.
☒ **A, B,** and **C** are incorrect. Changing the SSID does not allow you to directly control which systems can connect; it changes the name of the wireless network. Disabling DHCP on the wireless router cannot control which machines connect; it requires each device to have a manual TCP/IP configuration. Changing the wireless router admin password does not prevent connectivity to a wireless LAN.

2. ☑ **A** and **B.** Wi-Fi Protected Access (WPA) encrypts packets on a wireless network to prevent unauthorized viewing of data (Confidentiality), and it verifies that received data has not been tampered with (Integrity).
☒ **C** and **D** are incorrect. Availability relates to continuous access to data, not WPA. WPA secures wireless traffic; it does not check access rights to a network resource (authorization).

3. ☑ **D.** Wi-Fi Protected Access version 2 (WPA2) Enterprise uses an authentication server to control access to a wireless network.
☒ **A, B,** and **C** are not correct. Wired Equivalent Privacy (WEP) does encrypt traffic, but it cannot authenticate connecting users against an authentication server. Temporal Key Integrity Protocol (TKIP) secures wireless networks by changing the encryption key per packet. The question refers to an authentication server. WPA Personal simply uses a passphrase to secure the network; it cannot authenticate connecting users to a server.

4. ☑ **D.** Wireless isolation mode prevents wireless clients on the same Wireless LAN (WLAN) from seeing each other.
☒ **A, B,** and **C** are all incorrect. While they are relevant when securing a wireless network, none of them prevents a wireless client from seeing another client's network traffic.

5. ☑ **B.** War driving entails searching for wireless networks, often from within a moving vehicle.
☒ **A, C,** and **D** are incorrect. Although network scanning is occurring, the act of scanning for wireless networks is called war driving. War dialing involves using a modem to dial phone numbers until telephony equipment answers the call. War chalking refers to scanning for and charting (for example, writing in chalk on the sidewalk) open wireless networks.

6. ☑ **C.** Extensible Authentication Protocol (EAP) is a connecting device network authentication framework supporting methods such as PKI certificates, smartcards, and passwords. Wireless networks that support WPA or WPA2 commonly provide multiple EAP options to choose from for RADIUS authentication of connecting clients.

☒ **A, B,** and **D** are incorrect. Virus scanning checks for malware, hard disk encryption ensures only authorized persons can use data on a hard disk, and firewall rules control outbound network traffic.

7. ☑ **B.** Protected Extensible Authentication Protocol (PEAP) creates a secure channel for user authentication using a server-side PKI certificate initially; then a symmetric session key is used for the remainder of the session.

☒ **A, C,** and **D** are incorrect. Extensible Authentication Protocol (EAP) is a general framework for securing authentication traffic, but it does not specify whether PKI certificates are used. Lightweight Extensible Authentication Protocol (LEAP) is a Cisco wireless authentication protocol that does not involve PKI certificates; usernames are sent in clear text. Although similar to PEAP, Extensible Authentication Protocol – Transport Layer Security (EAP-TLS) requires the client and server to possess PKI certificates to secure authentication traffic.

8. ☑ **A.** Disabling the station set identifier (SSID) suppresses the wireless network name in beacon packets. When scanning for wireless networks, some tools will not display these networks, but Windows 8.1 displays them as Hidden Network.

☒ **B, C,** and **D** are incorrect. Media Access Control (MAC) filtering restricts which wireless client can connect by checking their network card hardware address (MAC address), but it does not control the display of wireless network names. MAC address filtering controls which wireless devices can connect to the wireless network. WEP and WPA encrypt wireless traffic but do not impact whether a wireless network is visible.

9. ☑ **A.** Counter mode CBC Message authentication Protocol (CCMP) is a WPA2 standard that uses an AES block cipher with counter mode. Counter mode makes pattern detection difficult, thus making this a strong protocol.

☒ **B, C,** and **D** are incorrect. Challenge Handshake Authentication Protocol (CHAP) is not a wireless encryption protocol; it is an authentication mechanism whereby credentials are not sent across the network. Wired Equivalent Privacy (WEP) is a deprecated wireless security protocol, but it does not use counter mode. Rivest Shamir Adleman (RSA) is a public key algorithm used for digitally signing and encrypting packets, but it does not use counter mode.

10. ☑ **C.** Omnidirectional antennae radiate radio signals in all directions, so a wireless router at one end of a building would allow connectivity from outside the building. Placing the wireless router in the center of the building would allow optimal wireless connectivity from within the building while minimizing radiation outside of the building.

☒ **A, B,** and **D** are incorrect. Wi-Fi Protected Access version 2 (WPA2) Personal requires each device to use a key, whereas WPA2 Enterprise uses an authentication server before allowing wireless network access. Using WPA2 Personal would make the network less secure. Although MAC addresses can be spoofed, MAC filtering is not useless since most users won't know or care about how to spoof a MAC address. The 802.11m standard does not apply to equipment; rather, it applies to the maintenance of 802.11 wireless documentation.

11. ☑ **A.** Wireless routers can be configured with a transmit power level (measured in milliwatts). Increasing this value can, to a point, provide better wireless access to clients. Decreasing this value reduces the wireless coverage area, for example, to only include a property where legitimate access is required.

☒ **B, C,** and **D** are incorrect because 802.3 defines the Ethernet standard, not a wireless encryption standard. Changing the default gateway address is pointless; it is still being delivered to clients automatically via Dynamic Host Configuration Protocol (DHCP). HyperText Transfer Protocol (HTTP) is the default protocol for connecting to and configuring a wireless router. HyperText Transfer Protocol Secure (HTTPS) would further secure a wireless network beyond HTTP.

12. ☑ **C.** A rogue access point is either a software or hardware wireless access point that can allow unauthorized wireless access to a secure network, or it can pose as a valid access point. In this case, a Windows 7 computer with a wireless card will advertise itself as a wireless network named AcmeWLAN.

☒ **A, B,** and **D** are incorrect. Users having Windows administrative access is not considered a security problem in all environments. Although it is true, the problem is not the password; the problem is the unauthorized wireless access point. The station set identifier (SSID) name is valid.

13. ☑ **D.** The Wi-Fi 2.4GHz range is divided into smaller bands (channels) that slightly overlap. If the wireless router is set to use channel 6 and other devices are interfering with it, select a channel furthest away from 6, perhaps channel 1 or 11.

☒ **A, B,** and **C** are incorrect. 802.11g and 802.11n can both use the 2.4GHz frequency range. Ceasing all wireless device use is an extreme solution to a simple problem; it is much easier to change the Wi-Fi channel. A higher-gain antenna would not solve interference problems, but it would increase your wireless coverage area.

14. ☑ **A.** Evil twin is the term used to describe the situation in the question. This is a security risk because users are tricked into connecting to what appears to be a legitimate wireless network when in fact all the network traffic can be controlled and redirected by a malicious user.

☒ **B, C,** and **D** are incorrect. Bad rogue is not an industry-standard term. War driving entails being mobile and scanning for wireless networks. War chalking entails charting (often with chalk on a sidewalk) open wireless networks.

15. ☑ **B.** Bluejacking refers to a Bluetooth user sending an anonymous message to another Bluetooth device such as a cell phone (assuming Bluetooth is enabled). Bluetooth is a short-range (10 meters) wireless technology running in the 2.4GHz range.

☒ **A, C,** and **D** are all incorrect because they are not industry-standard terms.

16. ☑ **B.** Bluesnarfing is the act of connecting to and accessing data from a device over a Bluetooth wireless connection. It is considered much more invasive than packet sniffing or port scanning.

☒ **A, C,** and **D** are incorrect. Bluejacking does not access data from a Bluetooth device; instead, bluejacking sends an unsolicited message to another Bluetooth device. The question specifies accessing data. Packet sniffing captures network traffic; it does not access data from a wireless device. Port scanning enumerates running services on a host, but it does not access data stored on the host.

17. ☑ **B.** Initialization vector (IV) attacks are specific to Wired Equivalent Privacy (WEP). The clear-text dynamic IV and static WEP key are included in each packet. Since the IV is a 24-bit value, there are only 16,777,216 possibilities (2 raised to the power of 24) that can be used with a WEP key. Given enough network traffic, an attacker can eventually derive the WEP key using freely available tools.

☒ **A, C,** and **D** are incorrect. Distributed Denial of Service (DDoS) attacks flood a host with useless traffic and are not specific to WEP. ARP poisoning modifies host ARP cache entries with a valid host IP address (for example, the default gateway IP) matched to the attacker's MAC address. This means the attacker would receive packets destined for the default gateway. ARP poisoning can happen on any wired or wireless network once an attacker gains network access. Dictionary attacks apply to any type of network (including wireless networks using WEP); they use a dictionary in an attempt to crack account passwords.

18. ☑ **A.** Disabling station set identifier (SSID) broadcasting results in clients not seeing the wireless network name when they are within range. Newer operating systems will detect a wireless network, but the name will not be displayed.

☒ **B, C,** and **D** are incorrect. Packet sniffing can be detected on the network because a network card is placed into promiscuous mode to capture traffic. This can be detected and controlled, for example, by disabling a switch port, but it has nothing to do with viewing wireless LANs. Reducing power levels or changing antenna placement on a wireless router might reduce the range from which the wireless network is visible, but it could prevent wireless devices (including those within range) from seeing the wireless network.

19. ☑ **B.** Any wireless devices using the 2.4GHz range, such as a microwave oven, could potentially interfere with an 802.11g Wi-Fi network.

☒ **A, C,** and **D** are incorrect. They do not use the 2.4GHz frequency range. Remote garage door openers usually operate in the 300MHz to 400MHz frequency range. Infrared remotes rely on line of sight for communication. Wi-Fi does not; it uses radio waves. Cell phones in general use the 800MHz to 2000MHz frequency range depending on the type of cell phone.

20. ☑ **B.** Extensible Authentication Protocol Transport Layer Security (EAP-TLS) uses public key cryptography to control network access. Cryptographic keys can be stored on smartcards. Smartcards are not used on servers; they are used on client stations, normally with a PIN, to authenticate to a server that has been configured with a public key certificate.

☒ **A, C,** and **D** are incorrect. Servers do not normally use smartcards; clients do. Microsoft Challenge Handshake Protocol (MS-CHAP) is not used with EAP-TLS; it can be used instead of EAP-TLS, although it is less secure.

21. ☑ **C.** Temporal Key Integrity Protocol (TKIP) is used by Wi-Fi Protected Access (WPA) for encryption and supersedes Wired Equivalent Privacy (WEP).

    ☒ **A, B,** and **D** are incorrect. The 802.11n standard in no way implies TKIP is used; rather, it is a Wi-Fi standard that improves upon the 802.11g Wi-Fi standard. TKIP addresses encryption implementation flaws in WEP. 802.1x specifies client network authentication and is not related to TKIP.

22. ☑ **C.** Like a hub, wireless clients share the network bandwidth on a wireless network, so the more wireless clients connected to the same network, the less bandwidth available per client.

    ☒ **A, B,** and **D** are incorrect. 802.11b runs at 11 Mbps, and 802.11g runs at 54 Mbps. Disabling wireless encryption and SSID broadcasting would not have as big of an impact on wireless network bandwidth as option C.

23. ☑ **C.** The IEEE 802.1x standard defines port-based authentication (including wireless) prior to allowing client network access.

    ☒ **A, B,** and **D** are incorrect. 802.11a and 802.11b are wireless standards, but they do not specify network authentication. 802.3 defines the wired Ethernet standard.

24. ☑ **A.** Unauthorized (rogue) wireless access points can either allow malicious wireless users unauthorized access to a wired network or fool unsuspecting users to make a connection to what appears to be a legitimate wireless network. There are many methods of detecting rogue access points; in this example the Basic Service Set Identifier (BSSID), or MAC address, of the access point is compared against a list of allowed BSSIDs.

    ☒ **B, C,** and **D** are incorrect. War driving is the action of scanning for wireless networks. The question states you are configuring valid access point (AP) MACs to prevent a threat. The questions states you are securing a Wi-Fi network, not a Bluetooth network.

25. ☑ **A** and **D.** Wi-Fi Protected Access (WPA) and WPA2 PreShared Key (PSK) are for home use. They both require the same passphrase be configured on the wireless router and connecting wireless clients.

    ☒ **B** and **C** are incorrect. WPA2 Enterprise and EAP-TLS are enterprise-class options. WPA2 Enterprise uses a RADIUS server to authenticate connecting wireless users. EAP-TLS authenticates connecting devices using public keys configured on both the client and the authenticating server.

26. ☑ **B.** MAC address filtering will prevent connections from unauthorized wireless clients.

    ☒ **A, C,** and **D** are incorrect. The user is not prompted with any further messages; incorrect WPA keys normally generate some type of error message. An external antenna would not make a difference since the wireless network appears at full strength. Because the user is clicking the visible wireless network, there is no need to enter the SSID; she can already see it.

27. ☑ **C.** Sending messages to users who did not ask for the message over a Bluetooth network is referred to as bluejacking.

☒ **A, B,** and **D** are incorrect. Bluetoothing and bluedriving are not standard industry terms. Bluesnarfing does not apply to this situation; only a message was sent. Bluesnarfing entails accessing private data on a Bluetooth device.

28. Captive portal: **C,** MIMO: **A,** Directional antenna: **D,** VPN: **B**

29. ☑ **B.** Near Field Communication (NFC) is a wireless technology whereby smart phone users with a specific app installed can transmit information (such as banking or credit card information) to another device in close proximity.

☒ **A, C,** and **D** are incorrect. Multiple Input Multiple Output (MIMO) uses multiple antennae to achieve greater wireless transmission throughput. Channel bonding transmits data over multiple channels simultaneously to achieve greater wireless transmission throughput. Wi-Fi hotspots can use captive portal that presents a user with an authentication web page before allowing Internet access.

30. ☑ **D.** Attackers can capture and resend wireless network traffic to an access point with the intent of cracking wireless encryption, using the appropriate cracking tools.

☒ **A, B,** and **C** are incorrect. Replay attacks can be issued against WPA networks, not only WEP. While captive portal requires authentication or the agreement of use terms prior to Internet access, this is not related to replay attacks. SSID broadcasting prevents the wireless network from being visible, but many tools will expose these networks. This is not related to replay attacks.

31. ☑ **A.** The Wi-Fi Protected Setup (WPS) standard was designed to allow home users to easily secure and connect to a wireless network but has since been found to be crackable.

☒ **B, C,** and **D** are incorrect. Bluetooth pairing codes are usually configured within the software on a Bluetooth device, and they allow Bluetooth devices to communicate with one another. WEP and WPA keys are never labeled on a sticker on wireless devices.

32. ☑ **D.** Multiple Input Multiple Output (MIMO) uses multiple antennas for faster wireless network speeds. Wi-Fi Protected Access version 2 (WPA2) authenticates users against a central authentication server (a RADIUS server). Secure Sockets Layer (SSL) can be enabled to encrypt administrative access to a wireless router. Media Access Control (MAC) filtering allows or prevents connectivity to only specific wireless devices with a specific MAC, or hardware address.

☒ **A, B,** and **C** are incorrect. Secure Shell (SSH) is a secure remote command-line mechanism unrelated to wireless networking technologies. Wired Equivalent Privacy (WEP) does not authenticate users against a network user account like Wi-Fi Protected Access (WPA2) does.

33. **WPA2 Personal.** Since there is no central authentication server on the network, WPA Enterprise, WPA2 Enterprise, and RADIUS are invalid options. WPA2 Personal requires only a passphrase, and it is considered more secure than WEP, WPA Personal, and disabled.

10
Authentication

QUESTIONS

Authentication involves verifying the identity of users and computers. This can be implemented at various levels, such as requiring authentication before gaining network or server access. Multifactor authentication requires more than one method of proving identity such as knowing a username and password, having a physical card, and knowing the PIN for that card. Network configuration in production environments will present you with many authentication options. This chapter prepares you to make informed decisions regarding these options.

1. Before accessing computer systems, a government agency requires users to swipe a card through a keyboard-embedded card reader and then provide a PIN. What is this an example of?

   A. Bi-factor authentication

   B. Biometric authentication

   C. Location-based authentication

   D. Multifactor authentication

2. Your traveling users require secure remote access to corporate database servers. What should you configure for them?

   A. Modem

   B. WLAN

   C. VPN

   D. Intranet

3. You are the network administrator for a national marketing firm. Employees have frequent lengthy telephone conference calls with colleagues from around the country. To reduce costs, you have been asked to recommend replacement telephony solutions. Which of the following might you suggest?

   A. Modem

   B. VoIP

   C. Internet text chat

   D. E-mail

4. You are an IT security consultant auditing a network. During your presentation of audit findings, one of your clients asks what can be used to prevent unauthorized LAN access. How do you answer the question?

   A. NAC

   B. Packet filtering firewall

   C. PKI

   D. SSL

5. What type of server authenticates users prior to allowing network access?

 A. File server

 B. Active Directory

 C. RADIUS

 D. Domain controller

6. Which of the following are examples of RADIUS clients? (Choose two.)

 A. VPN client

 B. 802.1x-capable switch

 C. Wireless router

 D. Windows 7 OS

 E. Linux OS

7. Which of the following are true regarding TACACS+? (Choose three.)

 A. It is compatible with TACACS.

 B. It is compatible with RADIUS.

 C. It is a Cisco proprietary protocol.

 D. It can be used as an alternative to RADIUS.

 E. TACACS+ uses TCP.

8. You are the network administrator for a UNIX network. You are planning your network security. A secure protocol must be chosen to authenticate all users logging in. Which is a valid authentication protocol choice?

 A. TCP

 B. Telnet

 C. Kerberos

 D. AES

9. A client asks you to evaluate the feasibility of a Linux client and server operating system environment. The primary concern is having a central database of user and computer accounts capable of secure authentication. What Linux options should you explore?

 A. NFS

 B. SSH

 C. Samba

 D. LDAP

10. You are configuring a Cisco network authentication appliance. During configuration, you are given a list of authentication choices. Which choice provides the best security and reliability?

    A. RADIUS

    B. TACACS

    C. TACACS+

    D. XTACACS

11. A user enters their logon name to gain network access. To which of the following terms would this example apply?

    A. Identification

    B. Authorization

    C. Auditing

    D. Authentication

12. A user enters a logon name and password to gain network access. Choose the best description to which this applies.

    A. Single-factor authentication

    B. Dual-factor authentication

    C. Multifactor authentication

    D. Quasifactor authentication

13. A corporation has invested heavily in the development of a much sought after product. To protect its investment, the company would like to ensure that only specific personnel can enter a research facility. Which of the following is considered the most secure?

    A. Building access card

    B. Voice scan

    C. Fingerprint scanner

    D. Retinal scanner

14. Which of the following is considered three-factor authentication?

    A. Building access card/voice recognition scan

    B. Building access card/username/password

    C. Username/password/smartcard

    D. Username/password/smartcard/PIN

15. To log on to a secured system, a user must enter a username, password, and passcode. The passcode is generated from a tiny handheld device and displayed on a tiny screen. What type of device is this?

    A. Smartcard

    B. PKI certificate

    C. Key fob

    D. VPN

16. Which of the following prevents users from having to specify logon credentials when accessing multiple applications?

    A. Single sign-on

    B. Remember my password

    C. Biometric authentication

    D. Trusted OS

17. Which authentication protocol replaces RADIUS?

    A. TACACS

    B. TACACS+

    C. XTACACS

    D. Diameter

18. Which of the following best describes the CHAP protocol?

    A. PKI certificates must be used on both ends of the connection.

    B. 802.1x equipment forwards authentication requests to a RADIUS server.

    C. Passwords are never sent over the network.

    D. SSL is used to encrypt the session.

19. You are configuring a WPA2 wireless network connection on a company laptop. The company has implemented a PKI. Which WPA2 network authentication method would be the best choice?

    A. MS-CHAP

    B. Local computer certificate

    C. WPA2 PSK

    D. SSO

20. Which of the following examples best illustrates authentication?

    A. A user accesses a shared folder to which they have been granted permission.

    B. A computer successfully identifies itself to a server prior to user logon.

    C. A network contains two network links to a remote office in case one fails.

    D. A network appliance encrypts all network traffic before transmitting it further.

21. A technician is troubleshooting user access to an 802.1x wireless network called CORP. The same computer was previously given an IP address on the 10.17.7.0/24 network, but now for some reason it has an IP address on the 10.16.16.0/24 network. DHCP is functioning correctly on the network. The technician reports the machine was recently reimaged, and the image uses DHCP. What is the most likely cause of the problem?

    A. The workstation has a static IP address on the 10.16.16.0/24 network.

    B. The technician needs to issue the ipconfig /renew command.

    C. The workstation time is incorrect.

    D. The workstation needs to have its PKI certificate reinstalled.

22. What type of security problem would Network Access Control best address?

    A. Dictionary attack

    B. ARP cache poisoning

    C. WEP

    D. SQL injection attack

23. A company intranet consists of various internal web servers each using different authentication stores. What would allow users to use the same username and password for all internal web sites?

    A. NAC

    B. SSO

    C. VPN

    D. Smartcard

24. While capturing network traffic, you notice clear-text credentials being transmitted. After investigating the TCP headers, you notice the destination port is 389. What type of authentication traffic is this?

    A. EAP

    B. EAP-TLS

    C. LDAP

    D. CHAP

25. You are evaluating public cloud storage solutions. Users will be authenticated to a local server on your network that will allow them access to cloud storage. Which identity federation standard could be configured to achieve this?

    A. LDAP

    B. SSL

    C. PKI

    D. SAML *SECURITY ASSERTION MARKUP LANGUAGE*

26. As the network administrator, you are asked to configure a secure VPN solution that uses multifactor authentication. Which of the following solutions should you recommend? (Choose two.)

    A. Key fob and password

    B. Username and password

    C. Fingerprint scanner

    D. Smartcard and password

27. You have been hired by a university to recommend IT solutions. Currently, students and faculty use proximity cards to access buildings on campus after hours, and they have usernames and passwords to log on to lab computers. The university would like to use PKI information unique to each user to allow access to campus buildings and to log on to workstations in labs. What should you recommend?

    A. Hardware token and password

    B. Common access card

    C. PKI private key

    D. PKI certificate authority

28. Android-based smart phones have been distributed to traveling employees for use with Google online services. You deploy the Google Authenticator app to the smart phones to allow user authentication based on the time as well as a unique code generated by the server. What type of authentication is this?

    A. Time-based one-time password

    B. Network time protocol authentication

    C. PAP

    D. CHAP

29. Your router ACL is as follows:

```
ip access-group 55 out
access-list 55 permit host 199.126.129.8
access-list 55 permit host 199.126.129.9
```

A workstation, PC1, with an IP address of 199.126.129.10 attempts to access a remote network and is prevented from doing so. Which statement accurately describes this scenario?

A. PC1 was explicitly denied access to the remote network.

B. PC1 was implicitly denied access to the remote network.

C. PC1 was explicitly granted access to the remote network.

D. PC1 was implicitly granted access to the remote network.

30. Which of the following authentication methods is based on something you do?

A. Handwriting

B. Entering the PIN for a smartcard

C. Retinal scan

D. Presenting a personal identification verification card

31. You are the Microsoft Active Directory administrator for an American government agency. The Active Directory domain in Los Angeles is configured to trust the Active Directory domain in Chicago, which in turn trusts the Active Directory domain in Orlando. Which term correctly describes the trust relationship between Los Angeles and Orlando?

A. Transitive trust

B. Wide area network trust

C. NTLM

D. NTLMv2

QUICK ANSWER KEY

1.	D	9.	D	17.	D	25.	D
2.	C	10.	C	18.	C	26.	A, D
3.	B	11.	A	19.	B	27.	B
4.	A	12.	A	20.	B	28.	A
5.	C	13.	D	21.	D	29.	B
6.	B, C	14.	D	22.	B	30.	A
7.	C, D, E	15.	C	23.	B	31.	A
8.	C	16.	A	24.	C		

IN-DEPTH ANSWERS

1. ☑ **D.** Multifactor authentication involves more than one item to authenticate to a system, such as something you have (a card) and something you know (a PIN).

   ☒ **A, B,** and **C** are incorrect. Bi-factor authentication is not a standard industry term (two-factor is, though). Biometric authentication requires a unique physical characteristic (something you are) such as a fingerprint or retinal scan. Somewhere you are (location-based authentication) uses your physical location or the device you are using as part of the authentication.

2. ☑ **C.** A virtual private network (VPN) creates an encrypted tunnel between a remote access client and a private network over the Internet. This would allow access to corporate database servers.

   ☒ **A, B,** and **D** are incorrect. A modem converts between computer digital signals and analog signaling used by some portions of the Public Switched Telephone Network (PSTN) to allow remote access to a private network, but a modem itself does not provide secure remote access. Wireless local area networks (WLANs) that you configure would have a short range (a few hundred feet) and would not work for traveling users. An intranet is an internal private network that uses Internet technologies such as TCP/IP and HTTP web servers; it is not related to traveling users.

3. ☑ **B.** Voice over Internet Protocol (VoIP) transmits digitized voice over a TCP/IP network such as the Internet. As such, the only cost to both parties is that of your Internet connection.

   ☒ **A, C,** and **D** are incorrect. A modem converts digital signals to analog, and vice versa; it is used to connect computers to the PSTN but is not well suited for multiple-party conference calls. Internet text chat and e-mail are not telephony solutions to conference calls.

4. ☑ **A.** Network Access Control (NAC) technology can be a hardware or software solution that requires user or device authentication prior to gaining network access.

   ☒ **B, C,** and **D** are incorrect. Packet filtering firewalls analyze packet headers to allow or block traffic already on the network; they don't control who (or what) gains access to the network in the first place. Unto itself, Public Key Infrastructure (PKI) does not control network access. PKI certificates can be used to authenticate and secure network traffic and can be used with NAC solutions. Secure Sockets Layer (SSL) encrypts traffic that is already on the network.

5. ☑ **C.** Remote Authentication Dial In User Service (RADIUS) servers are central user or device authentication points on the network. Authentication can occur in many ways, including Extensible Authentication Protocol (EAP) and Challenge Handshake Authentication Protocol (CHAP).

    ☒ **A, B,** and **D** are incorrect. File servers host shared file and folder resources; they rely on users and devices already having network access. Active Directory is a replicated database of network resources in a Microsoft domain environment, and it does not control network access; it partially controls network resource access. Domain controllers partake in Active Directory database replication.

6.   ☑ **B** and **C.** RADIUS clients are network devices such as switches, wireless routers, or VPN concentrators that authenticate connecting devices or users to a RADIUS authentication server to grant network access.

    ☒ **A, D,** and **E** are incorrect. Connecting clients such as Windows and Linux operating systems are not considered RADIUS clients; they are access clients. These access clients initially request network access to a RADIUS client, which in turn then checks against a RADIUS server to determine whether access is allowed.

7.   ☑ **C, D,** and **E.** Terminal Access Controller Access Control System (TACACS+) is a Cisco proprietary network access protocol that uses the reliable TCP transport mechanism. TACACS+ might be used instead of RADIUS because it encrypts the entire packet payload instead of only the password, as well as separating authentication, authorization, and accounting duties.

    ☒ **A** and **B** are incorrect. TACACS and TACACS+ are not compatible despite their namesake. TACACS is an old network access standard that was used primarily in UNIX network environments. RADIUS uses the best-effort UDP transport, whereas TACACS+ uses the more reliable TCP.

8.   ☑ **C.** Kerberos is an authentication protocol used by many vendors, including Microsoft with Active Directory services. Clients and servers must securely prove their identity to each other by way of a central third-party referred to as a key distribution center (KDC).

    ☒ **A, B,** and **D** are incorrect. TCP is a reliable connection-oriented TCP/IP transport protocol, but it does not perform authentication. Telnet transmits data in clear text, so it is not secure. It is used to allow administrative remote access to hosts running a Telnet daemon, usually in UNIX or Linux environments. Advanced Encryption Standard (AES) is a symmetric key encryption algorithm; it encrypts data transmissions, but it does not authenticate users on a network.

9.   ☑ **D.** A central database that can securely authenticate users or computers sounds like a Lightweight Directory Access Protocol (LDAP)–compliant database. LDAP transmissions can be clear text (TCP port 389) or encrypted (TCP port 636), and the LDAP database can also be replicated among servers. Encrypted LDAP transmissions are referred to as Secured LDAP. Microsoft Active Directory Services and Novell eDirectory are LDAP compliant.

☒ **A, B,** and **C** are incorrect. Network File System (NFS) is a UNIX-based file sharing protocol; there is no central database involved. SSH encrypts remote administrative shell access to a host running an SSH daemon, commonly UNIX or Linux. Samba is a Microsoft-compliant file and printer sharing technology in UNIX and Linux environments. Options A, B, and C may authorize access to LDAP authenticated users, but they themselves do not perform authentication.

10. ☑ **C.** TACACS+ is a Cisco proprietary protocol that authenticates connecting users over TCP to a remote authentication server.
☒ **A, B,** and **D** are incorrect. RADIUS uses UDP to authenticate users, and only the password in the packet payload is encrypted, unlike TACACS+. UDP is a connectionless, or best-effort, network transport whereby there are no packet receipt acknowledgments. TACACS+ supersedes them both.

11. ☑ **A.** Specifying a unique attribute of some kind (such as a logon name) is identification.
☒ **B, C,** and **D** are incorrect. Authorization to network resources can happen only after a user has been identified and authenticated. Although user logon can be audited, the logon process itself does not imply auditing. Authentication occurs as a result of correct identification. A logon name uniquely identifies one user from another; all users will be authenticated given they provide their unique credentials.

12. ☑ **A.** The logon name and password combination is known as single-factor authentication (something you know). Higher security environments either will require additional factors (such as a physical card) or will limit access when single-factor authentication is used.
☒ **B, C,** and **D** are incorrect. Dual-factor authentication means using two independent authentication methods such as a token card and username/password combination, whereas multifactor authentication can mean two or more methods of establishing identity. Quasifactor authentication is not an industry-standard term.

13. ☑ **D.** Retinal scanning is considered one of the most secure of biometric authentication methods. Retinal blood vessel patterns are unique to an individual and are extremely difficult to reproduce.
☒ **A, B,** and **C** are incorrect. An impersonator would only need to have the building access card in their possession. Voice and fingerprint scans are not as secure as retinal scanning; voice and fingerprint scans have been defeated by using high-fidelity MP3 players and by using valid lifted fingerprints.

14. ☑ **D.** The username and password combination is considered single-factor authentication. Possessing a smartcard along with knowing the PIN to use the smartcard results in Username/password/smartcard/PIN/Fingerprint scan (or multifactor) authentication.
☒ **A, B,** and **C** are incorrect because they are only two-factor authentication.

15. ☑ **C.** A key fob displays an authentication passcode that a user enters in addition to other data such as a username and password to gain access to a system or network resource.

☒ **A, B,** and **D** are incorrect. Smartcards do not have screens; they have an embedded chip containing personal identification data such as encryption keys or PKI digital certificates. A PKI certificate is not a hardware device; it is a software construct issued to a user or computer used to securely identify that entity and to secure transmissions. PKI information can also be stored on a card, much like a debit chip card. VPN concentrators are the device users connect to.

16. ☑ **A.** Single sign-on (SSO) enables access to many applications while requiring user authentication only once. SSO is often used when users access data from disparate systems to prevent multiple logons.

☒ **B, C,** and **D** are incorrect. Some applications offer to remember your password. This is a security risk and applies only to the application offering this option. Biometric authentication does not prevent the prompting of credentials when accessing applications; it simply provides another means of authentication. Trusted OS refers to an operating system that meets specific security requirements.

17. ☑ **D.** The Diameter protocol adds capabilities to the RADIUS protocol such as using TCP instead of UDP (more reliability) and being more scalable and flexible.

☒ **A, B,** and **C** are incorrect. The TACACS and XTACACS authentication protocols all predate RADIUS. TACACS+ does not succeed RADIUS; it is an alternative to RADIUS.

18. ☑ **C.** CHAP involves a three-way handshake to establish a session after which peers must periodically prove their identity by way of a changing value based on a shared secret. A shared secret (for example, a password) is known by both parties but is never sent over the network.

☒ **A, B,** and **D** are incorrect. PKI does not describe CHAP; it describes other authentication and security methods. An 802.1x infrastructure can use CHAP prior to allowing network access, but it does not have to. SSL is used to encrypt transmissions; CHAP is an authentication protocol.

19. ☑ **B.** A local computer certificate implies a PKI. A certificate is issued to users or computers and uniquely identifies those entities. It contains public and private key pairs used to secure network traffic and can be used with WPA2 wireless networks.

☒ **A, C,** and **D** are incorrect. MS-CHAP is a valid WPA2 network authentication method, but it is not a better choice than PKI certificate authentication. WPA2 PSK is not as secure an authentication method as PKI. SSO is not a configuration setting for WPA2 network authentication.

20. ☑ **B.** Authentication means proving your identity (user or computer). This can be done via username/password, smartcard, and PIN, or in this case, the computer might have a PKI certificate installed that gets validated against a server with a related PKI certificate.

☒ **A**, **C**, and **D** are incorrect. A user legitimately accessing a network resource describes authorization. Redundant network links relate to availability, not authentication. The question states all network traffic is encrypted; authentication is not implied here.

21. ☑ **D.** A computer PKI certificate can grant access to an 802.1x-configured wireless network. Without the certificate, the machine is either denied network access or, in this case, placed on a guest VLAN.

    ☒ **A**, **B**, and **C** are incorrect. A static IP address does not apply since the question states DHCP is in use. DHCP should have received a correct IP address on first boot after the image was applied, so ipconfig /renew should not be necessary. Unsynchronized clocks would not put the machine on a different subnet.

22. ☑ **B.** ARP cache poisoning involves an attacker modifying host ARP caches with the attacker's MAC address associated with a valid host IP, thus forcing network traffic to the attacker station. This can be difficult to prevent, so the key lies in controlling access to the network in the first place.

    ☒ **A**, **C**, and **D** are incorrect. Some ways to mitigate dictionary attacks are to use strong passwords and enable account lockout thresholds. WEP is a deprecated wireless encryption standard; NAC does not address WEP problems. The best way to address SQL injection attacks is for the developer to carefully validate user-submitted queries.

23. ☑ **B.** SSO enables users to use only a single username and password to access multiple network resources even if those network resources use different authentication sources.

    ☒ **A**, **C**, and **D** are incorrect. NAC determines which users or computers are given access to a network. A VPN would not enable the use of one set of credentials for intranet web servers. Since the question states the use of a username and password, smartcards are not applicable.

24. ☑ **C.** LDAP is a standard for accessing a network directory (database), in this case, for authentication purposes. LDAP uses TCP port 389 for clear-text transmissions and TCP port 636 for encrypted transmissions.

    ☒ **A**, **B**, and **D** are incorrect. EAP is an authentication framework with many specific authentication methods, but it is not tied to LDAP. EAP-TLS is a mechanism using Transport Layer Security (TLS) and PKI certificates for authentication. Certificates containing encryption and decryption keys are required on the server and client. CHAP is an authentication mechanism whereby the shared secret (often a password) is never sent across the network.

25. ☑ **D.** Security Assertion Markup Language (SAML) is an XML standard that defines how authentication and authorization data can be transmitted in a federated identity environment.

    ☒ **A**, **B**, and **C** are incorrect. Lightweight Directory Access Protocol (LDAP) is a protocol defining how to access a replicated network database. Secure Sockets Layer (SSL) provides a method to secure application-specific network transmissions. Public Key Infrastructure (PKI) is a hierarchy of digital security certificates that can be used with computing devices to provide data confidentiality, authentication, and integrity services.

26. ☑ **A** and **D.** Key fobs are physical devices with a small display showing a number that is synchronized with a server-side component. This number changes frequently and is used in conjunction with other authentication factors, such as a password, to ensure additional security. Smartcards contain circuitry used for the secure identification of a user in conjunction with a PIN. Both of these constitute multifactor authentication.

☒ **B** and **C** are incorrect. Username/password is considered single-factor authentication (something you know). Fingerprint scans are also considered single-factor authentication (something you are).

27. ☑ **B.** A common access card is used to gain access to more than one type of secured resource.

☒ **A, C,** and **D** are incorrect. Hardware tokens are physical devices with a small display showing a number that is synchronized with a server-side component. This number changes frequently and is used in conjunction with other authentication factors, such as a password, to ensure additional security. PKI private keys are unique to the user or computer to which they are issued. Private keys can be used to digitally sign data and to decrypt data. A PKI certificate authority is at the top of the PKI hierarchy and issues, renews, and revokes PKI certificates in that hierarchy.

28. ☑ **A.** Time-based one-time passwords (TOTP) use the current system time and a shared secret known by both the client and the server as input to a hashing algorithm. The shared secret could be a user password. The OTP is useful for only a short period of time and is recalculated often, unlike HMAC-based One Time Passwords (HOTP), which are longer lived authentication passwords.

☒ **B, C,** and **D** are incorrect. Network Time Protocol (NTP) is used to keep time in sync between computing devices; it is not used for authentication. Password Authentication Protocol (PAP) transmits credentials in clear text. Challenge Handshake Authentication Protocol (CHAP) is a three-phase authentication method that involves the server sending a challenge to the client.

29. ☑ **B.** Implicit denial means there is no specific denial to a resource; it is implied only. Because other hosts are specifically allowed access, PC1 is implicitly denied.

☒ **A, C,** and **D** are incorrect. Explicit denials list the specific object (PC1 in this case) that is to be denied access to a resource. PC1 was not granted access to anything.

30. ☑ **A.** Handwriting is unique to the person doing it (something you do).

☒ **B, C,** and **D** are incorrect. Smartcard authentication relates to something you have and something you know (the PIN). Retinal scans are considered something you are. Personal identification verification cards are used to control user access to resources such as buildings and computer systems.

31. ☑ **A.** Transitive trusts are created where one party trusts a remote party through a middle party.

☒ **B, C,** and **D** are incorrect. There is no such thing as a wide area network trust. NTLM and NTLMv2 are deprecated methods of providing confidentiality, integrity, and authentication.

11

Access Control

QUESTIONS

Access control allows a computer system to secure access to resources including the network itself, servers, shared folders, and printers, just to name a few. IT administrators must implement strong password policies, network access rules, and strong file and folder permissions in accordance with established security policies.

1. A network administrator must grant the appropriate network permissions to a new employee. Which of the following is the best strategy?

    A. Give the new employee user account the necessary rights and permissions.

    B. Add the new employee user account to a group. Ensure the group has the necessary rights and permissions.

    C. Give the new employee administrative rights to the network.

    D. Ask the new employee what network rights they would like.

2. In securing your network, you enforce complex user passwords. Users express concern about forgetting their passwords. What should you configure to allay those concerns?

    A. Password expiration

    B. Periodic password change

    C. Password hints

    D. Maximum password length

3. To quickly give a contractor network access, a network administrator adds the contractor account to the Windows Administrators group. Which security principle does this violate?

    A. Separation of duties

    B. Least privilege

    C. Job rotation

    D. Account lockout

4. James is the branch network administrator for ABC, Inc. Recently the company headquarters requested a network security audit, so James performed an audit himself using freely available Linux tools. What is the problem with James' actions?

    A. ABC, Inc., should have sent a network administrator from headquarters to perform the audit.

    B. The chief security officer should have conducted the audit.

    C. Freely available tools are not reliable and should not have been used.

    D. A third party should have been hired to conduct the audit.

5. A secure computing environment labels data with various security classifications. Authenticated users must have clearance to read this classified data. What type of access control model is this?

    A. Mandatory access control

    B. Discretionary access control

    C. Role-based access control

    D. Time-of-day access control

6. To ease giving access to network resources for employees, you decide there must be an easier way than granting users individual access to files, printers, computers, and applications. What security model should you consider using?

    A. Mandatory access control

    B. Discretionary access control

    C. Role-based access control

    D. Time-of-day access control

7. Linda creates a folder called Budget Projections in her home account and shares it with colleagues in her department. Which of the following best describes this type of access control system?

    A. Mandatory access control

    B. Discretionary access control

    C. Role-based access control

    D. Time-of-day access control

8. You require that users not be logged on to the network after 6 P.M. while you analyze network traffic during nonbusiness hours. What should you do?

    A. Unplug their stations from the network.

    B. Tell users to press CTRL-ALT-DEL to lock their stations.

    C. Configure time-of-day restrictions to ensure nobody can be logged in after 6 P.M.

    D. Disable user accounts at 6 P.M.

9. One of your users, Matthias, is taking a three-month sabbatical because of a medical condition, after which he will return to work. What should you do with Matthias' user account?

    A. Delete the account and re-create it when he returns.

    B. Disable the account and enable it when he returns.

    C. Export his account properties to a text file for later import and then delete it.

    D. Ensure you have a backup of his account details and delete his account.

10. During an IT security meeting, the topic of account lockout surfaces. When you suggest all user accounts be locked for 30 minutes after three incorrect logon attempts, your colleague Phil states this is a serious problem when applied to administrative accounts. What types of issues might Phil be referring to?

    A. Dictionary attacks could break into administrative accounts.

    B. Administrative accounts are much sought after by attackers.

    C. Administrative accounts are placed into administrative groups.

    D. DoS attacks could render administrative accounts unusable.

11. Your VPN appliance is configured to disallow user authentication unless the user or group is listed as allowed. Regarding blocked users, what best describes this configuration?

    A. Implicit allow

    B. Implicit deny

    C. Explicit allow

    D. Explicit deny

12. Margaret is the head of Human Resources for Emrom, Inc. An employee does not want to use his annual vacation allotment, but Margaret insists it is mandatory. What IT benefit is derived from mandatory vacations?

    A. Irregularities in job duties can be noticed when another employee fills that role.

    B. Users feel recharged after time off.

    C. Emrom, Inc., will not be guilty of labor violations.

    D. There is less security risk when fewer users are on the network.

13. What type of attack is mitigated by strong, complex passwords?

    A. DoS

    B. Dictionary

    C. Brute force

    D. DNS poisoning

14. A government contract requires your computers to adhere to mandatory access control methods and multilevel security. What should you do to remain compliant with this contract?

    A. Patch your current operating system.

    B. Purchase new network hardware.

    C. Use a trusted OS.

    D. Purchase network encryption devices.

15. Which term is best defined as an object's list of users, groups, processes, and their permissions?

    A. ACE

    B. ACL

    C. Active Directory

    D. Access log

16. Users complain that they must remember passwords for a multitude of user accounts to access software required for their jobs. How can this be solved?

    A. SSO

    B. ACL

    C. PKI

    D. Password complexity

17. What security model uses data classifications and security clearances?

    A. RBAC

    B. DAC

    C. PKI

    D. MAC   *MANDATORY ACCESS CONTROL*

18. A Windows server has an inbound firewall rule allowing inbound RDP as shown in Figure 11-1. Which term best describes this particular firewall rule?

    A. Explicit allow

    B. Explicit deny

    C. Implicit allow

    D. Implicit deny

FIGURE 11-1   Windows firewall rules

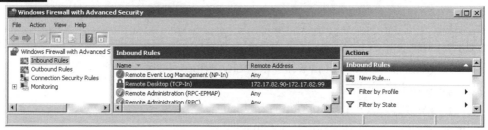

19. The permissions for a Windows folder are shown in Figure 11-2. Permission inheritance has been disabled. User RLachance attempts to access the folder Jones_Vs_Cowell. What is the result?

    A. RLachance is denied access because of explicit denial.

    B. RLachance is allowed access because of being in the Everyone group.

    C. RLachance is denied access because of implicit denial.

    D. RLachance is allowed access because of implicit allowal.

FIGURE 11-2

File system permissions for the Jones_Vs_Cowell folder

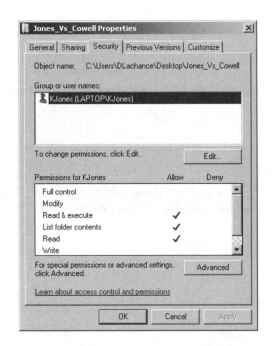

20. A Microsoft SQL database administrator creates a service account for the SQL server agent with the settings shown in Figure 11-3. What security problem exists with this configuration?

    A. The username does not follow a naming convention.

    B. The password is not long enough.

    C. The password never expires option is enabled.

    D. The account is disabled option is not enabled.

FIGURE 11-3

Creating a new user account

21. A network router has the following ACL:

```
ip access group 101 in
access-list 101 permit tcp any any eq 20
access-list 101 permit tcp any any eq 21
access-list 101 permit tcp any any eq 3389
```

Choose the correct description of the ACL configuration.

A. SMTP, SNMP, and RDP are explicitly allowed; all else is implicitly denied.

B. SMTP, SNMP, and RDP are implicitly allowed; all else is explicitly denied.

C. FTP and RDP are explicitly allowed; all else is implicitly denied.

D. FTP and RDP are implicitly allowed; all else is explicitly denied.

22. Which of the following is an example of physical access control?

A. Encrypting the USB flash drive

B. Disabling USB ports on a computer

C. Using cable locks to secure laptops

D. Limiting who can back up sensitive data

23. A technician notices unauthorized computers accessing the local area network. What solution should the technician consider?

A. Stronger passwords

B. Network encryption

C. VPN

D. NAC

24. A network administrator, Justin, must grant various departments read access to the Corp_ Policies folder and grant other departments read and write access to the Current_Projects folder. What strategy should Justin employ?

    A. Add all departmental users to the shared folder ACLs with the appropriate permissions.

    B. Create one group, add members, and add the group to the folder ACLs with the appropriate permissions.

    C. Create a Users group and an Administrators group with the correct members. Add the groups to the folder ACLs with the appropriate permissions.

    D. Create a group for each department and add members to the groups. Add the groups to the folder ACLs with the appropriate permissions.

25. What provides secure access to corporate data in accordance with management policies?

    A. SSL

    B. Technical controls

    C. Integrity

    D. Administrative controls

26. Which of the following are considered administrative controls? (Choose two.)

    A. Personnel hiring policy

    B. VPN policy

    C. Disk encryption policy

    D. Separation of duties

27. What is the difference between security clearances and classification labels? (Choose two.)

    A. There is no difference.

    B. Classification labels identify data sensitivity.

    C. Security clearances identify data sensitivity.

    D. Security clearances are compared with classification labels.

28. What security problem exists with the password policy shown in Figure 11-4?

    A. The maximum password age is too low.

    B. The minimum password age is too low.

    C. The minimum password length is too low.

    D. Passwords should be stored using reversible encryption.

FIGURE 11-4   Password policy settings

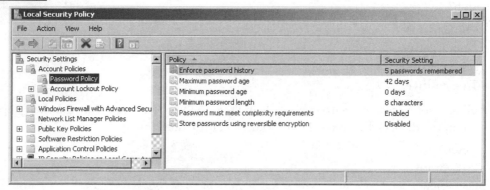

29. Using Figure 11-5, match the security terms on the left with the descriptions listed on the right.

FIGURE 11-5

Security terms and definitions

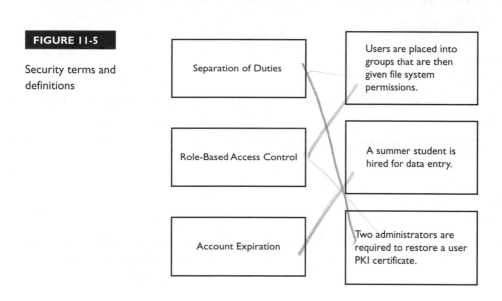

30. Complex passwords are considered which type of security control?

A. Management

B. Technical

C. Physical

D. Operational

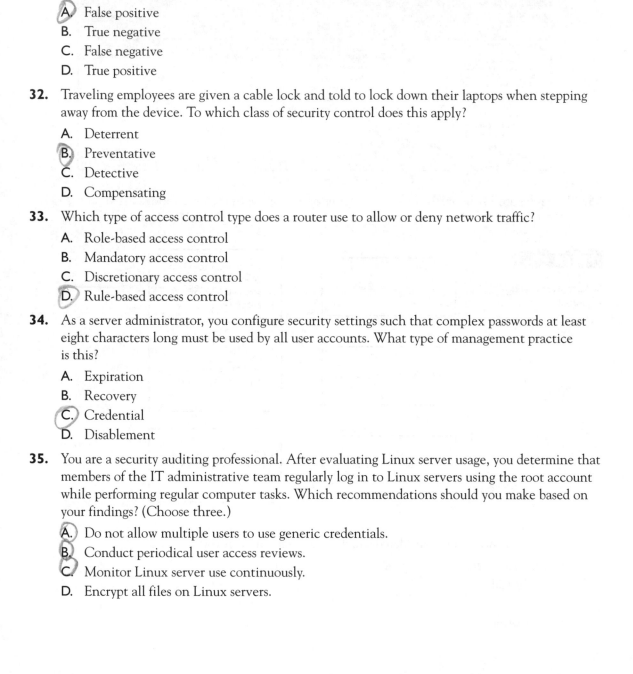

31. A legitimate e-mail message ends up being flagged as spam. Which term best describes this situation?

A. False positive

B. True negative

C. False negative

D. True positive

32. Traveling employees are given a cable lock and told to lock down their laptops when stepping away from the device. To which class of security control does this apply?

A. Deterrent

B. Preventative

C. Detective

D. Compensating

33. Which type of access control type does a router use to allow or deny network traffic?

A. Role-based access control

B. Mandatory access control

C. Discretionary access control

D. Rule-based access control

34. As a server administrator, you configure security settings such that complex passwords at least eight characters long must be used by all user accounts. What type of management practice is this?

A. Expiration

B. Recovery

C. Credential

D. Disablement

35. You are a security auditing professional. After evaluating Linux server usage, you determine that members of the IT administrative team regularly log in to Linux servers using the root account while performing regular computer tasks. Which recommendations should you make based on your findings? (Choose three.)

A. Do not allow multiple users to use generic credentials.

B. Conduct periodical user access reviews.

C. Monitor Linux server use continuously.

D. Encrypt all files on Linux servers.

QUICK ANSWER KEY

1. B	**10.** D	**19.** C	**28.** B
2. C	**11.** B	**20.** C	**29.** See Figure 11-6.
3. B	**12.** A	**21.** C	**30.** B
4. D	**13.** B	**22.** C	**31.** A
5. A	**14.** C	**23.** D	**32.** B
6. C	**15.** B	**24.** D	**33.** D
7. B	**16.** A	**25.** B	**34.** C
8. C	**17.** D	**26.** A, D	**35.** A, B, C
9. B	**18.** A	**27.** B, D	

FIGURE 11-6

Security terms and definitions—the answer

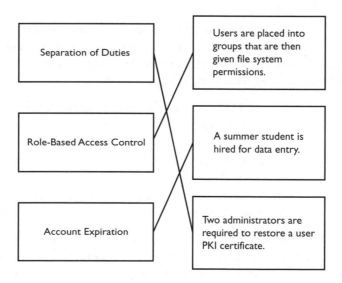

IN-DEPTH ANSWERS

1. ☑ **B.** The best strategy for assigning rights and permissions is to add users to groups. Working with rights and permissions for individual users becomes unmanageable beyond a small number of users. New employees can then simply be added to the appropriate group to acquire the needed access to network resources.

   ☒ **A, C,** and **D** are incorrect. Granting individual user rights and permissions becomes difficult to manage as the number of users grows. Granting new employees administrative rights to the network is a violation of all network security best practices—only grant the rights needed. Users may not know what rights they need, or they may ask for rights they do not need to perform their job.

2. ☑ **C.** Password hints remind users what their password is without revealing the actual password.

   ☒ **A, B,** and **D** are incorrect. Password expiration, periodic password change, and password lengths should not be configured differently even if users have difficulty remembering passwords.

3. ☑ **B.** The least privilege principle states users should be given only the rights needed to perform the duties and nothing more. Adding a contractor to the Administrators group grants too much privilege to the contractor.

   ☒ **A, C,** and **D** are incorrect. Separation of duties requires multiple people to perform a specific job. Job rotation is a strategy that exposes employees to various facets of a business and has nothing to do with security. Account lockout relates to security but is not violated by giving a user too many permissions.

4. ☑ **D.** No one person should have control of implementing, maintaining, and auditing an IT infrastructure—this violates the separation of duties principle and presents a conflict of interest.

   ☒ **A, B,** and **C** are incorrect. You should not have company employees conducting an audit. Many freely available tools are robust and reliable.

5. ☑ **A.** Mandatory access control (MAC) models can use security labels to classify data. These labels are then compared to a user's sensitivity level to determine whether access is allowed.

   ☒ **B, C,** and **D** are incorrect. Discretionary access control (DAC) models leave control of security to the data owner. Permissions are set at the individual object level as opposed to using data classification labels. Role-based access control places users in roles where those roles have been granted groups of permissions to perform a job function; roles were not mentioned in the question. Dates or times of allowed access were not mentioned in the question.

6. ☑ **C.** Role-based access control (RBAC) would allow you to group access privileges for files, printers, computers, and applications into a single entity (a role). Users needing these rights are then simply added as occupants of the appropriate role.

☒ **A, B,** and **D** are incorrect. Mandatory access control grants access based on security clearances given to users. Discretionary access control puts the control of giving access in the hands of the data owner (for example, a file owner can give permissions to others to that file). Time-of-day controls access based on time of day and are therefore incorrect in this case.

7. ☑ **B.** Discretionary access control puts the ability to grant other people access in the hands of data owners, in this case, Linda.

☒ **A, C,** and **D** are incorrect. Mandatory access control is security-policy driven, not user-driven. A role that groups the needed access rights is not required for access to a single folder. Linda has given rights to the folder, and those rights are in effect at any time of the day.

8. ☑ **C.** Network operating systems (NOSs) have the ability to control when users can and cannot log on, as well as ending existing logon sessions based on time of day.

☒ **A, B,** and **D** are incorrect. Unplugging stations involves physically visiting each station; there are better ways. Locking a workstation does not log the user out. Disabling user accounts at 6 P.M. is an extreme solution and may not affect existing logon sessions immediately (for example, a Windows Active Directory Kerberos ticket would have to first expire).

9. ☑ **B.** Disabling his account will prevent anyone from logging on with the account but will preserve all of the account settings. When he returns, simply enable the account.

☒ **A, C,** and **D** are incorrect. A user account should never be deleted when that user will be returning; instead, it should simply be disabled.

10. ☑ **D.** Denial-of-service (DoS) attacks render a legitimate network service unusable. Attempting three incorrect logon attempts every half hour to administrative accounts would effectively keep those accounts locked, thus preventing legitimate use of those accounts.

☒ **A, B,** and **C** are incorrect. Although these are all true, they are not issues resulting from account lockout settings.

11. ☑ **B.** Implicit denial means all are denied unless specifically allowed; there are no specific listings of users or computers that are denied.

☒ **A, C,** and **D** are incorrect. Implicit allowance implies all are allowed unless specifically denied. The questions asks about blocked users, not allowed users. The configuration does not specify who (or what) is blocked, so explicit deny is not applicable here.

12. ☑ **A.** It is easy for an employee to spot inconsistencies or irregularities when someone is on vacation.

☒ **B, C,** and **D** are incorrect. Users feeling recharged and adherence to labor regulations are important, but they are not the motivating factor in IT environments. Fewer users on the network does not imply less security risk.

13. ☑ **B.** Stronger passwords make it more difficult for dictionary password attacks to succeed. A stronger password is a minimum of eight characters, where those characters might be a combination of uppercase letters, lowercase letters, symbols, and numerals.

    ☒ **A**, **C**, and **D** are incorrect. They are not directly impeded by stronger passwords, like dictionary attacks are.

14. ☑ **C.** A trusted OS uses a secured OS kernel that supports mandatory access control (MAC), which applies security centrally to adhere with security policies. This type of OS is considered too strict for general use and is applicable in high-security environments.

    ☒ **A**, **B**, and **D** are incorrect. The question does not state details about the operating system being patched, so patching in itself is not the best answer. Purchasing new network equipment refers to acquiring or replacing network hardware, not computer hardware.

15. ☑ **B.** Access control lists (ACLs) detail which users, groups, or processes have permissions to an object, such as a file or folder.

    ☒ **A**, **C**, and **D** are incorrect. An individual entry in an ACL is known as an access control entry (ACE). Active Directory is Microsoft's replicated authentication database. Users and groups from Active Directory can appear in ACLs, but permissions themselves are not stored here; they are stored with the file system object. An access log simply lists request details (date, time, user, or computer) for a network resource such as a file.

16. ☑ **A.** Single sign-on (SSO) allows a user to authenticate once to multiple resources that would otherwise require separate logins.

    ☒ **B**, **C**, and **D** are incorrect. An ACL controls who and what has access to a particular resource. Although a public key infrastructure (PKI) can be used to authenticate instead of or in addition to usernames and passwords, PKI does not eliminate multiple password prompts; that is what SSO is for. Password complexity is likely to increase the burden that users are complaining about.

17. ☑ **D.** MAC is a security model that classifies data according to sensitivity that enables access to only those with proper clearance.

    ☒ **A**, **B**, and **C** are incorrect. RBAC assigns rights and permissions to roles. People occupying the role therefore acquire the role's access to resources. DAC allows the owner of a resource (for example, a file) to determine who else has access. Public key infrastructure (PKI) is a system of digital certificates used for authentication, data encryption, and digital signatures.

18. ☑ **A.** Computers with an IP address in the range of 172.17.82.90–172.17.82.99 are specifically for allowing Remote Desktop access; this is explicit allowance.

    ☒ **B**, **C**, and **D** are incorrect. Explicit denial would mean the firewall rule would block, not allow, Remote Desktop access. Implicit allow and implicit deny do not apply since there is a specific direct firewall rule allowing access.

19. ☑ **C.** Because permission inheritance is disabled, the permissions listed are the only ones in effect. User RLachance is not listed with any privileges and is therefore blocked from the Jones_Vs_Cowell folder because of implicit denial.

☒ **A, B,** and **D** are incorrect. RLachance is not explicitly denied any permission; RLachance is not even in the ACL. The Everyone group is not in the ACL. RLachance will not have any access to the Jones_Vs_Cowell folder because he is not listed; this is an implicit denial.

20. ☑ **C.** Administrators often enable the password never expires option on service accounts so that they are exempt from regular user password policies that force periodic password change. This presents a security problem, since the service account password remains the same indefinitely. Changing the password on a service account means changing the password for each service using that account. Windows Server 2008 R2 has a Managed Accounts option that resets service account passwords automatically.

☒ **A, B,** and **D** are incorrect. We do not know whether a naming convention is being followed. The password is eight characters long, the minimum accepted length. If the account is disabled, it cannot be used.

21. ☑ **C.** File Transfer Protocol (FTP) uses TCP ports 20 and 21. Remote Desktop Protocol (RDP) uses TCP port 3398. The ACL on the router explicitly allows this traffic in; all other traffic is implicitly denied.

☒ **A, B,** and **D** are incorrect. Simple Mail Transfer Protocol (SMTP) uses TCP port 25, Simple Network Management Protocol (SNMP) uses UDP port 161, and RDP uses TCP port 3389. FTP and RDP are not implicitly allowed; they are explicitly allowed.

22. ☑ **C.** Locking laptops down with a cable lock physically prevents the theft of laptops.

☒ **A, B,** and **D** are all incorrect because they are examples of software access control, not physical access control.

23. ☑ **D.** Network Access Control (NAC) is software or a network appliance that can verify that connecting computers are allowed to access the network. This can be done by checking PKI certificates, checking that antivirus software is installed and updated, and so on.

☒ **A, B,** and **C** are incorrect. Stronger passwords and network encryption protect user accounts and data transmissions, but they are applicable once a computer has gained access to the network, not before. VPNs do not apply to a local area network. Virtual private networks (VPNs) secure a data channel to a private network over an untrusted network.

24. ☑ **D.** Each department should have its own group with department employees as members. This facilitates granting group members access to the appropriate resources.

☒ **A, B,** and **C** are incorrect. Managing individual user permissions becomes difficult as the network grows. A single group will not work here since different sets of users require different sets of permissions to different shared folders. A users group and an administrators group will not suffice; each department should have its own group.

25. ☑ **B.** Technical controls include any hardware or software solution utilizing access control in adherence with established security policies.

    ☒ **A, C,** and **D** are incorrect. Secure Sockets Layer (SSL) provides application-specific transmission encryption to ensure data confidentiality. Integrity assures data is authentic and has not been tampered with. Administrative controls provide a foundation for how a business should be run.

26. ☑ **A** and **D.** Hiring correct personnel and ensuring no one employee has control of a business transaction (separation of duties) are part of creating a business management foundation; these are examples of administrative controls.

    ☒ **B** and **C** are incorrect. VPN and disk encryption policies deal with specific technologies and thus are considered technical controls.

27. ☑ **B** and **D.** Data sensitivity is referred to with classification labels. Security clearances are compared against these labels to determine whether access is granted.

    ☒ **A** and **C** are incorrect. There is a difference between the security clearances and classification labels. Security clearances do not identify data sensitivity; classification labeling does.

28. ☑ **B.** The minimum password age must be increased; otherwise, when a forced password change occurs every 42 days, users can immediately cycle through five passwords to eventually set their password to an old, easy-to-remember password.

    ☒ **A, C,** and **D** are incorrect. Increasing the maximum password age could be considered a security problem. Eight-character passwords are accepted throughout the industry as acceptable. Storing passwords using reversible encryption is a backward-compatible option that stores passwords in what is comparable to plain text.

29. See Figure 11-7. Requiring two administrators to restore a single user's PKI certificate constitutes separation of duties. Role-based access control can be implemented by adding users to groups and then assigning those groups permissions. Summer students require their user accounts for a limited time, so an account expiration date should be set on their accounts.

30. ☑ **B.** Technical security controls are put in place to protect computing resources such as files, web sites, databases, and so on. Passwords prevent everybody from accessing network resources.

    ☒ **A, C,** and **D** are incorrect. Management controls are written policies that determine acceptable activities and how they should be conducted. Physical controls such as door locks and fences protect organizational assets from threats. Operational controls such as data backups ensure business continuity.

31. ☑ **A.** A false positive is triggered when an occurrence is incorrectly determined to be malicious.

    ☒ **B, C,** and **D** are incorrect. A true negative means an occurrence is considered normal activity and not malicious. False negatives are problems that do not get detected, such as zero-day exploits. True positive means an occurrence that is malicious has been detected.

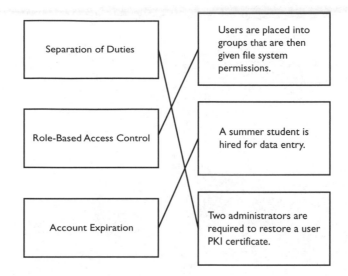

FIGURE 11-7

Security terms and definitions—the answer

32. ☑ **B.** Preventative security controls prevent security breaches, such as the theft as a laptop.

☒ **A, C,** and **D** are incorrect. Deterrent controls discourage malicious or illegal actions but do not necessarily prevent them from happening. Detective controls recognize malicious activity and generate a notification. Compensating controls are used when other specific security requirements cannot be met but are mitigated through a different type of control.

33. ☑ **D.** Routers use rules to determine whether to allow or deny network traffic.

☒ **A, B,** and **C** are incorrect. Role-based access control assigns rights to roles or groups. Occupants of the role or group inherits those rights. Mandatory access control uses classification labels for resources to determine resource access. Discretionary access control uses an access control list (ACL) listing who has which specific permissions to a resource.

34. ☑ **C.** The management of usernames, passwords, security certificates and so on, is referred to as credential management.

☒ **A, B,** and **D** are incorrect. Expiry can be set on user accounts for temporary accounts. Recovery entails setting the state of a user account or computer system to a previous functional state. Disabling user accounts is appropriate for users who are on leave.

35. ☑ **A, B,** and **C.** Each member of the IT team should use their own user account when performing regular computer tasks. Periodically reviewing user access and server usage will ensure security controls are effective for the Linux servers.

☒ **D** is incorrect. Encrypting files increases file security, but it is not related to the security audit findings stated in the question.

12

Introduction to Cryptography

'S

... used in various forms for thousands of years. It is the act of scrambling
... such that only intended people can read it. Modern cryptography feeds plain text through
encryption algorithms resulting in cipher text. Symmetric encryption uses a single key for encryption
and decryption, whereas asymmetric uses mathematically related keys to secure data. This chapter
explores the difference between the most common encryption standards.

1. A network technician notices TCP port 80 traffic when users authenticate to their mail server.
    What should the technician configure to protect the confidentiality of these transmissions?

    A. MD5

    B. SHA-256

    C. SHA-512

    D. HTTPS

2. Which of the following allows secured remote access to a UNIX host?

    A. SSH   SECURE SHELL   PORT 22

    B. SSL

    C. SSO

    D. SHA

3. An IT manager asks you to recommend a LAN encryption solution. The solution must
    support current and future software that does not have encryption of its own. What should
    you recommend?

    A. SSL

    B. SSH

    C. IPSec

    D. VPN

4. Which protocol supersedes SSL?

    A. TLS

    B. SSO

    C. TKIP

    D. VPN

5. Which TCP port would a firewall administrator allow so that users can access SSL-enabled web sites?

- A. 443
- B. 80
- C. 3389
- D. 69

6. Data integrity is provided by which of the following?

- A. 3DES
- B. RC4
- C. AES
- D. MD5   MESSAGE   DIGEST 5

7. You are configuring a network encryption device and must account for other devices that may not support newer and stronger algorithms. Which of the following lists encryption standards from weakest to strongest?

- A. DES, 3DES, RSA   DIGITAL ENCRYPTION, 3 DIG, RIVEST, SHAMIR ADLEMAN
- B. 3DES, DES, AES
- C. RSA, DES, Blowfish
- D. RSA, 3DES, DES

8. Which of the following uses two mathematically related keys to secure data transmissions?

- A. AES
- B. RSA
- C. 3DES
- D. Blowfish

9. Your company has implemented a PKI. You would like to encrypt e-mail messages you send to another employee, Amy. What do you require to encrypt messages to Amy?

- A. Amy's private key
- B. Amy's public key
- C. Your private key
- D. Your public key

10. You decide that your LAN computers will use asymmetric encryption with IPSec to secure LAN traffic. While evaluating how this can be done, you are presented with an array of encryption choices. Select the correct classification of cryptography standards.

A. Asymmetric
RSA
AES

Symmetric
DES
3DES

B. Symmetric
3DES
DES

Asymmetric
Blowfish
RSA

C. Symmetric
3DES
DES

Asymmetric
RC4
RSA

D. Symmetric
AES
3DES

Asymmetric
RSA

11. Data is provided confidentially by which of the following?

A. MD5
B. Disk encryption
C. E-mail digital signatures
D. SHA

12. Which symmetric block cipher supersedes Blowfish?

A. TwoFish
B. FourFish
C. RSA
D. PKI

13. A user connects to a secured online banking web site. Which of the following statements is incorrect?

  A. The workstation public key is used to encrypt data transmitted to the web server. The web server private key performs the decryption.

  B. The workstation session key is encrypted with the server public key and transmitted to the web server. The web server private key performs the decryption.

  C. The workstation-generated session key is used to encrypt data sent to the web server.

  D. The workstation-generated session key is used to decrypt data received by the web server.

14. Which term describes the process of concealing messages within a file?

  A. Trojan

  B. Steganography

  C. Encryption

  D. Digital signature

15. Which term best describes the assurance that a message is authentic and neither party can dispute its transmission or receipt?

  A. Digital signature

  B. Encryption

  C. PKI

  D. Nonrepudiation   *CANNOT DENY*

16. You are a developer at a software development firm. Your latest software build must be made available on the corporate web site. Internet users require a method of ensuring they have downloaded an authentic version of the software. What should you do?

  A. Generate a file hash for the download file and make it available on the web site.

  B. Make sure Internet users have antivirus software installed.

  C. Configure the web site to use TLS.

  D. Make sure the web server has antivirus software installed.

17. Which cryptographic approach uses points on a curve to define public and private key pairs?

  A. RSA

  B. DES

  C. ECC   *ELIPTIC CURVE CRYPTOGRAPHY*

  D. PKI

18. Your company currently uses an FTP server, and you have been asked to make FTP traffic secure using SSL. What should you configure?
    - A. FTPS *FILE XFER PROTOCOL SECURE*
    - B. SFTP
    - C. IPSec
    - D. TLS

19. On which protocol is SCP built?
    - A. FTP *SECURE COPY*
    - B. SSL
    - C. SSH
    - D. ICMP

20. Which of the following are true regarding ciphers? (Choose two.)
    - A. Block ciphers analyze data patterns and block malicious data from being encrypted.
    - B. Stream ciphers encrypt data one byte at a time.
    - C. Block ciphers encrypt chunks of data.
    - D. Stream ciphers encrypt streaming media traffic.

21. Which of the following are block ciphers? (Choose two.)
    - A. DES *DIGITAL ENCRYPTION STANDARD*
    - B. RSA
    - C. RC4
    - D. AES *ADVANCED ENCRYPTION STANDARD*

22. What type of encryption has been configured in Figure 12-1?
    - A. Asymmetric
    - B. Symmetric
    - C. SSL
    - D. RSA

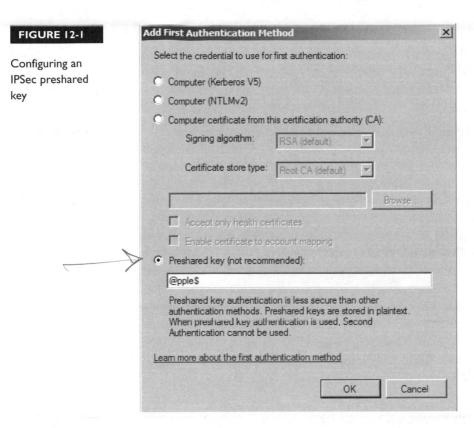

FIGURE 12-1

Configuring an
IPSec preshared
key

23. Which of the following are message digest algorithms? (Choose two.)

    A. 3DES

    B. RIPEMD   *RACE INTERITY PRIMITIVE EVALUATION MESSAGE DIGEST*

    C. Blowfish

    D. HMAC   *HASH BASED MESSAGE AUTHENTICATION CODE*

24. A military institution requires the utmost in security for transmitting messages during wartime. What provides the best security?

    A. AES

    B. 3DES

    C. One-time pad

    D. RSA

25. When hardening a VPN, what should you consider? (Choose two.)

    A. Enabling PAP

    B. Disabling PAP *PASSWORD AUTHENTICATION PROTOCOL*

    C. Disabling EAP-TLS

    D. Enabling EAP-TLS *EXTENSIBLE AUTHENTICATION PROTOCOL — TRANSPORT LAYER SECURITY*

26. Encrypting and digitally signing e-mail with public and private keys can be done with which technology?

    A. 3DES

    B. DES

    C. Blowfish

    D. PGP *PRETTY GOOD PRIVACY*

27. Which of the following is considered the least secure?

    A. MS-CHAP v2

    B. NTLM v2

    C. EAP-TLS

    D. PAP

28. A user digitally signs a sent e-mail message. What security principle does this apply to?

    A. Least privilege

    B. Integrity

    C. Confidentiality

    D. Authorization

29. Which of the following are true regarding user private keys? (Choose two.)

    A. It is used to encrypt sent messages.

    B. It is used to decrypt received messages.

    C. It is used to create digital signatures.

    D. It is used to verify digital signatures.

30. You are the IT directory for a company with military contracts. An employee, Sandra, leaves the company, and her user account is removed. A few weeks later somebody requires access to Sandra's old files but is denied access. After investigating the issue, you determine that Sandra's files are encrypted with a key generated from a passphrase. What type of encryption is this?

    A. WEP

    B. Asymmetric

    C. Symmetric

    D. RSA

31. Which of the following best describes the Diffie-Hellman protocol?

   (A) It is a key exchange protocol for asymmetric encryption.

   B. It is a symmetric encryption algorithm.

   C. It is a key exchange protocol for symmetric encryption.

   D. It is a hashing algorithm.

32. Which of the following apply to symmetrical keys? (Choose two.)

   A. The public key is used for encryption.

   B. The private key is used for decryption.

   (C) The same key is used for encryption and decryption.

   (D) They are exchanged out-of-band.

33. Which of the following are two common negotiation protocols used by TLS? (Choose two.)

   A. Quantum cryptography

   (B) DHE *DIFFIE HILLMAN*

   C. RSA

   (D) ECDHE *ELIPTIAL CURVE DIFFIE HILLMAN*

34. What is another name for an ephemeral key?

   A. PKI private key

   B. SHA

   (C) Session key *SHORT LIVED SUCH AS DIFFIE HILLMAN OR ECDHE*

   D. PKI public key

35. During the monthly IT meeting in your office, your IT manager, Julia, expresses concern about weak user passwords on corporate servers and how they might be susceptible to brute-force password attacks. When allaying Julia about her concerns, which term might you use?

   A. Key forging

   B. Key escrow

   (C) Key stretching *CONVERT WEAK KEYS SUCH AS PASSWORDS*

   D. Key forwarding

36. Match the cryptographic terms to the appropriate scenario:

Security Policy Terms	Scenarios
Perfect forward secrecy _B_	A. An Ethernet switch must be securely managed from the command line.
File hashing _C_	B. You must secure a human resources web server such that temporary session keys are used to secure the transmissions.
Quantum cryptography _D_	C. A law enforcement forensic analyst must ensure that hard disk data has not been tampered with.
SSH _A_	D. A security analyst must recommend a method of encrypting data that is not based on mathematics, but instead, photon properties.

QUICK ANSWER KEY

1.	D	**11.**	B	**21.**	A, D	**31.**	A
2.	A	**12.**	A	**22.**	B	**32.**	C, D
3.	C	**13.**	A	**23.**	B, D	**33.**	B, D
4.	A	**14.**	B	**24.**	C	**34.**	C
5.	A	**15.**	D	**25.**	B, D	**35.**	C
6.	D	**16.**	A	**26.**	D	**36.**	Perfect forward secrecy: **B**, File hashing: **C**, Quantum cryptography: **D**, SSH: **A**
7.	A	**17.**	C	**27.**	D		
8.	B	**18.**	A	**28.**	B		
9.	B	**19.**	C	**29.**	B, C		
10.	D	**20.**	B, C	**30.**	C		

IN-DEPTH ANSWERS

1. ☑ **D.** TCP port 80 is HyperText Transfer Protocol (HTTP) network traffic. Web browsers use HTTP to connect to web servers. In this case, users are using web-based e-mail that is not encrypted. HyperText Transfer Protocol Secure (HTTPS) uses either Secure Sockets Layer (SSL) or Transport Layer Security (TLS) to encrypt HTTP traffic. This requires the installation of a digital certificate on the server.

   ☒ **A, B**, and **C** are incorrect. They are cryptographic hashing algorithms, which do not encrypt, or protect the confidentiality, of information; they validate data integrity. Data is fed to a hashing algorithm resulting in a *hash* (sometimes called a *message digest*) that represents the encoded data. Any change in the data will result in a different hash.

2. ☑ **A.** Secure Shell (SSH) listens on TCP port 22 and is used commonly on UNIX and Linux hosts to allow secure remote administration. An SSH daemon must be running on the server, and an SSH client (such as Putty) is required to make the connection. Unlike its predecessor, Telnet, SSH encrypts network traffic.

   ☒ **B, C**, and **D** are incorrect. Secure Sockets Layer (SSL) encrypts higher-level protocols such as HyperText Transfer Protocol (HTTP) or Simple Mail Transfer Protocol (SMTP). Single sign-on (SSO) allows access to multiple applications without prompting to authenticate to each one. Secure Hash Algorithm (SHA) is a specific hashing algorithm used to verify that data has not been tampered with. It is not tied to being used for remote admin access for UNIX and Linux.

3. ☑ **C.** IP Security (IPSec) is not specific to an application; all network traffic is encrypted and authenticated. Both sides of the secured connection must be configured to use IPSec.

   ☒ **A, B**, and **D** are incorrect. SSL can be applied to higher-level protocols such as Simple Mail Transfer Protocol (SMTP) or HyperText Transfer Protocol (HTTP). Secure Shell (SSH) is a secure remote administration mechanism. Virtual private networks (VPNs) do encrypt all traffic including applications that don't support encryption, but a VPN is not a local area network (LAN) solution; it is a wide area network (WAN) solution.

4. ☑ **A.** Transport Layer Security (TLS) replaces Secure Sockets Layer (SSL). For example, TLS offers more secure data authentication to ensure data has not been tampered with while in transit.

   ☒ **B, C**, and **D** are incorrect. SSO, TKIP, and VPNs do not supersede SSL. SSO enables authenticating only once to allow access to multiple applications. Temporal Key Integrity Protocol (TKIP) is a wireless security enhancement to Wired Equivalent Privacy (WEP). Virtual private networks (VPNs) do not supersede SSL, although there are SSL VPN solutions available. VPNs allow secure remote access to a LAN across an untrusted network.

5. ☑ **A.** Secure Sockets Layer (SSL) users TCP port 443.

☒ **B, C,** and **D** are incorrect. HyperText Transfer Protocol (HTTP) uses port 80, Remote Desktop Protocol (RDP) uses port 3389, and Trivial File Transfer Protocol (TFTP) uses UDP port 69, not TCP.

6. ☑ **D.** Message Digest 5 (MD5) is a hashing algorithm that computes a digest from provided data. Any change in the data will invalidate the digest; thus, data integrity is attained.

☒ **A, B,** and **C** are incorrect. Symmetric encryption algorithms provide confidentiality, not integrity. Triple Digital Encryption Standard (3DES) is a 168-bit encryption standard. RC4 and Advanced Encryption Standard (AES) are symmetric ciphers whose bit strengths come in various lengths.

7. ☑ **A.** Digital Encryption Standard (DES) is a 56-bit cipher, and 3DES is a 168-bit cipher; both are symmetric encryption algorithms. RSA (named after its creators, Rivest, Shamir, and Adleman) is a public and private key (asymmetric) encryption and digital signing standard whose bit strength varies. The bit length of a cipher is not the only factor influencing its strength; the specific implementation of the cryptographic functions also plays a role.

☒ **B, C,** and **D** are incorrect because 3DES is a stronger standard than DES. RSA is stronger than DES. RSA is considered more secure than 3DES or DES.

8. ☑ **B.** RSA is an asymmetric cryptographic algorithm that uses mathematically related public and private key pairs to digitally sign and encrypt data.

☒ **A, C,** and **D** are incorrect. AES, 3DES, and Blowfish are symmetric encryption standards. Symmetric encryption means the same key that encrypts a message is used to decrypt that message. The problem this presents is how to securely get the key to other parties.

9. ☑ **B.** A public key infrastructure (PKI) implies the use of public and private key pairs. To encrypt messages for Amy, you must have her public key. This can be installed locally on a computer or published centrally on a directory server. The related private key, which only Amy should have access to, is used to decrypt the message.

☒ **A, C,** and **D** are incorrect. Amy's private key is used to decrypt received messages encrypted with her public key. You need your private key to digitally sign messages, not to send encrypted messages. Your public key is used by others to encrypt data they send to you, or it can be used to verify items you digitally sign with your private key.

10. ☑ **D.** Advanced Encryption Standard (AES) and Triple Digital Encryption Standard (3DES) are cryptographic standards using symmetric algorithms. This means a single key is used to both encrypt and decrypt. RSA (named after its creators, Rivest, Shamir, and Adleman) is an asymmetric encryption algorithm. This means two mathematically related keys (public and private) are used to secure data; normally, a public key encrypts data, and a private key decrypts it.

☒ **A, B**, and **C** are incorrect. AES is not asymmetric and neither is Blowfish. RC4 is symmetric, not asymmetric.

11. ☑ **B.** Encryption provides data confidentiality. Only authorized parties have the ability to decrypt disk contents.

☒ **A, C**, and **D** are incorrect. MD5, digital signatures, and SHA provide data integrity. This assures a recipient that data is authentic and has not been tampered with.

12. ☑ **A.** TwoFish is a symmetric block cipher that replaces Blowfish.

☒ **B, C**, and **D** are incorrect. There is no such cipher as FourFish. RSA is an asymmetric standard. PKI is a term referring to the use of public and private key pairs (asymmetric); it is not a symmetric block cipher.

13. ☑ **A.** It is not the workstation public key that is used; it is the server's. The workstation-generated session key is encrypted with the server public key and transmitted to the web server where a related private key decrypts the message to reveal the session key.

☒ **B, C**, and **D** are incorrect. The question asks you to identify the incorrect statement. Once the unique session key is known to the server, it is used to encrypt and decrypt data between the two hosts.

14. ☑ **B.** Steganography hides messages within files. For example, a message could be hidden within an inconspicuous JPEG picture file.

☒ **A, C**, and **D** are incorrect. A Trojan is malware masking itself as a useful file or software. Encryption makes no attempt to hide the fact that data is encrypted. Digital signatures are used to verify the integrity and authenticity of data. No attempt is made to conceal a message.

15. ☑ **D.** Nonrepudiation means neither the sending nor receiving party can dispute the fact that a transmission occurred. The recipient is assured of data authenticity and integrity via a digital signature applied with the sender's private key.

☒ **A, B**, and **C** are incorrect. Digital signatures do assure a recipient that a message is authentic, but nonrepudiation is a better answer. Encryption ensures data confidentiality but does not ensure data is authentic. Public key infrastructure (PKI) is a general term describing a security framework that does include message authentication and nonrepudiation.

16. ☑ **A.** File hashing performs a calculation on a file resulting in what is called a *hash*. Changing a file in some way and then performing the same calculation would result in a different hash. This is one way to verify that the file is the correct version.

☒ **B, C**, and **D** are incorrect. As a software developer, you cannot control whether Internet users have antivirus software installed. Antivirus software on a server is always important but is not related to file hashing. While Transport Layer Security (TLS) could be used to secure the Internet traffic to the web site, it cannot check for file tampering.

17. ☑ **C.** Elliptic Curve Cryptography (ECC) is public key cryptography based on points on an elliptic curve.

☒ **A, B,** and **D** are incorrect. RSA is an asymmetric cryptographic standard. DES is incorrect because it is a symmetric standard. PKI does involve public and private key pairs but has nothing specifically to do with elliptic curve points.

18. ☑ **A.** File Transfer Protocol Secure (FTPS) can use Secure Sockets Layer (SSL) to secure FTP traffic.

☒ **B, C,** and **D** are incorrect. Secure File Transfer Protocol (SFTP) refers to tunneling FTP traffic through a Secure Shell (SSH) encrypted session. IP Security (IPSec) cannot use SSL; it is an alternative to SSL. IPSec performs at a lower level in the Open Systems Interconnect (OSI) model, which means IPSec can secure network traffic for higher-level applications that do not encrypt. SSL is application specific. Transport Layer Security (TLS) supersedes SSL.

19. ☑ **C.** Secure Copy (SCP) is a secure way of copying files between computers over an SSH session.

☒ **A, B,** and **D** are incorrect. File Transfer Protocol (FTP) is not secured and is not related to SCP. SCP is not built on Secure Sockets Layer (SSL); therefore, SSL is incorrect. Internet Control Message Protocol (ICMP) has nothing to do with security. ICMP reports on network congestion and the reachability of network nodes.

20. ☑ **B** and **C.** Stream ciphers encrypt data a bit or a byte at a time, whereas block ciphers encrypt segments (blocks) of data at one time in various block sizes.

☒ **A** and **D** are incorrect. Block ciphers do not block malicious data from being encrypted. Stream ciphers are not designed to encrypt only streaming media traffic.

21. ☑ **A** and **D.** Block ciphers encrypt data a block at a time (rather than a bit or byte at a time). Digital Encryption Standard (DES) and Advanced Encryption Standard (AES) are both block ciphers.

☒ **B** and **C** are incorrect. RSA and RC4 are stream ciphers; they encrypt data a bit or byte at a time.

22. ☑ **B.** Configuring the same preshared key on both sides of a connection defines symmetric (same key) encryption.

☒ **A, C,** and **D** are incorrect. Different related keys (public and private) would be used for asymmetric encryption. Asymmetric encryption uses public and private key pairs, not a preshared key. SSL and RSA are not configured with preshared keys.

23. ☑ **B** and **D.** RACE Integrity Primitives Evaluation Message Digest (RIPEMD) and Hash-based Message Authentication Code (HMAC) are both cryptographic hashing functions.

☒ **A** and **C** are incorrect. They are encryption functions, not hashing (message digest) functions.

24. ☑ **C.** One-time pads are used to combine completely random keys with plain text resulting in cipher text, after which one-time pads are not used again. Both communicating parties must have the same one-time pads, which presents a problem if communicating with a large number of entities. No amount of computing power or time can increase the likelihood of breaking this type of cipher text.

    ☒ **A, B,** and **D** are incorrect. AES, 3DES, and RSA encryption do not provide the utmost in security compared to one-time pads.

25. ☑ **B and D.** Password Authentication Protocol (PAP) should be disabled. PAP sends unencrypted passwords across the network during authentication. Extensible Authentication Protocol – Transport Layer Security (EAP-TLS) should not be disabled when hardening VPNs; it is considered very secure because of its mutual authentication of both VPN client and VPN server.

    ☒ **A and C** are incorrect. PAP should be considered only as a last resort; even then it may violate security policies in place. EAP-TLS should not be disabled when hardening a VPN; it is considered very secure.

26. ☑ **D.** Pretty Good Privacy (PGP) uses public and private key pairs to encrypt and digitally sign messages.

    ☒ **A, B,** and **C** are incorrect. 3DES, DES, and Blowfish are symmetric algorithms. Symmetric algorithms use the same key to encrypt and decrypt data, not related public and private key pairs.

27. ☑ **D.** Password Authentication Protocol (PAP) is considered insecure because it does not encrypt transmitted credentials.

    ☒ **A, B,** and **C** are incorrect. Microsoft Challenge Handshake Authentication Protocol (MS-CHAP v2) does not send credentials, even in encrypted form, over the network at all because it hashes credentials on both sides of a connection. This of course requires both parties to have knowledge of a shared secret to compute the hash. New Technology LAN Manager (NTLM) hashes data on both sides of a connection similarly to CHAP and is therefore more secure than PAP. Extensible Authentication Protocol – Transport Layer Security (EAP-TLS) is the most secure of the presented choices. This is because it requires both the client and the server to possess a certificate used for authentication.

28. ☑ **B.** Integrity is achieved when digitally signing an e-mail message. The sender's private key creates the unique signature, which is verified on the receiving end using the sender's related public key. If the message has not changed since it was sent, the signature will be considered valid.

    ☒ **A, C,** and **D** are not correct. The principle of least privilege ensures users have only the rights they need to complete a task. Confidentiality would apply only if the user had encrypted the e-mail message. Authorization occurs when an authenticated entity is granted access to a particular network resource.

29. ☑ **B and C.** Because the recipient's public key is used to encrypt a message, the related private key is used for decryption. Digitally signing a message must assure the recipient that it came from who it says it came from. Because only the owner of a private key has access to it, the private key is used to create digital signatures. The related public key verifies the validity of that signature.

☒ **A and D** are incorrect. The public key of the recipient of the message is required to encrypt a message to them. The recipient then decrypts the message using the related private key. In modern systems, this process is completely transparent. Verifying digital signatures is performed using the sender's public key.

30. ☑ **C.** Symmetric encryption uses the same key for encryption and decryption. In this case, if the same passphrase is used, the data can be decrypted.

☒ **A, B, and D** are incorrect. Wired Equivalent Privacy (WEP) is for wireless networks, not file encryption. Asymmetric and RSA are not applicable because only a single key is being used in this example. Asymmetric encryption (RSA is asymmetric) uses two related keys.

31. ☑ **A.** Diffie-Hellman is a secure key exchange protocol used for asymmetric encryption.

☒ **B, C, and D** are incorrect. Diffie-Hellman is neither used for symmetric encryption nor is it a hashing algorithm.

32. ☑ **C and D.** The same symmetrical key is used on both sides of a secured connection, and the keys are exchanged out-of-band. (Outside of the normal message communication channel, for example, the key is communicated over the telephone or in person on a USB flash drive.) Keys exchanged within the normal communication channel, as is the case with the Diffie-Hellman protocol, is referred to as *in-band key exchange*.

☒ **A and B** are incorrect. Public and private keys are different (asymmetrical), whereas using the same key for encryption and decryption is considered symmetrical encryption.

33. ☑ **B and D.** Diffie-Hellman Ephemeral (DHE) and Elliptic Curve Diffie-Hellman Ephemeral (ECDHE) are commonly used with Transport Layer Security (TLS) to provide perfect forward secrecy.

☒ **A and B** are incorrect. Public and private keys are different (asymmetrical), whereas using the same key for encryption and decryption is considered symmetrical encryption.

34. ☑ **C.** Ephemeral keys are short-lived keys, such as a unique session key. Diffie-Hellman Ephemeral (DHE) and Elliptic Curve Diffie-Hellman Ephemeral (ECDHC) are common key negotiation protocols.

☒ **A**, **B**, and **C** are incorrect. Public key infrastructure (PKI) public and private keys are not considered short-lived, or session-specific, unlike random public key (ephemeral key) generation, which is referred to as perfect forward secrecy. Secure Hashing Algorithm (SHA) is a hashing algorithm and not a temporary key.

35. ☑ **C.** Key stretching converts weak keys such as passwords into stronger keys that are less susceptible to brute-force attacks. Bcrypt and PBKDF2 are common key strengthening algorithms.

☒ **A**, **B**, and **D** are incorrect. Key forging and key forwarding are not terms related to the strength of passwords or keys. Key escrow refers to a trusted third party having a copy of decryption keys.

36. Perfect forward secrecy: **B**, File hashing: **C**, Quantum cryptography: **D**, SSH: **A**

13
Managing a PKI Infrastructure

QUESTIONS

Sensitive data exchange on any network will benefit from a public key infrastructure (PKI). A PKI provides security using digital certificates. Certificate authorities (CAs) issue certificates to valid parties for the purpose of confidentially (encryption), integrity (digital signatures and hashing), authentication (user or device), and nonrepudiation (no disputing of private key usage). Each certificate contains a unique, mathematically related public and private key pair in addition to other data such as the certificate expiration date. Compromised certificates can be revoked and their serial numbers published with a certificate revocation list (CRL).

1. After importing a user certificate file to an e-mail program, a user finds she cannot digitally sign sent e-mail messages. What are some possible reasons for this? (Choose two.)

   A. The public key is not in the certificate.

   B. The private key is not in the certificate.

   C. The certificate was not created for e-mail usage.

   D. The PKI is not in the certificate.

2. Which of the following would not be found in a digital certificate?

   A. Public key

   B. Private key

   C. Digital signature of issuing CA

   D. IP address of PKI server

3. You are providing consulting services to a legal firm that has a PKI. They would like to enable document workflow where documents are sent electronically to the appropriate employees within the firm. You are asked whether there is a way to prove that documents were sent from the user listed in the From field. Of the following, what would you recommend?

   A. File encryption

   B. Digital signatures

   C. E-mail encryption

   D. Certificate revocation list

4. As a security auditor, you are focusing on hardening an existing PKI. Which of the following should you consider? (Choose two.)

   A. Take the CA offline.

   B. Do not make public keys publicly accessible.

   C. Configure a recovery agent.

   D. Encrypt all digital certificates.

5. Your colleagues report that there is a short time frame where a revoked certificate can still be used. Why is this?   *CERTIFICATE REVOCATION LIST*
   - A. The CRL is published periodically.
   - B. The CRL is published immediately but must replicate to all hosts.
   - C. The CRL lists only revoked certificate serial numbers; it is not used in any way.
   - D. The CRL is dependent on network bandwidth.

6. Which of the following best describes the term *key escrow*?
   - A. A trusted third party with decryption keys in case the original keys have expired
   - B. A trusted third party with decryption keys in addition to existing original keys
   - C. An account that can be used to encrypt private keys
   - D. An account that can be used to encrypt data for any user

7. Which PKI component verifies the identity of certificate requestors before a certificate is issued?
   - A. Public key
   - B. RA   *REGISTRATION AUTHORITY*
   - C. PKI
   - D. CRL

8. A user reports that they are unable to authenticate to the corporate VPN while traveling. You have configured the VPN to require X.509 user certificate authentication. After investigating the problem, you learn that the user certificate has expired. Which of the following presents the quickest secure solution?
   - A. Create a new user certificate and configure it on the user computer.
   - B. Disable X.509 certificate authentication for your VPN.
   - C. Reduce the CRL publishing frequency.
   - D. Set the date back on the VPN appliance to before the user certificate expired. *CANNOT BE DONE*

9. When users connect to an intranet server by typing **https://intranet.acme.local**, their web browser displays a warning message stating the site is not to be trusted. How can this warning message be removed while maintaining security?
   - A. Configure the web server to use HTTP instead of HTTPS.
   - B. Install the intranet server private key on all client workstations.
   - C. Use TCP port 443 instead of TCP port 80.
   - D. Install the trusted root certificate in the client web browser for the issuer of the intranet server certificate.

10. A web server's security is being configured as shown in Figure 13-1. Identify the configuration error.

    A. The physical web site path should not be on drive C:
    B. HTTPS web sites must use port 443.
    C. Port 444 must be used for HTTP, not HTTPS.
    D. An SSL certificate must be selected.

FIGURE 13-1

Web site
configuration

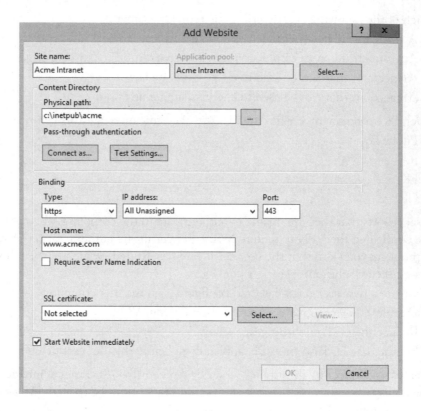

11. An HTTPS-secured web site requires the ability to restrict which workstations can make a connection. Which option is the most secure?

    A. Configure the web site to allow connections only from the IP addresses of valid workstations.
    B. Configure the web site to allow connections only from the MAC addresses of valid workstations.
    C. Configure the web site to use user authentication.
    D. Configure the web site to require client-side certificates.

12. Which of the following is untrue regarding certificates containing private keys?
    A. They can be used to encrypt mail sent to others.
    B. They can be used to encrypt hard disk contents.
    C. They should be password protected.
    D. They can be used to digitally sign mail sent to others.

13. For which purpose would a computer digital certificate be used? (Choose the best answer.)
    A. Network access control
    B. IPSec
    C. Both of the above
    D. Neither of the above

14. You are responsible for enabling SSL on an e-commerce web site. What should you do first?
    A. Install the web server digital certificate.
    B. Enable SSL on the web server.
    C. Create a CSR and submit it to a CA. *CERTIFICATE SIGNING REQUEST CERTIFICATE AUTHORITY*
    D. Configure the web server to use port 443.

15. While generating a certificate signing request for a web site, you enter the information listed here. Users will connect to the web site by typing **https://www.acme.com**. Identify the configuration error.
    Expiry: 12 months
    Bit length: 2048
    Common Name: 215.66.77.88
    Organization: Acme Inc.
    OU: Sales
    Country: US
    State: TN
    City: Memphis

    A. The expiry date is one year away.
    B. The bit length should be 128.
    C. The common name should be www.acme.com.
    D. The State field must not be abbreviated.

16. A national company with headquarters in Dallas, Texas, is implementing a PKI. There are corporate locations in 12 other major U.S. cities. Each of those locations has a senior network administrator. Which option presents the best PKI solution?
    - A. Install a root CA in Dallas. Create subordinate CAs for each city and use these to issue certificates for users and computers in that city. Take the root CA offline.
    - B. Install a root CA in Dallas. Issue certificates for users and computers in all locations.
    - C. Install a root CA in Dallas. Issue certificates for users and computers in all locations. Take the root CA offline.
    - D. Install a root CA in Dallas and each city. Issue certificates for users and computers using each city root CA. Take the root CAs offline.

17. A work colleague has sent you a digital certificate file to install on your computer so that you can encrypt e-mail messages to him. What error was made in Figure 13-2 when the file was generated?
    - A. There should not be a private key password.
    - B. A private key should never be shared with others.
    - C. The option Enable Strong Private Key Protection must be enabled.
    - D. The option Include All Extended Properties must be disabled.

18. To secure your server, you would like to ensure server hard disk data cannot be accessed if the hard disks are stolen. What should you do?
    - A. Configure EFS.
    - B. Configure TPM with PKI encryption keys.
    - C. Configure NTFS security.
    - D. Configure a power-on password.

19. Which security objectives are met by PKI? (Choose two.)
    - A. Least privilege
    - B. Integrity
    - C. Nonrepudiation
    - D. DMZ

FIGURE 13-2

Certificate Import Wizard

---

20. Your company, Acme, Inc., conducts business with a supplier, Widgets, Inc. Both companies have an existing PKI with departmental subordinate CAs. Certain Widgets departments require access to specific secured Acme web servers that require client-side certificates before access is granted. What solution should you propose?

   A. Acme administrators should create a new root CA for Widgets and issue certificates to those employees needing access to the Acme web server.

   B. Acme administrators should create a new subordinate CA for Widgets and issue certificates to those employees needing access to the Acme web server.

   C. The Acme web servers should be cross-certified with the appropriate Widgets subordinate CAs.

   D. The appropriate Widgets and Acme departmental CAs should be cross-certified.

21. Which types of keys are commonly used for e-commerce web sites?
    - A. Public, private, session
    - B. Public and private
    - C. Public, private, TPM
    - D. Public, private, PKI

22. The CA signature exists in all digital certificates that it issues. Which key does the CA use to create its signature?
    - A. Private
    - B. Public
    - C. Symmetric
    - D. Asymmetric

23. In a PKI, what role does the CA play? (Choose two.)
    - A. Revokes certificates
    - B. Uses its private key to digitally sign certificates
    - C. Uses its public key to digitally sign certificates
    - D. Controls access to the network using certificates

24. To which does the X.509 standard apply?
    - A. LDAP
    - B. PKI certificates
    - C. Biometric authentication
    - D. A type of network transport

25. Using Figure 13-3, match the appropriate term listed on the left to the requirement listed on the right. (Not all terms will be used.)

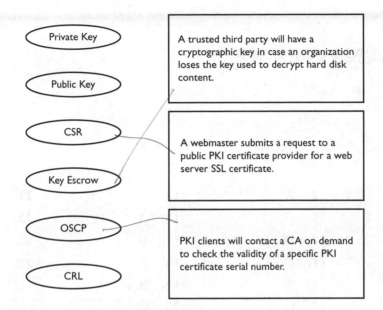

FIGURE 13-3

PKI terms and
scenarios

QUICK ANSWER KEY

1. B, C	**8.** A	**15.** C	**22.** A
2. D	**9.** D	**16.** A	**23.** A, B
3. B	**10.** D	**17.** B	**24.** B
4. A, C	**11.** D	**18.** B	**25.** See Figure 13-4.
5. A	**12.** A	**19.** B, C	
6. B	**13.** C	**20.** C	
7. B	**14.** C	**21.** A	

FIGURE 13-4

PKI terms and scenarios—the answer

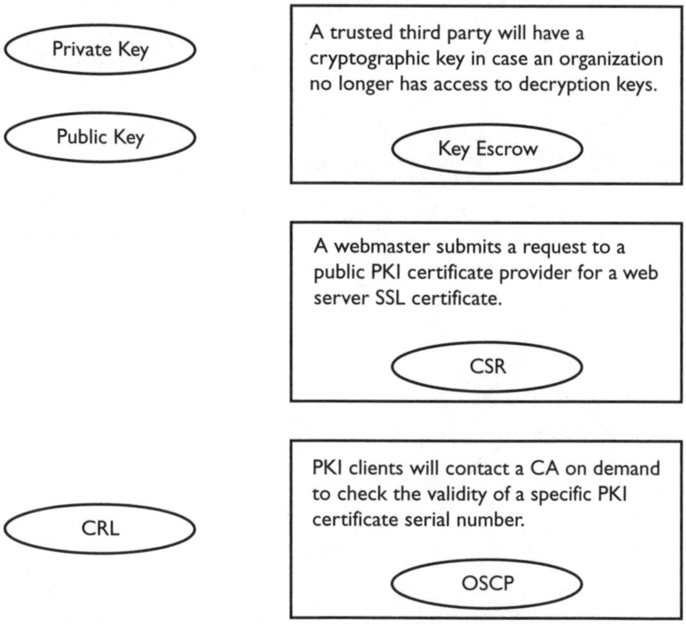

Private Key

Public Key

CRL

A trusted third party will have a cryptographic key in case an organization no longer has access to decryption keys.

Key Escrow

A webmaster submits a request to a public PKI certificate provider for a web server SSL certificate.

CSR

PKI clients will contact a CA on demand to check the validity of a specific PKI certificate serial number.

OSCP

IN-DEPTH ANSWERS

1. ☑ **B** and **C.** A private key is used to create digital signatures, and the related public key verifies the authenticity of that signature. A certificate lacking a private key cannot be used to digitally sign e-mail messages. Depending on how the certificate file was created, the private key may have been omitted. This is sometimes done when you send your public key to another party so that they can encrypt messages to you. Certificates can be created for specific uses, such as e-mail.

    ☒ **A** and **D** are incorrect. Public keys do not create digital signatures; they verify them. A public key infrastructure (PKI) is a collection of certificates generated from a certificate authority (CA) to establish a chain of trust. Each certificate contains data such as the issuer, the subject to whom the certificate was issued, an expiration date, public keys, optionally private keys, and so on.

2. ☑ **D.** A PKI server does not write its IP address within certificates it issues; however, it does write its digital signature with a private key.

    ☒ **A**, **B**, and **C** are incorrect. A digital certificate would contain public and private keys as well as the signature of the issuing CA.

3. ☑ **B.** Digital signatures are created with the sender's private key (to which only they have access) and verified with the corresponding public key. This is the best solution for workflow documents in this scenario.

    ☒ **A**, **C**, and **D** are incorrect. Encrypting files or messages conceals the data from unauthorized parties but does nothing to verify its authenticity. The certificate revocation list (CRL) periodically publishes a list of invalidated certificates to ensure the PKI does not accept these revoked certificates for any use.

4. ☑ **A** and **C.** The CA is used to issue and renew X.509 certificates and should be taken offline when not in use for security purposes. Normally, subordinate CAs are used to issue certificates. Recovery agents have the ability to recover encrypted data when the original private key is unavailable. Failure to configure this could result in no access to important data.

    ☒ **B** and **D** are incorrect. Public keys are designed to be made publicly available. Digital certificates are not normally themselves encrypted.

5. ☑ **A.** The CRL is not published immediately; it is published either manually or on a schedule, so there may be a small time frame where revoked certificates can still be used.

    ☒ **B**, **C**, and **D** are incorrect. The CRL is not published immediately when a certificate is revoked; it is published on a periodic interval. Once the CRL is published, it is referenced by clients. Network bandwidth does not affect when the CRL is published.

6. ☑ **B.** Key escrow refers to a trusted third party with a copy of decryption keys. A court order may be necessary to use these keys under certain circumstances.

   ☒ **A, C,** and **D** are incorrect. Keys within expired PKI certificates are unusable. Key escrow is not used to encrypt private keys. Generic accounts should never be used, especially for user data encryption.

7. ☑ **B.** A registration authority (RA) is an optional PKI component that performs requestor verification before certificates are issued.

   ☒ **A, C,** and **D** are incorrect. Public keys verify digital signatures created with the corresponding private key; they do not verify the identity of a certificate requestor. PKI itself is not a PKI component. The CRL is not involved with the issuance of digital certificates; instead, the CRL is a published list of revoked certificates.

8. ☑ **A.** X.509 certificates cannot be renewed if they have expired; a new certificate must be created.

   ☒ **B, C,** and **D** are incorrect. Disabling VPN certificate authentication is not necessary and does not address the issue. Reducing the CRL publishing frequency means that the list of revoked certificates is updated more frequently; this has no effect on expired certificates. Do not set the date back on VPN appliances; VPN logs will have incorrect date and time stamps, and some VPN clients that could previously connect may no longer be able to connect.

9. ☑ **D.** The web browser must trust the digital signature in the intranet web server certificate; this is the digital signature of the server certificate issuer. If a client trusts the signer, it then trusts all certificates signed by the signer. In addition, the server certificate must be valid, meaning it must not have expired, and it must not be listed in the CRL. The subject name in the server certificate must match the URL entered by the user.

   ☒ **A, B,** and **C** are incorrect. Using HTTP instead of HTTPS would not maintain security; it would make the connection less secure because the traffic would not be encrypted. The problem is not with HTTP or HTTPS but rather that the client workstation does not trust the server's certificate. Client workstations do not need the server private key to trust the web site. Only the owner of a private key should have access to it. HTTPS implies that TCP port 443 is already being used.

10. ☑ **D.** To configure HTTPS, a digital certificate must be selected. The certificate (among other things) contains a public and private key pair used to secure HTTP traffic.

   ☒ **A, B,** and **C** are incorrect. While the default web site directory should not be used for security reasons, the web site residing on drive C: does not constitute a configuration error. HTTP and HTTPS can use any unused port configured by the administrator; however, straying from the default port 80 for HTTP and port 443 for HTTPS requires users to enter the port number as part of the URL.

11. ☑ **D.** Client-side digital certificates must be installed on each workstation to access the web site. The web server must also be configured to allow access only from workstations with appropriate certificates installed.

☒ **A, B,** and **C** are incorrect. IP addresses and MAC addresses are easy to spoof. Usernames and passwords can be learned much more easily than forging a digital certificate.

12. ☑ **A.** Private keys are not used to encrypt message to others; for that you must have the recipient's public key.

☒ **B, C,** and **D** are incorrect. These statements are all true.

13. ☑ **C.** Computer digital certificates can be used to authenticate the computer to another device such as with an 802.1x network switch that forwards authentication requests to an authentication server (network access control). IPSec can use computer certificates to ensure secure communication takes place between network hosts.

☒ **A, B,** and **D** are incorrect. Computer certificates can be used not only for network access control or IPSec but for both purposes as well as many others.

14. ☑ **C.** Creating a certificate signing request (CSR) and submitting it to a CA is the first step that must be completed. There are various Internet certificate authorities such as VeriSign and Entrust with varying pricing structures. Then the CA digitally signed certificate must be installed on your web server. Finally, you must configure your web site to use the digital certificate.

☒ **A, B,** and **D** are incorrect. These cannot be done until a CA-approved CSR exists. Also, secured web sites do not have to use port 443.

15. ☑ **C.** The common name in a web server certificate must match the name that will be typed in as the uniform resource locator (URL) hostname; otherwise, client web browsers will not trust the web site.

☒ **A, B,** and **D** are incorrect. Twelve months is normally how long web server certificates are valid. 2048 is a valid bit strength selection for the public and private key pair. Web browsers use 128-bit session keys to secure transactions, but the client-generated session key will be transmitted to the server initially after having been encrypted with the web server's 2048-bit public key. The state name can be abbreviated.

16. ☑ **A.** Because there is IT expertise in each city, create a subordinate CA for each city and issue certificates using these CAs for their respective cities. The root CA should be taken offline for security purposes. If a single subordinate CA is compromised, you should revoke that certificate. This will invalidate all certificates issued by this CA. The other subordinate city CAs and their issued certificates would still be valid.

☒ **B, C,** and **D** are incorrect. If the root CA is compromised, all certificates must be revoked. Taking the root CA offline is a step in the right direction, but in a large distributed environment you should consider using subordinate CAs. A PKI solution within a company should allow a chain of trust such that certificates in one part of the company trust certificates in another part of the company.

17. ☑ **B.** Under no circumstances should you send others your private key; otherwise, they can decrypt messages sent to you and create digital signatures on your behalf.
☒ **A, C,** and **D** are incorrect. If a private key is exported to a digital certificate file, you must specify a password for the file. The options for enabling strong key protection and including extended properties are optional.

18. ☑ **B.** Trusted Platform Module (TPM) is a firmware security solution that can use PKI certificate keys to encrypt and decrypt hard disk contents. TPM-encrypted disks placed in a different computer (with or without a TPM chip) are unreadable.
☒ **A, C,** and **D** are incorrect. EFS will not adequately secure hard disk data in this scenario. If server hard disks are stolen, user account passwords could be hacked, which could allow access to Encrypting File System (EFS)–encrypted data. NTFS file system security can be circumvented by taking ownership of files and folders. A power-on password applies to a single computer, not another computer where stolen hard disks might be hooked up.

19. ☑ **B** and **C.** Integrity proves data is authentic and came from who it says it came from. Nonrepudiation means neither party can dispute a transmission occurred or who it came from because only the owner of a private key has access to it; the private key is used to create unique digital signatures used for data integrity. Both of these are met by a PKI.
☒ **A** and **D** are incorrect. Least privilege refers to granting only the rights needed to perform a specific duty. A demilitarized zone (DMZ) is a network sitting between a private LAN and the Internet. Hosts in a DMZ are reachable from the Internet. Neither least privilege nor DMZ is directly related to PKI.

20. ☑ **C.** Cross-certifying the appropriate subordinate CAs with the correct Acme web servers would allow only required Widgets departmental users to use their existing certificates to authenticate to the Acme web servers.
☒ **A, B,** and **D** are incorrect. Creating a new root or subordinate CA involves more management effort than cross-certification. In this scenario, access is required only to specific Acme web servers, not all of them. Cross-certifying entire subordinate CAs does not allow you to control to which specific servers Widgets employees could be authenticated.

21. ☑ **A.** The web server sends its public key to the client. The client encrypts its self-generated session key with the server public key. The server decrypts the message with its private key, thus exposing the session key to the server. The symmetric session key is then used for the remainder of the session to encrypt data.

☒   **B, C,** and **D** are incorrect. Public and private key pairs are used to securely transmit a session key, so three keys are involved. TPM is not involved with securing e-commerce data. PKI is not a key; it is a system of using digital certificates for authentication, integrity, confidentiality, and nonrepudiation.

22.   ☑   **A.** The CA's private key creates the digital signature that exists in issued certificates.
☒   **B, C,** and **D** are incorrect. The public key is used to verify a signature. Symmetric and asymmetric are terms used to classify key types; they are not specific keys used with digital signatures.

23.   ☑   **A** and **B.** The CA can revoke certificates that are no longer trusted, and it uses its private key to digitally sign all certificates it issues—this establishes a chain of trust.
☒   **C** and **D** are incorrect. Signatures are verified with the public key. The CA cannot directly control access to the network. Network appliances can use PKI certificates issued by CAs to accomplish this.

24.   ☑   **B.** The X.509 standard stems from the 1980s. It defines a hierarchy of certificate authorities that issue, renew, and revoke certificates.
☒   **A, C,** and **D** are incorrect. The Lightweight Directory Access Protocol (LDAP) is used to access a network database (directory), often for authentication purposes. Biometric authentication is a mechanism for authenticating a user based on a physical trait such as a voice or fingerprint. X.509 is not a network transport mechanism.

25.   ☑   See Figure 13-5. Key escrow refers to a trusted third party possessing cryptographic keys in case an organization cannot use its cryptographic key because of disaster or a security incident. A certificate signing request (CSR) is generated when initially beginning the process of acquiring a web server SSL certificate. The CSR is then submitted to the PKI CA for approval and digital signing. The online certificate status protocol (OCSP) queries a CA for a single PKI certificate serial number instead of downloading a list of all revoked certificate serial numbers, as is the case with a CRL.

FIGURE 13-5

PKI terms and
scenarios—the
answer

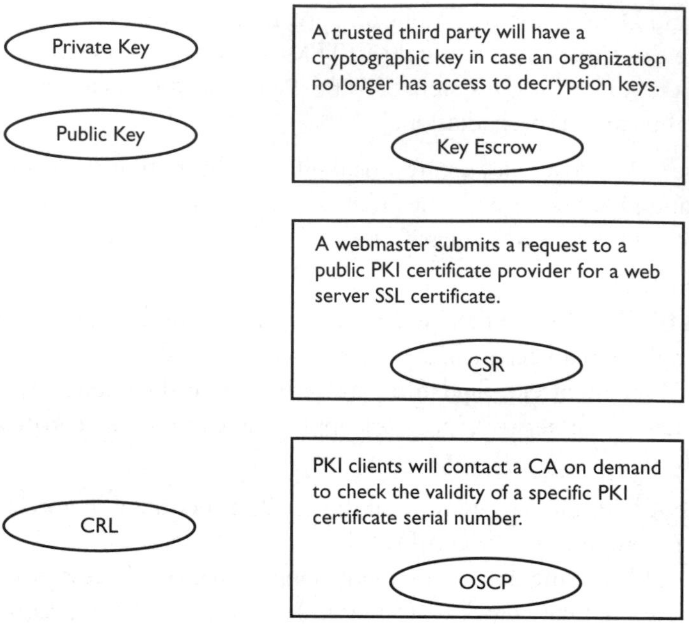

Private Key

Public Key

A trusted third party will have a cryptographic key in case an organization no longer has access to decryption keys.

Key Escrow

A webmaster submits a request to a public PKI certificate provider for a web server SSL certificate.

CSR

CRL

PKI clients will contact a CA on demand to check the validity of a specific PKI certificate serial number.

OSCP

14

Physical Security

QUESTIONS

Security breaches can be perpetrated remotely across a network or physically on the premises. The effects of physical security, from barricades, locks, and guards, must not be underestimated. Many security breaches today are the result of poor physical security.

Climate controls including temperature, humidity, and ventilation play a crucial role in ensuring the ongoing availability of computer systems. Poor ventilation in a server room could result in physical servers shutting down because of high temperatures.

1. What can be done to locally secure switches and routers? (Choose two.)
    A. Configure ACLs.
    B. Use SSH instead of Telnet.
    C. Set a console port password.
    D. Disable unused ports.

2. Which of the following would not be a physical security concern?
    A. Printer
    B. USB flash drive
    C. Workstation
    D. USB mouse

3. You are configuring an uninterruptible power supply (UPS) for your three servers such that in the event of a power failure, the servers will shut down gracefully. Which term best describes this configuration?
    A. Fail open
    B. Fail safe
    C. False positive
    D. False negative

4. In the event of a physical security breach, what can you do to secure data in your server room? (Choose three.)
    A. Install a UPS.
    B. Use TPM.
    C. Prevent booting from removal devices.
    D. Lock the server chassis.

5. What can limit the data emanation from electromagnetic radio frequencies?

   A. Faraday cage

   B. Antistatic wrist strap

   C. ESD mat

   D. ESD boots

6. How can security guards verify whether somebody is authorized to access a facility? (Choose two.)

   A. Employee ID badge

   B. Username and password

   C. Access list

   D. Smartcard

7. Which of the following is the first step in preventing physical security breaches?

   A. Firewall

   B. IDS

   C. Perimeter fencing

   D. Door keypad lock

8. While reviewing facility entry points you decide to replace existing doors with ones that will stay locked during power outages. Which term best describes this feature?

   A. Fail secure

   B. Fault tolerant

   C. Fail safe

   D. UPS

9. What advantages do human security guards have over video surveillance systems? (Choose two.)

   A. Human security guards have more detailed memory than saved video surveillance.

   B. Human security guards can notice abnormal circumstances.

   C. Human security guards can detect smells.

   D. Human security guards can recall sounds more accurately than saved video surveillance.

10. A data center IT director requires the ability to analyze facility physical security breaches after they have occurred. Which of the following present the best solutions? (Choose two.)

   A. Motion sensor logs

   B. Laser security system

   C. Mantrap

   D. Software video surveillance system

11. Which of the following physical access control methods do not normally identify who has entered a secure area? (Choose two.)

    A. Mantrap
    B. Hardware locks
    C. Fingerprint scan
    D. Smartcard

12. You would like to minimize disruption to your IT infrastructure. Which of the following environmental factors should you monitor? (Choose three.)

    A. Air flow
    B. Tape backups
    C. Server hard disk encryption
    D. Humidity
    E. Power

13. Your company has moved to a new location where a server room is being built. The server room currently has a water sprinkler system in case of fire. Regarding fire suppression, what should you suggest?

    A. Keep the existing water sprinkler system.
    B. Purchase a smoke detection waterless fire suppression system.
    C. Keep the existing water sprinkler system and install a raised floor.
    D. Place a fire extinguisher in the server room.

14. A data center administrator uses thermal imaging to identify hot spots in a large data center. She then arranges rows of rack-mounted servers such that cool air is directed to server fan inlets and hot air is exhausted out of the building. Which of the following terms best define this scenario?

    A. HVAC
    B. Form factoring
    C. Hot and cold aisles
    D. Data center breathing

15. Which access control method electronically logs entry into a facility?

    A. Picture ID card
    B. Security guard and log book
    C. IPSec
    D. Proximity card

16. You have received the email message depicted here. Which item should be further investigated to potentially maximize server room security?

Subject: Construction of new server room
Hi Glen,
How was your week at Defcon in Vegas?
Our contractor has supplied the following details regarding server room construction and configuration. If you agree, could you please sign off and return to me?
Dan

- A. Cipher lock for server room door
- B. Anti-static floor finishing
- C. Raised floor with under-floor air distribution
- D. Removal of single window to be covered by wall
- E. Wall mounted IP phone
- F. Preserve existing drop ceiling
- G. UPS
- H. Server room environmental controls
- I. Eight-foot server room entry door

17. A top-secret pharmaceutical research laboratory building uses CAT 6 network cabling. The company requires no disruption or interception of Bluetooth, network, and video monitor transmissions. What should the company consider?

- A. Wireless networking with WPA2 Enterprise
- B. EMI shielding for the building
- C. Fiber-optic cabling
- D. IPSec

18. You are consulting with a client regarding a new facility. Access to the building must be restricted to only those who know an access code. What might you suggest?

- A. Cipher lock
- B. Deadbolt lock
- C. Smartcard
- D. Biometric authentication

19. Over the last month servers have been mysteriously shutting down for no apparent reason. Servers restart normally only to eventually shut down again. Servers are fully patched, and virus scanners are up to date. Which of the following is the most likely reason for these failures?

A. The server room temperature is too hot.

B. The server room temperature is too cool.

C. The servers are infected with a virus.

D. The servers have operating system flaws.

20. What should be done in facility parking lots to ensure employee safety?

A. Install a barricade.

B. Install proper lighting.

C. Install an exit sign.

D. Install a first-aid kit.

21. Which of the following statements regarding wired networks are correct? (Choose two.)

A. They are slower than wireless networks.

B. They are faster than wireless networks.

C. Cable runs should be installed in conduits.

D. Cable runs should be exposed to facilitate troubleshooting.

22. You are considering options for securing windows in your facility. Which of the following might you consider?

A. WPA

B. PDS *PROTECTED DIST. SYS.*

C. Closed-circuit sensor

D. ID badge

E. CCTV

QUICK ANSWER KEY

1.	C, D	**7.**	C	**13.**	B	**19.**	A
2.	D	**8.**	A	**14.**	C	**20.**	B
3.	B	**9.**	B, C	**15.**	D	**21.**	B, C
4.	B, C, D	**10.**	A, D	**16.**	F	**22.**	C
5.	A	**11.**	A, B	**17.**	B		
6.	A, C	**12.**	A, D, E	**18.**	A		

IN-DEPTH ANSWERS

1. ☑ **C** and **D.** A console port allows a local user to plug a cable into the router or switch to locally administer the device. A strong password is recommended. Disabling unused switch ports and router interfaces prevents unauthorized people from gaining access to the device or the network.

   ☒ **A** and **B** are not local security measures. Access control lists (ACLs) on routers determine what type of traffic is allowed or denied. Secure Shell (SSH) is an encrypted remote command-line administrative tool. Telnet passes data across the network in clear text.

2. ☑ **D.** A Universal Serial Bus (USB) mouse does not store data and does not grant access to data, so it is not a security concern.

   ☒ **A**, **B**, and **C** are all valid security concerns. Printers can retain print job information and statistics in volatile or nonvolatile memory. USB flash drives are small and easily stolen or forgotten. User workstations could have sensitive data on their disks, and they can give access to network resources. Each of these three items must be accounted for when considering physical security.

3. ☑ **B.** Fail safe is a term meaning a response to a failure will result in the least amount of damage. For example, during a power outage, servers connected to the uninterruptible power supply (UPS) will have enough power to shut down properly.

   ☒ **A**, **C**, and **D** are incorrect. Fail open would mean if the firewall failed, instead of analyzing traffic to determine whether it is allowed in or out, all network traffic would be free to flow. False positives and false negatives relate to intrusion detection systems (IDSs) or security systems. A false positive occurs when a system reports there is a problem when in fact there is none.

4. ☑ **B**, **C**, and **D.** Trusted Platform Module (TPM) is a chip used with hard disk encryption. Data on disks taken from one TPM system and placed in another TPM or non-TPM machine will not be accessible. Preventing removable media boot is critical because there are many free tools that can reset administrative passwords this way. Physically locking the server chassis further deters an intruder from stealing physical hard disks.

   ☒ **A** is incorrect. An uninterruptible power supply (UPS) provides power during an outage but does nothing to secure data.

5. ☑ **A.** Faraday cages enclose electronic equipment to prevent data emanation or to protect components from external static charges.

   ☒ **B**, **C**, and **D** are important when touching electrical components. Each of these items is designed to put the user and the equipment at equal charge to prevent the flow of static electricity, but they do not prevent actual data emanation.

6. ☑ **A and C.** An employee ID badge allows physical verification that somebody is allowed to access a building. An access list defines who is allowed to access a facility.

   ☒ **B and D** cannot be verified by security guards. Usernames and passwords can authenticate a user to a computer system, as can a smartcard. Smartcards contain an embedded microchip. Users enter a PIN in conjunction with using their smartcard.

7. ☑ **C.** The first step in physical security involves perimeter fencing to prevent intruders from getting on the property.

   ☒ **A and B** are not physical security mechanisms. Firewalls allow or block network traffic based on configured rules. Intrusion detection systems (IDSs) analyze network traffic for suspicious activity and either log or take action for this incident. Door keypad locks do apply to physical security, but one must first get on the property to get to a door, so D is not correct.

8. ☑ **A.** Fail secure systems ensure that a component failure (such as a power source) will not compromise security, as in this case (the doors will stay locked).

   ☒ **B, C, and D** are incorrect. Fault tolerance (sometimes referred to as fail safe) ensures that a system can continue functioning despite a failure of some type. For example, a server may spread file and error recovery data across multiple disks. In the event of a disk failure, data can be reconstructed from the remaining disks. An uninterruptable power supply (UPS) provides temporary power to devices when there is a power outage.

9. ☑ **B and C.** Video surveillance systems cannot detect smells or notice anything out of the ordinary like a human security guard could.

   ☒ **A and D** are incorrect. Video surveillance with sound can be analyzed frame by frame, resulting in a much more detailed analysis.

10. ☑ **A and D.** Motion sensor logs can track a perpetrator's position more accurately than most video systems; however, software video surveillance can be played back and used to physically identify unauthorized people. To conserve disk space, most solutions record only when there is motion.

    ☒ **B and C** are incorrect. Laser security systems rely on laser beams being interrupted and do not work well with detailed analysis after the fact. Mantraps are small rooms controlling access to a building where the first door must be closed before the second will open. They offer little in terms of post-analysis.

11. ☑ **A and B.** Mantraps are designed to trap trespassers in a restricted area. Some mantrap variations use two sets of doors, one of which must close before the second one opens. Traditional mantraps do not require access cards. Hardware locks simply require possession of a key. Neither reveals the person's identity.

    ☒ **C and D** are incorrect. Fingerprints identify the user via biometric authentication. Smartcard authentication identifies the user through a unique code or PKI certificate in a smartcard.

12. ☑ **A, D,** and **E.** Enterprise-class environmental monitoring solutions track a variety of items such as air flow, humidity, and power availability. Any of these variables could create unfavorable conditions in a server room resulting in server downtime.

    ☒ **B** and **C** are incorrect. Tape backups provide a copy of important data should server hard disks fail. Server hard disk encryption protects hard disk data should the server hard disks be physically stolen.

13. ☑ **B.** Assuming local building codes allow, you should suggest waterless fire suppression systems because they will not damage or corrode computer systems or components like water will.

    ☒ **A, C,** and **D** are incorrect. Water sprinkler systems will damage or destroy computer equipment and data and should be avoided when possible. While important, placing a fire extinguisher in the server room is not the only thing you should recommend; water damage devastates computer systems.

14. ☑ **C.** Hot and cold aisles are an important consideration in data center cooling. Equipment layout and raised floors to distribute cold air are a few examples of the specifics involved.

    ☒ **A, B,** and **D** are incorrect. Heating Ventilation Air Conditioning (HVAC) generally refers to air flow and environmental control within a room or building. Form factoring and data center breathing are fictitious terms.

15. ☑ **D.** Proximity cards must be within a few inches to read the card number and either allow or deny access to a facility. All access is logged electronically without the need of a physical log book or security guard.

    ☒ **A, B,** and **C** are incorrect. Picture ID cards identify people. Security guards do not log facility access electronically. IP Security (IPSec) is a mechanism by which packets are authenticated and encrypted; there is no correlation to physical site security.

16. ☑ **F.** The existing drop ceiling should not be used since it presents a potential entry point into the server room.

    ☒ **A, B, C, D, E, G, H,** and **I** are incorrect. These server room changes do not require further investigation as they already increase server room security.

17. ☑ **B.** Electromagnetic interference (EMI) can disrupt network transmissions. CAT 6 cabling consists of four twisted copper wire pairs. As such, CAT 6 is susceptible to wiretap eavesdropping. Video screen emissions can be captured with the correct equipment. All of these factors put a top-secret facility at risk. The best solution is to shield the entire facility.

    ☒ **A, C,** and **D** are incorrect. Wireless networking will not solve any problems, and it will make things worse. Wireless networking always presents more security risks than a wired network. Fiber-optic cabling will keep network transmissions secure and free from interference, but Bluetooth and video monitor emissions would still be a security issue. IP Security (IPSec) does nothing to quell electromagnetic interference or prevent screen emissions. IPSec encrypts and authenticates network data.

18. ☑ **A.** Cipher locks are electronic keypads whereby authorized people enter an access code to gain access to a room or a building. All the user needs to know is an access code; no physical card is required.

☒ **B, C,** and **D** do not meet the client requirement of users knowing an access code. A deadbolt lock requires possession of a key, a smartcard is a physical object a user must have, and biometric authentication does not require knowledge of an access code.

19. ☑ **A.** A hot server room is most likely the problem since the servers are fully patched and properly protected. A Heating Ventilation Air Conditioning (HVAC) technician should be consulted.

☒ **B, C,** and **D** are incorrect. A hot server room is most likely the problem since the servers are patched and protected.

20. ☑ **B.** Proper lighting in parking lots reduces the likelihood of attacks or muggings perpetrated against employees.

☒ **A, C,** and **D** are incorrect. Installing a barricade in front of or around a building could prevent damage from vehicles, but it does not ensure employee safety in parking lots. A first-aid kit is not standard practice for parking lot safety. Signage, such as exit signs, helps ensure user safety, along with valid escape routes and regular fire drills. Unless dealing with an interior parking lot, exit signs would not be needed.

21. ☑ **B** and **C.** Generally speaking, wired networks are faster than wireless networks. Protected Distribution System (PDS) dictates that cables should not be easily physical accessible. This reduces the likelihood of tampering and eavesdropping.

☒ **A** and **D** are incorrect. Wireless networks are generally considered to be slower than wired networks. Wired network cables should not be physically exposed because this presents a security risk as well as a potential tripping hazard.

22. ☑ **C.** Closed-circuit sensors use a variety of mechanisms such that when a window is open, an alarm is triggered.

☒ **A, B, D,** and **E** are incorrect. Wi-Fi Protected Access (WPA) is a wireless security standard. Protected Distribution System (PDS) is a security standard that protects physical cables from tampering. ID badges are used to identify authorized personnel in a facility. Closed-circuit television (CCTV) is a standard security monitoring tool, but it is not the best windows-securing option.

15
Risk Analysis

QUESTIONS

Risk analysis determines the possible threats a business could face and how to effectively minimize their impact. Quantitative risk analysis results in a prioritized list of risks by dollar amount, whereas qualitative risk analysis uses a relative prioritizing system to rate risks to one another. Failure to properly perform a risk analysis could result in violation of laws, a loss of customer trust, or even bankruptcy in the event of the realization of risks.

1. You are conducting a risk analysis for a stock brokerage firm in Miami, Florida. What factors should you consider? (Choose two.)

   A. Server downtime because of earthquakes

   B. Destruction of government regulation documentation because of fire

   C. Server downtime because of power outages

   D. Customer invoicing data destroyed because of fire

2. You are responsible for completing an IT asset report for your company. All IT-related equipment and data must be identified and given a value. What term best describes what you must next do?

   A. Asset identification

   B. Risk assessment

   C. Risk mitigation

   D. Threat analysis

3. You are identifying security threats to determine the likelihood of virus infection. Identify potential sources of infection. (Choose two.)

   A. USB flash drives

   B. USB keyboard

   C. Smartcard

   D. Downloaded documentation from a business partner web site

4. During a risk analysis meeting you are asked to specify internal threats being considered. Choose which item is not considered an internal threat from the list that follows.

   A. Embezzlement

   B. Hackers breaking in through the firewall

   C. Employees using corporate assets for personal gain

   D. Users plugging in personal USB flash drives

5. A client conveys their concern to you regarding malicious Internet users gaining access to corporate resources. What type of assessment would you perform to determine this likelihood?

A. Threat assessment

B. Risk analysis

C. Asset identification

D. Total cost of ownership

6. You are an IT consultant performing a risk analysis for a seafood company. The client is concerned with specific cooking and packaging techniques the company uses being disclosed to competitors. What type of security concern is this?

A. Integrity

B. Confidentiality

C. Availability

D. Authorization

7. After identifying internal and external threats, you must determine how these potential risks will affect business operations. What is this called?

A. Risk analysis

B. Fault tolerance

C. Availability

D. Impact analysis

8. When determining how best to mitigate risk, which items should you consider? (Choose two.)

A. Insurance coverage

B. Number of server hard disks

C. How fast CPUs in new computers will be

D. Network bandwidth

9. You are listing preventative measures for potential risks. Which of the following would you document? (Choose three.)

A. Larger flat-screen monitors

B. Data backup

C. Employee training

D. Comparing reliability of network load balancing appliances

10. An insurance company charges an additional $200 monthly premium for natural disaster coverage for your business site. What figure must you compare this against to determine whether to accept this additional coverage?

    A. ALE
    B. ROI
    C. Total cost of ownership
    D. Total monthly insurance premium

11. Which of the following is true regarding qualitative risk analysis?

    A. Only numerical data is considered.
    B. ALE must be calculated.
    C. Threats must be identified.
    D. ROI must be calculated.

12. Which values must be calculated to derive annual loss expectancy? (Choose two.)

    A. Single loss expectancy
    B. Annual rate of occurrence
    C. Monthly loss expectancy
    D. Quarterly loss expectancy

13. You are the server expert for a cloud computing firm named Cloud Nine Computing. Management would like to set aside funds to respond to server downtime risks. Using historical data, you determine the probability of server downtime is 17 percent. Past data suggests the server would be down for an average of one hour and that $3,000 of revenue can be earned in one hour. You must calculate the annual loss expectancy (ALE). Choose the correct ALE.

    A. $300
    B. $510
    C. $3,000
    D. $36,000

    $ X SERVER DOWN TIME
    .17 x 3000 = 51

14. Your boss asks you to calculate how much money the company loses when critical servers required by employees are down for 2 hours. You have determined that the probability of this happening is 70 percent. The company has 25 employees each earning $18.50 per hour. Choose the correct value.

    A. $12.95
    B. $18.50
    C. $323.75
    D. $3,885

    .7 multi by 25 x 18.5

15. Your company is considering having the e-mail server hosted by Hosted Solutions, Inc., to reduce hardware and mail server technician costs at the local site. What type of document formally states the reliability and recourse if the reliability is not met?

A. BPA *BLANKET PURCHASE AG*
B. MOU *MEMO OF UNDERSTANDING*
C. SLA *SERVICE LEVEL AGREEMENT*
D. ISA *INTERNET SERVICE AGREEMENT*

16. Which term best describes monies spent to minimize the impact that threats and unfavorable conditions have on a business?

A. Risk management
B. Security audit
C. Budgetary constraints
D. Impact analysis

17. Which risk analysis approach makes use of ALE?

A. Best possible outcome
B. Quantitative
C. ROI
D. Qualitative

18. You are presenting data at a risk analysis meeting. During your presentation you display a list of ALE values sorted ranked by dollar amount. Bob, a meeting participant, asks how reliable the numeracy used to calculate the ALE is. What can you tell Bob?

A. The numbers are 100 percent reliable.
B. The numbers are 50 percent reliable.
C. ALEs are calculated using probability values that vary.
D. ALEs are calculated using percentages and are accurate.

19. Which of the following should be performed when conducting a qualitative risk assessment? (Choose two.)

A. Asset valuation
B. ARO *ANNUAL RATE OF OCCURRENCE*
C. SLE *SINGLE LOSS EXPECTANCY*
D. Ranking of potential threats

20. You are the IT security analyst for Big John's Gourmet Foods. Big John's plans to open a plant in Oranjestad, Aruba, next year. You are meeting with a planning committee in the next week and must come up with questions to ask the committee about the new location so you can prepare a risk analysis report. Which of the following would be the most relevant questions to ask? (Choose two.)

    A. How hot does it get in the summer?
    B. How reliable is the local power?
    C. What kind of physical premise security is in place?
    D. How close is the nearest highway?

21. Your corporate web site is being hosted by an Internet service provider. How does this apply to the concept of risk?

    A. Risk avoidance
    B. Risk transference
    C. Risk analysis
    D. Increase in ALE

22. Which of the following regarding risk management is true?

    A. Funds invested in risk management could have earned much more profit if spent elsewhere.
    B. ALEs are only estimates and are subject to being inaccurate.
    C. IT security risks are all handled by the corporate firewall.
    D. Qualitative risk analysis results are expressed in dollar amounts.

23. Your competitors are offering a new product that is predicted to sell well. After much careful study, your company has decided against launching a competing product because of the uncertainty of the market and the enormous investment required. Which term best describes your company's decision?

    A. Risk analysis
    B. Risk transfer
    C. Risk avoidance
    D. Product avoidance

24. How can management determine which risks should be given the most attention?

    A. Threat vector
    B. Rank risks by likelihood
    C. Rank risks by probable date of occurrence
    D. Rank risks by SLE

25. Recently your data center was housed in Albuquerque, New Mexico. Because of corporate downsizing, the data center equipment was moved to an existing office in Santa Fe. The server room in Santa Fe was not designed to accommodate all the new servers arriving from Albuquerque, and the server room temperature is very warm. Because this is a temporary solution until a new data center facility is built, management has decided not to pay for an updated air conditioning system. Which term best describes this scenario?

    A. Risk transfer

    B. Risk avoidance

    C. Risk acceptance

    D. Risk reduction

26. Which factors could influence your risk management strategy?

    A. Government regulations

    B. Moving operations to a new building

    C. The purchase of a newer firewall solution

    D. None of the above

    E. All of the above

27. You are a member of an IT project team. The team is performing an IT risk analysis and has identified assets and their values as well as threats and threat mitigation solutions. What must be done next?

    A. Perform a cost-benefit analysis of proposed risk solutions.

    B. Calculate the ALE values.

    C. Decide which vulnerabilities exist.

    D. There is nothing more to do.

28. To reduce the likelihood of internal fraud, an organization implements policies that ensure more than one person is responsible for a financial transaction from beginning to end. Which of the following best describes this scenario?

    A. Probability

    B. Mitigation solution

    C. Impact analysis

    D. Threat analysis

29. What is the difference between risk assessment and risk management?

    A. They are the same thing.

    B. Risk assessment identifies and prioritizes risks; risk management is the governing of risks to minimize their impact.

    C. Risk management identifies and prioritizes risks; risk assessment is the governing of risks to minimize their impact.

    D. Risk assessment identifies threats; risk management controls those threats.

30. Identify the two drawbacks to quantitative risk analysis compared to qualitative risk analysis. (Choose two.)

    A. Quantitative risk analysis entails complex calculations.

    B. Risks are not prioritized by monetary value.

    C. Quantitative analysis is more time-consuming than qualitative.

    D. It is difficult to determine how much money to allocate to reduce a risk.

31. Which of the following represent methods by which sensitive organizational information could be unintentionally leaked? (Choose two.)

    A. Encrypted cloud backup

    B. Social network apps on mobile phones

    C. E-mail

    D. NTFS file permissions

32. As an IT administrator, you are responsible for creating user accounts for newly hired employees. New hires must have a picture ID to obtain a network/e-mail account, and they must be given a PKI card that they assign a PIN to. Which term applies to the described process?

    A. Onboarding

    B. Offboarding

    C. Data ownership

    D. User-adding

33. Using Figure 15-1, match the terms on the left to the correct scenario on the right.

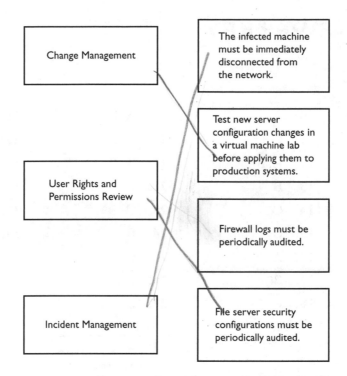

FIGURE 15-1

Risk mitigation
strategies

Change Management

The infected machine must be immediately disconnected from the network.

Test new server configuration changes in a virtual machine lab before applying them to production systems.

User Rights and Permissions Review

Firewall logs must be periodically audited.

Incident Management

File server security configurations must be periodically audited.

QUICK ANSWER KEY

1. C, D	**10.** A	**19.** A, D	**28.** B
2. A	**11.** C	**20.** B, C	**29.** B
3. A, D	**12.** A, B	**21.** B	**30.** A, C
4. B	**13.** B	**22.** B	**31.** B, C
5. A	**14.** C	**23.** C	**32.** A
6. B	**15.** C	**24.** B	**33.** See Figure 15-2.
7. D	**16.** A	**25.** C	
8. A, B	**17.** B	**26.** E	
9. B, C, D	**18.** C	**27.** B	

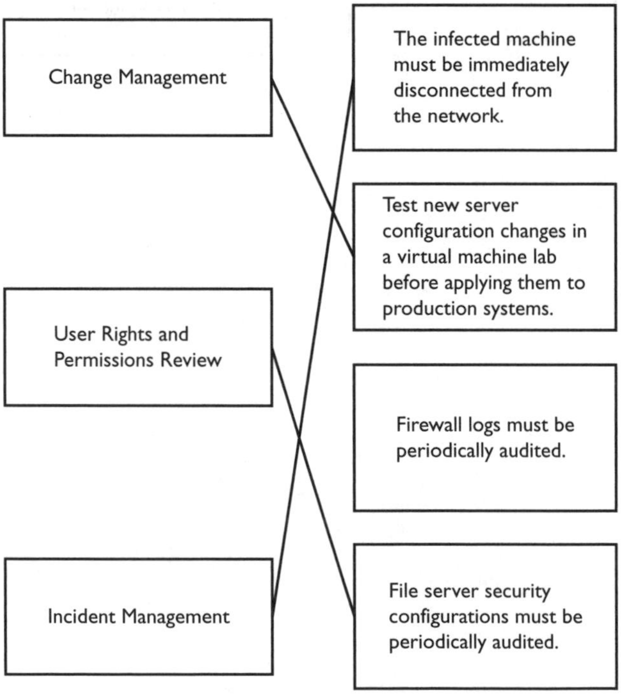

FIGURE 15-2

Risk mitigation strategies—the answer

Change Management

The infected machine must be immediately disconnected from the network.

Test new server configuration changes in a virtual machine lab before applying them to production systems.

User Rights and Permissions Review

Firewall logs must be periodically audited.

Incident Management

File server security configurations must be periodically audited.

IN-DEPTH ANSWERS

1. ☑ **C** and **D.** Risk analysis includes calculating plausible risks such as server downtime because of power outage and such as loss of equipment and data because of fire.
   ☒ **A** and **B** are incorrect. The likelihood of earthquakes in this part of the world is minimal. Government regulations documentation can be easily reacquired, so there is no risk in losing it.

2. ☑ **A.** Asset identification involves identifying assets (including data) and associating a value with them. This can then be used to justify expenditures to protect these assets.
   ☒ **B, C,** and **D** are incorrect. Risk assessment is the identification of threats, but the next step in this case is asset identification. Risk mitigation minimizes the impact of perceived risks. Threat analysis does not involve identifying IT hardware with a cost.

3. ☑ **A** and **D.** USB flash drives could have files downloaded from the Internet or copied from less secure machines that could infect your network. Business partner documentation downloaded from the Internet could potentially be infected.
   ☒ **B** and **C** are incorrect. USB keyboards and smartcards are not likely sources of malware.

4. ☑ **B.** Hackers breaking in through a firewall would be considered an external threat.
   ☒ **A, C,** and **D** are incorrect. Anything involving employees and security would be considered a potential internal threat.

5. ☑ **A.** Determining how an entity can gain access to corporate resources would require a threat assessment.
   ☒ **B, C,** and **D** are incorrect. Risk analysis is a general term that includes conducting a threat assessment, but threat assessment is a more specific and applicable answer. Asset identification involves determining what items (tangible and nontangible) are of value and associating a dollar value with those items. Cost of ownership allows consumers to determine the true cost of a product or service.

6. ☑ **B.** Confidentiality means keeping data hidden from those who should not see it, such as competitors.
   ☒ **A, C,** and **D** are incorrect. Integrity verifies the authenticity of data; it does not conceal it. Availability ensures a resource is available as often as possible, for example, clustering a database server. Authorization grants access to a resource once the identity of an entity has been verified through authentication.

7. ☑ **D.** Determining the effect that materialized risks have on the operation of a business is called impact analysis. It is often used to determine whether expenditures against these risks are justified.

☒   A, B, and C are incorrect. Risk analysis is too general a term in this case; impact analysis is a more specific answer. Fault tolerance can reduce the impact if a disk fails, but it is very specific; the question refers to more than a single risk. Availability ensures resources are available as often as possible to minimize risks, but it does not determine how risks affect a business.

8.   ☑   A and B. Assessing risk includes determining what is and is not covered by various types of insurance coverage and whether the cost of those insurance premiums is justified. The number of server hard disks is definitely risk related. The likelihood of hard disk data loss is minimized when there are multiple hard disks configured properly, such as RAID 1 (disk mirroring).
☒   C and D are incorrect. CPU speed and network bandwidth are not directly related to risk assessment; they are related to performance.

9.   ☑   B, C, and D. Backing up data minimizes the risk of losing data. Employee training reduces the likelihood of errors or disclosure of confidential information. Choosing the most reliable network load balancing appliance can reduce the risk of network traffic congestion.
☒   A is incorrect. Larger flat-screen monitors are not related to risk prevention.

10.   ☑   A. The annual loss expectancy (ALE) value is used with quantitative risk analysis approaches to prioritize and justify expenditures that protect from potential risks. For example, an ALE value of $1,000 might justify a $200 annual expense to protect against that risk.
☒   B, C, and D are incorrect. The return on investment (ROI) calculates how efficient an investment is (does the benefit of a product or service outweigh the cost?). The total cost of ownership exposes all direct and indirect dollar figures associated with a product or service. Using the total monthly premium value to determine whether to accept the additional insurance coverage would be meaningless; it must be compared against the probability of natural disasters in your area.

11.   ☑   C. Qualitative risk analysis categorizes risks (threats) with general (not hard numerical) terms and numerical ranges, for example, a risk falling between 1 (small risk) to 10 (big risk). For this to happen, threats must first be identified.
☒   A, B, and D are incorrect. Although numerical data is important in both quantitative and qualitative risk assessments, it is not only numerical data that is considered; the scale of the risks and their effects and how responses to risks are handled are also considered. Annual loss expectancy (ALE) is a specific dollar figure used in quantitative analysis. Qualitative analysis uses a relative measurement scale to rank risks. Return on investment (ROI) cannot be determined until a risk analysis has been done.

12.   ☑   A and B. Annual loss expectancy (ALE) is derived by multiplying the annual rate of occurrence (ARO) by the single loss expectancy (SLE).
☒   C and D are incorrect. Monthly and quarterly loss expectancy are not used to calculate the ALE.

13. ☑ **B.** Annual loss expectancy (ALE) is calculated by multiplying the annual rate of occurrence (ARO – .17) by the single loss expectancy (SLE – 3,000). So, .17 multiplied by 3,000 equals 510.
☒ **A, C,** and **D** are incorrect. ALE = ARO multiplied by SLE.

14. ☑ **C.** This question is asking you to calculate the annual loss expectancy (ALE). Multiply the probability (annual rate of occurrence) by the dollar amount associated with a single failure (single loss expectancy), so .7 multiplied by (25*18.5) equals 323.75.
☒ **A, B,** and **D** are incorrect. ALE = ARO multiplied by SLE.

15. ☑ **C.** A service level agreement (SLA) formally defines what type of service a customer can expect and what type of recourse is available should that level of service not be provided.
☒ **A, B,** and **D** are incorrect. Blanket purchase agreements (BPAs) are agreements covering recurring services or supplies. A memorandum of understanding (MOU) details agreements between two parties involved in some kind of business affair. Internet service agreements (ISAs) are contractual documents detailing the expected service from an Internet provider.

16. ☑ **A.** Risk assessment means determining the impact that threats and less than optimal conditions can have on a business or agency. Risk management involves setting aside the funds to account for these eventualities. Determining the amount of money to set aside may involve many detailed calculations.
☒ **B, C,** and **D** are incorrect. A security audit may be one factor influencing how monies are to be spent to protect a business, but a risk analysis is used to determine how a reasonable amount of funds must be set aside to deal with risks after all factors (perhaps including a security audit) have been considered. Budgetary constraints do not describe the definition presented in the question. An impact analysis specifically determines the effect threats and unfavorable circumstances have on the operation of a business, but, like a security audit, it would be one of many factors influencing what the appropriate number of dollars to mitigate these issues would be.

17. ☑ **B.** The annual loss expectancy (ALE) is a specific figure derived from the probability of a loss and the cost of one occurrence of this loss. Because specific dollar values (quantities) are used to prioritize risks, this falls into the category of quantitative risk analysis.
☒ **A, C,** and **D** are incorrect. Best possible outcome is not a risk analysis approach. Return on investment cannot be calculated prior to a risk analysis being completed. Qualitative risk analysis approaches uses a relative ranking scale to rate risks instead of using specific figures.

18. ☑ **C.** Annual loss expectancy (ALE) values use the probability of a loss in conjunction with the cost of a single incident. Probability values are rarely accurate, but because the future cannot be predicted, they are acceptable. Probability values can be arrived at by referring to past historical data.

☒   **A, B**, and **D** are incorrect. When dealing with probabilities, you cannot state a definite percentage of accuracy. Although the ALE is calculated using a percentage (probability of annual rate of occurrence), you cannot tell Bob that the ALE is accurate.

19.   ☑   **A** and **D.** Qualitative risk analysis assesses the likelihood of risks that will impede normal business operations and prioritizes (ranks) them relative to one another. Assets that must be protected from identified risks must have an assigned value to determine whether the cost of risk mitigation is justified.

☒   **B** and **C** are incorrect. Annual rate of occurrence (ARO) and single loss expectancy (SLE) use specific dollar figures (quantitative) to calculate the ALE. Annual loss expectancy (ALE) = annual rate of occurrence (ARO) multiplied by single loss expectancy (SLE).

20.   ☑   **B** and **C.** A reliable power source is critical for IT systems. Unreliable power would mean a different plant location or the use of a uninterruptible power supply (UPS) and power generators. Physical security should always be considered during risk analysis

☒   **A** and **D** are incorrect. Summer temperatures might be relevant, but power reliability will deal with this since reliable power means reliable heating, ventilation, and air conditioning (HVAC). Unless toxic waste or something similar is being transported on the nearest highway, this is not relevant.

21.   ☑   **B.** Risk transference shifts some or all of the burden of risk to a third party.

☒   **A, C**, and **D** are incorrect. Risk avoidance is not applicable in this case; risk avoidance removes threats. Risk analysis is the practice of identifying and ranking threats jeopardizing business goals in order to allocate funds to mitigate these threats. The annual loss expectancy (ALE) is a dollar value associated with the probability of a failure.

22.   ☑   **B.** Annual loss expectancy (ALE) figures are considered inaccurate because part of their calculation is based on probabilities.

☒   **A, C**, and **D** are incorrect. Assuming risk analysis was conducted properly, the allocated funds to minimize the impact of risk are probably better invested where they are than in other endeavors. Firewalls do not handle all IT security risks. Qualitative risk analysis reports do not express results in dollar values; instead, risks are weighed against each other and ranked.

23.   ☑   **C.** Deciding to invest heavily in a new product for an uncertain market is a gamble. Deciding against it would be classified as risk avoidance.

☒   **A, B**, and **D** are incorrect. Risk analysis is not as specific an answer as risk avoidance. Risk transfer would imply some or all risk is assumed by another party. Product avoidance is a fictitious risk management term.

24.   ☑   **B.** Whether qualitative or quantitative risk analysis is done, once data has been properly considered, risks should be ranked by likelihood.

☒   **A, C**, and **D** are incorrect. A threat vector is a tool or mechanism used by an attacker to exploit a system. In some cases, ranking threats by date can be beneficial, but this is usually factored in when ranking by priority. The single loss expectancy (SLE) is a dollar value associated with a single failure. The annual loss expectancy (ALE) uses the SLE as well as a probability of the incident occurring, resulting in a dollar figure. ALE figures can be sorted by dollar value to determine which threats should be given the most attention, but the SLE by itself is not enough.

25. ☑ **C.** Accepting the potential consequences of a threat is referred to as risk acceptance. The amount of money to minimize the risk is not warranted, as was the case of a temporary data center in Santa Fe.

☒ **A, B,** and **D** are incorrect. Risk transfer shifts risk consequence responsibility to another party. Risk avoidance refers to the disregard of an opportunity because of the risk involved. Risk reduction is the application of mitigation techniques to minimize the occurrence of threats.

26. ☑ **E.** Government regulations might involve the privacy of client information, which could mean a new or more prevalent security risk. It is always important to review agreement requirements to ensure that compliance and performance standards are being met. A new building might have better security than an old one, which may reduce the physical security risks. Newer firewall solutions generally have better protection than older solutions (if configured and maintained properly), which again could reduce risk.

☒ **D** is incorrect. All listed items could influence your risk management strategy.

27. ☑ **B.** The annual loss expectancy (ALE) values must be calculated now that threats have been identified and assets have been valued.

☒ **A, C,** and **D** are incorrect. A cost-benefit analysis can be done only once ALE values have been calculated. ALE values give you something to compare threat mitigation costs against to determine whether expenditures are warranted. Deciding which vulnerabilities exist has already been done at this stage. There is much more to be done (ALE, cost-benefit analysis, and so on).

28. ☑ **B.** The implementation of policies for the internal control of transactions encompasses mitigation solutions. The threat is identified, and a solution is put into place.

☒ **A, C,** and **D** are incorrect. Probability is a factor used to calculate the annual loss expectancy (ALE). An impact analysis determines the effect various threats can have on business operations. A threat analysis defines threats and possible solutions.

29. ☑ **B.** Risk assessment requires identification and prioritization of risks using either a relative ranking scale or objective numeric data. Managing those risks involves minimizing their impact on the business.

☒ **A, C,** and **D** are incorrect. Risk assessment and management are not the same thing. Risk assessment identifies and prioritizes risks, while risk management governs risks to minimize their impact. Threat analysis identifies threats, not risk assessment or risk management.

30. ☑ **A** and **C.** Quantitative risk analysis involves complex, time-consuming calculations. Results are expressed in specific percentages or monetary values despite that probability figures are used to arrive at these results.

⊠ **B** and **D** are incorrect. Prioritizing risks applies to qualitative risk analysis where risks are ranked relative to each other but not necessarily by dollar value. Quantitative risk analysis strives to provide a specific dollar amount to facilitate allocating funds.

31. ☑ **B** and **C.** Users could inadvertently post work-related messages, images, or documents through a social networking app. Organizational data could be in an e-mail message body or attached as a file. Data loss prevention (DLP) software can be configured to monitor and enforce this.

    ⊠ **A** and **D** are incorrect. Cloud backup does not present a data leakage problem, especially if it is encrypted. NTFS file permissions unto themselves do not present a DLP problem.

32. ☑ **A.** Adding new users to an identity management system is referred to as onboarding.

    ⊠ **B, C,** and **D** are incorrect. Offboarding is the removal of a user from an identity management system. Data ownership refers to a cloud service level agreement (SLA) stipulating that data ownership is retained by the cloud customer. User-adding is a fictitious term.

33. ☑ See Figure 15-3. Testing new server configurations before applying those changes to production systems falls under change management. Auditing file servers relates to user rights and permission reviews. Removing infected machines from the network is related to incident management.

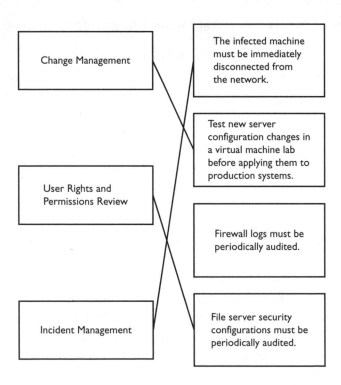

FIGURE 15-3

Risk mitigation strategies—the answer

16

Disaster Recovery and Business Continuity

QUESTIONS

Unfavorable circumstances can temporarily or permanently cripple a business. A disaster recovery plan attempts to minimize the impact that these circumstances, whether caused by nature or by humans, have on a business. The plan should include incident assessment, and it should specify who performs which tasks under specific circumstances.

1. In the event of a server hard disk failure, you have been asked to configure server hard disks as depicted in Figure 16-1. What type of disk configuration is this?

   A. RAID 0
   B. RAID 1
   C. RAID 5
   D. RAID 5+1

FIGURE 16-1

Hard disk
configuration

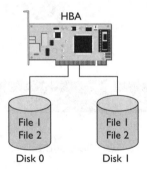

2. A team leader assigns Ron, a server administrator, the task of determining the business and financial effects that a failed e-mail server would have if it was down for two hours. What type of analysis must Ron perform?

   A. Critical systems and components identification
   B. Business impact analysis
   C. Security audit
   D. Risk assessment

3. An urban law enforcement agency leases a new space in another part of town complete with a functioning computer network mirroring the current live site. A high-speed network link constantly synchronizes data between the two sites. What type of site is the new leased location?

   A. Frost site
   B. Cold site
   C. Warm site
   D. Hot site

4. An urban law enforcement agency leases a new space in another part of town complete with a functioning computer network mirroring the current live site. Data backups from the primary site are copied to the new leased location every two days. What type of site is the new leased location?

   A. Frost site

   B. Cold site

   C. Warm site

   D. Hot site

5. Turtle Airlines has hired you to ensure its customer reservation system is always online. The software runs and stores data locally on the Linux operating system. What should you do?

   A. Install two Linux servers in a cluster. Cluster the airline software, with its data being written to shared storage.

   B. Install a new Linux server. Ensure the airline software runs from the first server. Schedule airline data to replicate to the new Linux server nightly.

   C. Configure the Linux server with RAID 5.

   D. Configure the Linux server with RAID 1.

6. A busy clustered web site regularly experiences congested network traffic. You must improve the web site response time. What should you implement?

   A. Ethernet switch

   B. Network load balancing

   C. Fibre Channel switch

   D. Proxy server

7. Your primary e-mail server uses three hot-swappable hard disks in a RAID 5 configuration. When one disk fails, you have other disks readily available in the server room that you simply plug in while the server is still running. Which term best describes this scenario?

   A. Disk clustering

   B. Hardware fault tolerance

   C. Disk striping

   D. Disk mirroring

8. Your server backup routine consists of a full backup each Friday night and a nightly backup of all data changed since Friday's backup. What type of backup schedule is this?

   A. Full

   B. Full and incremental

   C. Full and differential

   D. Fully incremental

9. The chief security officer at a national bank chain will be retiring next year, and an IT security employee must be groomed to fill that position. What term encompasses this procedure?

    A. Retirement

    B. Job rotation

    C. Succession planning

    D. Disaster recovery

10. You are a network engineer for a Los Angeles law firm. After the 1989 earthquake, an emphasis on continued business operation after future earthquakes dominated the Los Angeles business community. What type of plan focuses on ensuring that personnel, customers, and IT systems are minimally affected after a disaster?

    A. Risk management

    B. Fault tolerant

    C. Disaster recovery

    D. Business continuity

11. A server is configured with three hard disks as per Figure 16-2. What type of configuration is this?

    A. RAID 0

    B. RAID 1

    C. RAID 5

    D. RAID 5+1

FIGURE 16-2

Hard disk configuration

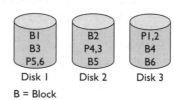

Disk 1 Disk 2 Disk 3

B = Block
P = Parity

12. Windows Server 2012 backups are scheduled as follows: full backups on Saturdays at 3 a.m. and incremental backups weeknights at 9 p.m. Write verification has been enabled. Backup tapes are stored offsite at a third-party location. What should be done to ensure the integrity and confidentially of the backups? (Choose two.)

A. Have a different person than the backup operator analyze each day's backup logs.

B. Ensure the user performing the backup is a member of the Administrators group.

C. Encrypt the backup media.

D. Use SSL to encrypt the backup media.

13. You are an IT network architect. Your firm has been hired to perform a network security audit for Acme Shipping Inc. One of Acme's warehouses has a server room containing one Windows server and two Linux servers. After interviewing the server administrators, you learn they have no idea what to do if the Linux servers cease to function. What is needed here?

A. Disaster recovery plan

B. Risk analysis

C. Windows servers

D. Server clustering

14. Which items should be considered when ensuring high availability for an e-commerce web site? (Choose two.)

A. Using TPM to encrypt server hard disks

B. Using redundant Internet links

C. Network load balancing

D. Upgrading the server CMOS to the latest version

15. Which items should be considered when creating a disaster recovery plan? (Choose three.)

A. Determine which class of IP addresses are in use.

B. Rank risks.

C. Disable unused switch ports.

D. Assign recovery tasks to personnel.

E. Establish an alternate location to continue business operations.

16. As part of your disaster recovery planning, you create a prioritized list of professionals who can be contacted in the event of a flood. Who are they? (Choose three.)

A. Property restoration specialist

B. Document restoration specialist

C. Server backup specialist   *TO LATE*

D. Server restoration specialist

17. What should be used to make informed decisions regarding your specific disaster recovery plan?

   A. DRP template freely downloaded from a web site

   B. ROI analysis *RETURN ON INVESTMEN*

   C. TCO analysis *TOTAL COST OF OWNERSHIP*

   D. Business impact analysis

18. Identify the disaster recovery plan errors. (Choose two.)

   A. Perform a business impact analysis first.

   B. Base your DRP on a downloaded template. *DISASTER RECOVERY PLAN*

   C. Data backups are never tested; it costs the company too much money.

   D. Keep existing backup solutions in place even though the software is two versions out of date.

19. You are creating a DRP for a small, independent car dealership. There are four employees who each use a desktop computer; there are no servers. All company data is stored on the four computers. A single high-speed DSL link is shared by all users. What are the best DRP solutions? (Choose two.)

   A. Store data with an online data storage service.

   B. Ensure employees know exactly what to do in the event of a disaster.

   C. Purchase faster desktops.

   D. Purchase a file server.

20. Mark is the server specialist for Big Game Hunting Inc. While installing a new server data hard disk, Mark spills his cup of coffee on the old server data hard disk. What should Mark do?

   A. Use a blow-dryer to dry the hard disk.

   B. Immerse the hard disk in warm water to remove the coffee.

   C. Place the hard disk in an air-sealed container.

   D. Contact a network specialist.

21. You are working with management to justify the cost of a warm site versus a cold site. What factors can help justify the cost of a warm site? (Choose two.)

   A. Large revenue loss during short downtime

   B. Small revenue loss during long downtime

   C. Customer contracts tolerating no more than 8 hours downtime

   D. Customer contracts tolerating no more than 72 hours downtime

22. Your senior network administrator has decided that the five physical servers at your location will be virtualized and run on a single physical host. The five virtual guests will use the physical hard disks in the physical host. The physical host has the hard disks configured with RAID 1. Identify the flaw in this plan.

   A. The physical server should be using RAID 5.

   B. The physical hard disks must not reside in the physical host.

   C. You cannot run five virtual machines on a physical host simultaneously.

   D. The physical host is a single point of failure.

23. Your company is virtualizing DNS, DHCP, web, and e-mail servers at your location. Each of the four virtual machines will be spread out across two physical hosts. Virtual machines are using virtual hard disks, and these files exist on a SAN. Choose the best virtual machine backup strategy that will allow the quickest granular restore.

   A. Back up the virtual machine hard disks at the SAN level.

   B. Install a backup agent in each virtual machine and perform backups normally.

   C. Duplicate your SAN disk array so that backups are not necessary.

   D. All four virtual machines must run on the same physical host to be backed up.

24. What should you do when storing server backup tapes offsite?

   A. Encrypt backed-up data.

   B. Generate file hashes for each backed-up file.

   C. Place backup tapes in static shielding bags.

   D. It is a security violation to store backup tapes offsite.

25. You are the administrator for a virtual Windows 2012 Server running Active Directory Domain Services (AD DS). Abnormal server behavior and finally a server freeze leads you to believe that the server has a virus infection. What should you do?

   A. Revert to an earlier virtual machine snapshot prior to the virus infection.

   B. Format the hard disk, reinstall the server, and restore from tape.

   C. Refer to your DRP. *DISASTER RECOVERY PLAN*

   D. Refer to your ARP. *FICTICIOUS*

26. What is the purpose of a disaster recovery plan? (Choose two.)

   A. To minimize economic loss

   B. To have a premeditated reaction to public relations blunders

   C. To install confidence in shareholders

   D. To earn a high rate of return annually

27. Which of the following would appear on a DRP?

    A. Prioritized list of critical computer systems

    B. Single points of failure

    C. Employee birth dates

    D. Dollar value associated with an hour of downtime

28. You are the network administrator for a small IT consulting firm. All servers are located at the single site. After testing the DRP and receiving management approval, you e-mail a copy to all employees for their reference in the event of a disaster. Identify the problem.

    A. The e-mail should have been encrypted.

    B. The e-mail should have been digitally signed.

    C. Only executives should have received the message.

    D. The mail server might not be available in the event of a disaster.

29. You are the network administrator for a small IT consulting firm. All servers are hosted externally. After analyzing threats, creating a DRP, and receiving management approval, you e-mail a copy to all employees for their reference in the event of a disaster. Identify the problem.

    A. The e-mail should have been encrypted.

    B. The DRP plan was not tested.

    C. The e-mail should have been digitally signed.

    D. Only executives should have received the message.

30. Which of the following regarding disaster recovery are true? (Choose two.)

    A. Once the plan is complete, it need never be revisited.

    B. Once the plan is complete, it must have management approval.

    C. The plan is never complete; it must evolve with the business.

    D. The plan should include only IT systems.

31. Using Figure 16-3, match the descriptions on the left to the corresponding terms on the right.

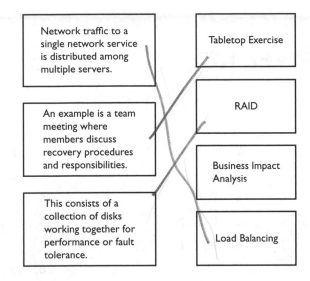

FIGURE 16-3

Disaster recovery and business continuity terminology

32. You are a server administrator for a public cloud provider. To ensure compliance with customer SLAs, you must use reliable hard disks in your hardware to host the virtual environment used by cloud customers. Which of the following terms best describes the reliability of hard disks?

    A. MTBF *MEAN TIME BETWEEN FAIL*
    B. MTTF *MEAN TIME TO FAILURE*
    C. MTTR *MEAN TIME TO RECOVER*
    D. RPO   *RECOVERY POINT OBJECTIVE*

33. As the IT director, you are comparing public cloud providers. Your company will no longer house on-premises mail or application servers. Which factors under your control must you consider to ensure mail and applications are always available to users?

    A. Updates applied to cloud provider servers
    B. Redundant network links
    C. RAID level used on cloud provider servers
    D. MTTF for cloud provider server hard disks

QUICK ANSWER KEY

1. B	12. A, C	23. B
2. B	13. A	24. A
3. D	14. B, C	25. C
4. C	15. B, D, E	26. A, C
5. A	16. A, B, D	27. A
6. B	17. D	28. D
7. B	18. B, C	29. B
8. C	19. A, B	30. B, C
9. C	20. C	31. See Figure 16-4.
10. D	21. A, C	32. B
11. C	22. D	33. B

FIGURE 16-4

Disaster recovery and business continuity terminology—the answer

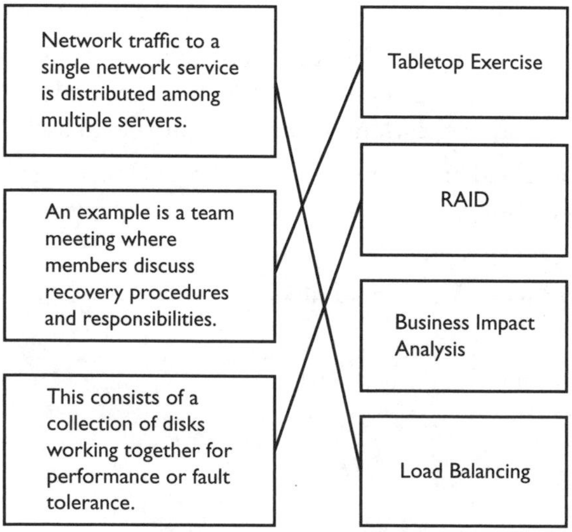

IN-DEPTH ANSWERS

1. ☑ **B.** Redundant Array of Independent Disks (RAID) level 1 refers to disk mirroring. When data is written to one disk, it is duplicated on the second disk. In the event of a single disk failure, the second disk can take over.

   ☒ **A, C,** and **D** are incorrect. RAID 0 involves striping data across multiple disks to increase performance, but there is no fault tolerance since a single disk failure would result in the loss of all data. RAID 5 stripes data across disks but distributes parity (recovery) data on disks so that a single disk failure means data can still be reconstructed. RAID 5+1 is a mirrored RAID 5 array.

2. ☑ **B.** A business impact analysis, also referred to as a business impact assessment, identifies the effect unwanted events have on the operation of a business.

   ☒ **A, C,** and **D** are incorrect. Identifying critical systems and components is part of determining assets and their worth when performing a risk analysis. A security audit tests how effective security policy implementation is for safeguarding corporate assets. Risk assessments identify assets and their related threats and potential losses; these can be used to create security policies and are an integral part of the overall business impact assessment (BIA).

3. ☑ **D.** Hot sites offer the least downtime but at the most cost.

   ☒ **A, B,** and **C** are incorrect. A frost site is not a valid term. Cold sites are backup sites that are not immediately functional but are cheaper to maintain than hot sites. Warm sites require little time to be fully operational. In the question, data is being constantly synchronized between the sites, so the backup site is immediately functional.

4. ☑ **C.** Warm sites are functional only once critical data is available.

   ☒ **A, B,** and **D** are incorrect. Cold sites are not equipped with a functional computer network mirroring the original site; they are often nothing more than leased space. Because the data is copied only every two days, this does not constitute a hot site.

5. ☑ **A.** Clustering software between two servers will allow the customer reservation system to function even if one server fails because the data is not stored within a single server; it exists on shared storage that both cluster nodes can access.

   ☒ **B, C,** and **D** are incorrect. Scheduling nightly data replication does not ensure the airline software is always online. RAID 1 (mirroring) and RAID 5 (striping with distributed parity) are useless if the server fails.

6. ☑ **B.** Network load balancing (NLB) can distribute network traffic to multiple servers hosting the same content to improve performance.

   ☒ **A, C,** and **D** are incorrect. Most networks already use Ethernet switches. Fibre Channel switches are used in a storage area network (SAN) environment, not local area networks (LANs) or wide area networks (WANs). A proxy server retrieves Internet content for clients and then optionally caches it for later requests; it would not improve performance here.

7. ☑ **B.** Hardware fault tolerance allows a hardware component to fail while not completely impeding data access. A single disk failure in a RAID 5 configuration means the failed disk can be hot-swapped with a functional disk. Because RAID 5 stripes data across disks in the array and parity is distributed across disks, user requests for data can be reconstructed dynamically in RAM until the data is reconstructed on the replaced disk.

☒ **A, C,** and **D** are incorrect. Disk clustering is not a proper term. Disk striping offers no fault tolerance, only performance increases. Disk mirroring is not applicable since the question states RAID 5 is in use.

8. ☑ **C.** Differential backups will archive data that has changed since the last full backup. Restoring data means first restoring the full backup and then the latest differential.

☒ **A, B,** and **D** are incorrect. Incremental backups archive data changed since the last incremental backup. Fully incremental is a fictitious term.

9. ☑ **C.** Succession planning involves identifying and preparing individuals to fill specific job roles.

☒ **A, B,** and **D** are incorrect. Job rotation could help prepare an individual to fill a key role, but succession planning is a much better answer. Job rotation doesn't guarantee that an individual will know all aspects of each area the chief security officer is required to know. Disaster recovery involves business continuity in the event of unfavorable circumstances; it has nothing to do with preparing an employee to fill a key role.

10. ☑ **D.** Business continuity is considered the key goal to which disaster recovery plays a part. Disaster recovery (DR) normally involves implementing steps taken to get the business operational. Business continuity ensures business operation after the successful implementation of the DR.

☒ **A, B,** and **C** are incorrect. Risk management refers to minimizing the impact potential risks could have on the primary goal of a business. Fault tolerance is not a type of plan; fault tolerance falls under the umbrella of risk management. Disaster recovery involves methodically returning the business to normal operation and is a component of a business continuity plan.

11. ☑ **C.** Distributing data and parity information across disks is referred to as RAID level 5.

☒ **A, B,** and **D** are incorrect. RAID 0 (striping) writes data across disks without parity, so there is a performance benefit but no fault tolerance. RAID 1 (mirroring) duplicates data written on the first disk to the second disk in case one disk fails. RAID 5+1 mirrors a RAID 5 configuration for additional fault tolerance.

12. ☑ **A and C.** To reduce the likelihood of tampering, a different person should review backup logs. For confidentiality, backup tapes stored offsite should be encrypted.

☒ **B and D** are incorrect. There is no need to be a member of the Administrators group, but there is a need to be in the Backup Operators group. SSL encrypts network traffic, not stored data.

13. ☑ **A.** Disaster recovery plans outline exactly who must do what in case unfavorable events occur.

☒ **B, C,** and **D** are incorrect. A risk analysis identifies threats to assets and prioritizes those threats, but actions taken in a disaster are included in a disaster recovery plan. Windows servers are not needed here; a disaster recovery plan is. Clustering the Linux servers would only make matters worse if they ceased functioning because clustering introduces more complexity. The administrators should get Linux training, and a DRP addressing the Linux servers should be crafted.

14. ☑ **B** and **C.** High availability makes a resource available as often as is possible. Redundant Internet links allow access to the web site even if one Internet link fails. Network load balancing (which could use the redundant Internet links) distributes traffic evenly either to server cluster nodes or through redundant network links.

☒ **A** and **D** are incorrect. Trusted Platform Module (TPM) encrypts hard disk contents. While this addresses confidentiality, it does not address high availability. CMOS upgrades may improve or give new hardware capabilities to the web server, but this does not directly address high availability. If the CMOS update corrects a problem with RAID configurations, then it would address high availability, but the possible answers do not list this.

15. ☑ **B, D,** and **E.** Risks should be ranked to determine which are the most probable. The most attention should be given to the most likely threats. Personnel must be assigned tasks according to the DRP to minimize confusion and downtime. An alternate site (cold, warm, or hot) should at least be considered. Larger businesses or agencies may be able to justify the cost of maintaining an alternate site.

☒ **A, C,** and **D** are incorrect. IP address classes have no impact on creating DRPs. Although unused switch ports should always be disabled, this would not be considered when crafting a DRP.

16. ☑ **A, B,** and **D.** Property restoration specialists efficiently restore the state of a facility so that a business can continue to operate. Their responsibilities include HVAC, electricity, water, lighting, and so on. Document restoration specialists have expertise in retrieving damaged data, whether it is physical (paper documents) or digital. Server restoration specialists are trained in quickly getting servers up and running to their previous state. A disaster recovery plan is required for server restoration specialists to efficiently perform their duties.

☒ **C.** Server backup is not a consideration after a disaster has occurred, but server restoration is.

17. ☑ **D.** A business impact analysis identifies which risks will affect business operations more than others. This is valuable in determining how to recover from a disaster.

☒ **A, B,** and **C** are incorrect. Freely downloadable DRP templates are generic and will not address your specific business or IT configuration. Return on investment (ROI) determines the efficiency of an investment (is the cost justified?). Total cost of ownership (TCO) identifies the true cost of a product or service. Neither the ROI nor TCO is tied directly to your DRP like a business impact analysis is.

18. ☑ **B and C.** Your DRP should be much more specific than what a downloaded template can provide. DRPs are not worth their investment if their success has not been proven through testing.
☒ **A and D** are incorrect. A DRP takes the business impact analysis into account. Backed-up software that is two versions out of date might still function correctly; often there are risks involved with immediately using the newest software.

19. ☑ **A and B.** Online data storage would be an affordable solution to safeguard business data. Users must know what to do in the event of a catastrophe to ensure the timely resumption of business.
☒ **C and D** are incorrect. Faster computers will not have an impact on a DRP for a small business. Purchasing a file server is not justified given the small number of employees and a single site; online data storage could be justified.

20. ☑ **C.** Mark must ensure the coffee does not dry onto any electrical components. An air-sealed container is a good solution, followed by immediately contacting a data recovery specialist.
☒ **A, B, and D** are incorrect. A blow-dryer will dry the coffee onto electrical components and disk surfaces and could damage the hard disk. You should never immerse hard disks in water. Instead of contacting a network specialist, you should contact a data recovery specialist.

21. ☑ **A and C.** Some businesses could lose large sums even in a short period of downtime. Calculating these figures enables intelligent decisions to be made regarding justifying the cost of an alternate site. Your business may have customer contracts requiring minimal downtime in the event of a disaster. The cost of the loss of this business could be factored into justifying the cost of an alternate (warm) site.
☒ **B and D** are incorrect. Losing a small amount of money even if long downtime is experienced cannot justify requiring a warm alternate site. Seventy-two hours is enough time to bring a cold site online to resume business services.

22. ☑ **D.** If the single physical host experiences a failure, all five virtual machine will be unavailable. A second server should be clustered with the first, and virtual guests should use shared disk storage versus local disk storage.
☒ **A, B, and C** are incorrect. RAID 5 would not solve the problem of the disks being in a single server. Even if shared storage were used, the physical server would still be a single point of failure. Given enough hardware resources, many more than five virtual guests can run simultaneously on a virtualization server.

23. ☑ **B.** If granular restores are required, backing up each virtual machine using a backup agent installed in each virtual machine is the best choice.
☒ **A, C, and D** are incorrect. Backing up the SAN means backing up virtual hard disks used by the virtual machines. This presents some difficulty if you must restore specific (granular) files. Backups are always necessary no matter what. If virtual hard disks are on a SAN, all four virtual machines do not have to be running on the same physical host.

24. ☑ **A.** Backup tapes stored offsite must be encrypted to ensure data confidentiality.

☒ **B, C,** and **D** are incorrect. Generating file hashes for every backed-up file would take a long time. The benefit of file hashing is to ensure the file has not changed (been tampered with), which is not as useful as encryption—encrypted files cannot be altered without the proper decryption key. Static shielding bags protect electrical components from electrostatic discharge; they do nothing for backup tapes. Offsite backup tape storage is a critical component in a disaster recovery plan.

25. ☑ **C.** A DRP specifies who should do what in case of a disaster, such as in the case of an infected server.

☒ **A, B,** and **D** are incorrect. Snapshots should not be used on servers that rely on date and time stamps for their operation. Formatting, reinstalling, and tape restore may be what the DRP requires be done, but the best answer is to refer to your DRP. ARP is a fictitious term in the disaster recovery realm.

26. ☑ **A** and **C.** Minimizing downtime, reducing customer disruption, and avoiding economic loss are the reasons for a disaster recovery plan. Shareholder confidence is solidified when an efficient, well-thought-out disaster recovery plan is in place.

☒ **B** and **D** are incorrect. A better term for this situation might be damage control. Earning high rates of return defines an ideal investment, not the purpose of a disaster recovery plan.

27. ☑ **A.** Prioritized lists of critical computer systems allow minimal downtime.

☒ **B, C,** and **D** are incorrect. Single points of failure would be identified in a risk analysis. Employee birth dates have nothing to do with a disaster recovery plan. Downtime and dollar values are calculated during risk analysis.

28. ☑ **D.** The only copy of the disaster recovery plan exists on a mail server that users may not have access to when they need it most. Alternate storage locations and physical copies must be considered.

☒ **A, B,** and **C** are incorrect. Although good advice, encrypted and signed e-mail is not a problem in this scenario. A comprehensive DRP must be made known to applicable employees.

29. ☑ **B.** A disaster recovery plan changes with the business and must be tested to ensure its success.

☒ **A, C,** and **D** are incorrect. For example, an IT DRP must be known by all IT employees.

30. ☑ **B** and **C.** Without management support and approval, a disaster recovery plan will not succeed. The plan must be revisited periodically to ensure it is in step with changes in the business.

☒ **A** and **D** are incorrect. Disaster recovery plans must be periodically revisited. Besides IT systems, disaster recovery can also include facility restoration and employee relocation.

31. ☑ See Figure 16-5. To improve performance, load balancing distributes network traffic to a farm, or collection, of servers offering the same network service. The server that is the least busy and up and running is normally the server that would handle a current request. Tabletop exercises help disaster recovery (DR) committees ensure the business continuity plan (BCP)

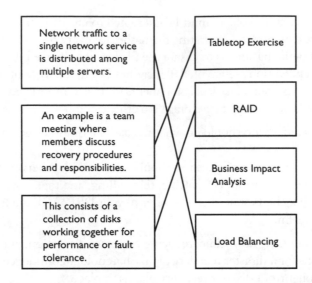

meets the organizational DR goals, including determining the responsibilities of all involved parties. Redundant Array of Independent Disks (RAID) groups physical disks together as logical disks seen by the operating system. This is done to improve disk performance and/or provide redundancy in case of disk failure.

32. ☑ **B.** Mean time to failure (MTTF) is a statistical measurement applied to nonrepairable items (such as hard disks). It denotes the average useful life of a device given that a specific number of those devices are in use.

☒ **A, C,** and **D** are incorrect. Mean time between failures (MTBF) is the measure of time between each subsequent failure of a repairable device. Hard disks are not considered repairable; when they fail, they are replaced. Mean time to recovery (MTTR) measures the amount of time it takes to return a device, system, or network to normal functionality. The recovery point objective (RPO) is the amount of time that can elapse after a failure before system and data resume normal operation, so a six-hour RPO means data backups can never be more than six hours old. The recovery time objective (RTO) differs in that it denotes the amount of time it will take after an unexpected failure for systems to resume normal operation. Unlike RPO, it does not specify how old the data can be.

33. ☑ **B.** Redundant network links to the Internet will ensure that if one Internet connection fails, the other can be used to access mail and application services in the cloud.

☒ **A, C,** and **D** are incorrect. Updating servers, RAID disk configuration, and MTTF are not your concern; they are the responsibility of the cloud provider.

17

Introduction to Computer Forensics

QUESTIONS

Digital footprints are left with all electronic devices we use daily from our cars to cell phones to personal computers. Computer forensics refers to the documentation, acquisition, and preservation of this digital data for use as evidence. Care must be taken to ensure that the proper steps are taken to legally perform data acquisition.

1. What must be determined by the first responder to an incident?

   A. The severity of the event
   B. Which other personnel must be called in
   C. The dollar amount associated with the incident
   D. Who is at fault

2. After seizing computer equipment alleged to have been involved in a crime, it is left in a corridor unattended for ten minutes while officers subdue a violent suspect. The seized equipment is no longer admissible as evidence because of what violation?

   A. Order of volatility
   B. Damage control
   C. Chain of custody
   D. Time offset

3. A warrant has been issued to investigate a server believed to be used to swap credit card information by organized crime. Following the order of volatility, which data should you collect first?

   A. Electronic memory (RAM)
   B. Hard disk
   C. USB flash drive
   D. CMOS

4. A server configured with a RAID-5 array must be properly imaged to preserve the original state of the data. You decide against imaging each physical hard disk in the array. Which two tasks must you perform? (Choose two.)

   A. Change the server CMOS boot order.
   B. Image the array as a single logical disk.
   C. Ensure your imaging solution supports RAID.
   D. Update the firmware for the RAID controller.

5. While capturing network traffic, you notice an abnormally excessive number of outbound SMTP packets. To determine whether this is an incident that requires escalation, what else should you consult?

   A. The contents of your inbox

   B. The mail server log

   C. The mail server documentation

   D. The web server log

6. You decide to work late on a Saturday night to replace wiring in your server room. Upon arriving, you realize there has been a break-in and server backup tapes appear to be missing. What should you do as law enforcement officials arrive?

   A. Clean up the server room.

   B. Sketch a picture of the broken-into premises on a notepad.

   C. Alert officials that the premise has surveillance video.

   D. Check the surrounding area for the perpetrator.

7. Which of the following best visually illustrates the state of a computer at the time it was seized by law enforcement?

   A. Digital photograph of the motherboard

   B. Screenshot

   C. Visio network diagram

   D. Steganography

8. Choose the correct order of volatility when collecting digital evidence:

   A. Hard disk, DVD-R, RAM, swap file

   B. Swap file, RAM, DVD-R, hard disk

   C. RAM, DVD-R, swap file, hard disk

   D. RAM, swap file, hard disk, DVD-R

9. What can a forensic analyst do to reduce the number of files that must be analyzed on a seized disk?

   A. Write a Visual Basic script.

   B. Delete files thought to be operating system files.

   C. Ensure the original disk is pristine and use a hash table on a copy of the files.

   D. Ensure the original disk is pristine and use a script to process a copy of the files.

10. A professional who is present at the time of evidence gathering can be summoned to appear in court or to prepare a report on their findings for use in court. What is this person referred to as?

   A. Plaintiff

   B. Defendant

   C. Auditor

   D. Forensic expert witness

11. Which of the following best describes chain of custody?

   A. Delegating evidence collection to your superior

   B. Preserving, protecting, and documenting evidence

   C. Capturing a system image to another disk

   D. Capturing memory contents before hard disk contents

12. In working on an insider trading case, you are asked to prove that an e-mail message is authentic and was sent to another employee. Which items should you consider? (Choose two.)

   A. Was the message encrypted?

   B. Was the message digitally signed?

   C. Are user public keys properly protected?

   D. Are user private keys properly protected?

13. What type of evidence would be the most difficult for a perpetrator to forge?

   A. IP address

   B. MAC address

   C. Cell phone SIM card

   D. Documents on a USB flash drive

14. What is the purpose of disk forensic software? (Choose two.)

   A. Using file encryption to ensure copied data mirrors original data

   B. Using file hashes to ensure copied data mirrors original data

   C. Protecting data on the original disks

   D. Creating file hashes on the original disks

15. You are preparing to gather evidence from a cell phone. Which of the following is false?

   A. CDMA mobile devices do not use SIM cards.

   B. CDMA mobile devices store user data on the mobile device.

   C. GSM mobile devices do not use SIM cards.

   D. GSM mobile devices use SIM cards.

16. You must analyze data on a digital camera's internal memory. You plan to connect your forensic computer to the camera using a USB cable. What should you do to ensure you do not modify data on the camera?

    A. Ensure the camera is turned off.

    B. Flag all files on the camera as read-only.

    C. Log in with a nonadministrative account on the forensic computer.

    D. Use a USB write-blocking device.

17. What can be used to ensure seized mobile wireless devices do not communicate with other devices?

    A. SIM card

    B. Faraday bag

    C. Antistatic bag

    D. GPS jammer

18. Robin works as a network technician at a stock brokerage firm. To test network forensic capturing software, she plugs her laptop into an Ethernet switch and begins capturing network traffic. During later analysis, she notices some broadcast and multicast packets as well as only her own computer's network traffic. Why was she unable to capture all network traffic on the switch?

    A. She must enable promiscuous mode on her NIC.

    B. She must disable promiscuous mode on her NIC.

    C. Each switch port is an isolated collision domain.

    D. Each switch port is an isolated broadcast domain.

19. A network intrusion detection device captures network traffic during the commission of a crime on a network. You notice NTP and TCP packets from all network hosts in the capture. You must find a way to correlate captured packets to a date and time to ensure the packet captures will be considered as admissible as evidence. What should you do? (Choose two.)

    A. Nothing. NTP keeps time in sync on a network. *NETWORK TIME PROTOCOL*

    B. Nothing. Packet captures are time stamped.

    C. Without digital signatures, date and time cannot be authenticated.

    D. Without encryption, date and time cannot be authenticated.

20. You arrive at a scene where a computer must be seized as evidence. The computer is powered off and has an external USB hard drive plugged in. What should you do?

    A. Turn on the computer.

    B. Unplug the external USB hard drive.

    C. Thoroughly document the state of the equipment.

    D. Place the computer in a Faraday bag.

21. You are asked to examine a hard disk for fragments of instant messaging conversations as well as deleted files. How should you do this?

    A. Use bit stream copying tools.

    B. Log in to the computer and copy the original hard drive contents to an external USB hard drive.

    C. Map a drive across the network to the original hard drive and copy the contents to an external USB hard drive.

    D. View log files.

22. Which type of file is most likely to contain incriminating data?

    A. Password-protected Microsoft Word file

    B. Encrypted Microsoft Word file

    C. Digitally signed Microsoft Word file

    D. File hash of Microsoft Word file

23. How can a forensic analyst benefit from analyzing metadata? (Choose three.)

    A. JPEG metadata can reveal specific camera settings.

    B. Microsoft Word metadata can reveal the author name.

    C. Microsoft Excel metadata can reveal your MAC address.

    D. PDF metadata can reveal the registered company name.

24. Which of the following rules must be followed when performing forensic analysis? (Choose two.)

    A. Work only with the original authentic data.

    B. Work only with a copy of data.

    C. Seek legal permission to conduct an analysis.

    D. Seek your manager's permission to conduct an analysis.

25. Refer to Figure 17-1. You must determine whether network traffic captured on interface E0 on Router A appears authentic or spoofed. You are analyzing a packet destined for Server A. The source MAC address in the packet is 00:34:D6:9B:08:8C, and the source IP address is 200.0.0.55. For a legitimate packet, which of the following statements is correct?

    A. The source MAC address should be 00:14:D6:9B:08:8C.

    B. The source IP address cannot be from the 200.1.1.0/24 network.

    C. The source IP address should be 200.1.1.254.

    D. The source IP address should be 1.1.0.1.

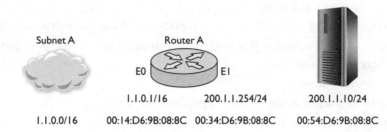

FIGURE 17-1

Network traffic analysis

26. The IT director is creating the following year's budget. You are asked to submit forensic dollar figures for your IT forensic team. Which one item should you not submit?

   A. Travel expenses

   B. Man hour expenses

   C. Training expenses

   D. ALE amounts

27. Users report at 9:30 A.M. severely degraded network performance since the workday began at 8 A.M. After network analysis and a quick discussion with your IT security team, you conclude a worm virus has infected your network. What should you do to control the damage? (Choose two.)

   A. Determine the severity of the security breach.

   B. Unplug SAN devices.

   C. Shut down all servers.

   D. Shut down Ethernet switches.

28. A suspect deletes incriminating files and empties the Windows recycle bin. Which of the following statements are true regarding the deletion? (Choose two.)

   A. The files cannot be recovered.

   B. The files can be recovered.

   C. Deleted files contain all of their original data until the hard disk is filled with other data.

   D. Deleted files contain all of their original data until the hard disk is defragmented.

29. The local police suspect a woman is using her computer to commit online fraud, but she encrypts her hard disk with a strong passphrase. Law enforcement would like to access the data on the encrypted disk to obtain forensic evidence. What tasks should be done? (Choose two.)

    A. Harness the processing power of thousands of Internet computers and attempt to crack the encryption passphrase.

    B. Obtain a warrant.

    C. Install a packet sniffer on the suspect's network.

    D. Install a keylogger to capture the passphrase.

30. A seized USB flash drive contains only natural scenic pictures. Law enforcement officers were convinced incriminating data was stored on the USB flash drive. What else should be done?

    A. Decrypt the USB flash drive.

    B. Format the USB flash drive.

    C. Check for steganographic hidden data.

    D. Analyze the USB flash drive log.

31. Richard, a meteorologist, is using specialized algorithms to develop climate projection models based on 30TB of weather data collected over the years. Which term best describes this scenario?

    A. Climate analysis

    B. Massive data analysis

    C. Weather analysis

    D. Big data analysis

32. In Figure 17-2, match the incident response definitions on the left to the terms on the right.

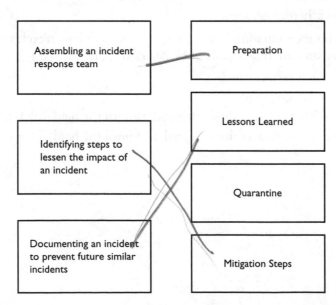

FIGURE 17-2

Incident response definitions and terms

Assembling an incident response team

Identifying steps to lessen the impact of an incident

Documenting an incident to prevent future similar incidents

Preparation

Lessons Learned

Quarantine

Mitigation Steps

33. One of the servers in your data center will no longer boot after being flooded with network traffic from a malicious user. What should you refer to so that the server returns to normal operation?

A. Reconstitution procedures

B. Operating system installation manual

C. Acceptable use policy

D. SLA

34. A user complains that the performance on their workstation has degraded to the point that they cannot get any work done. After investigating the problem, you run a virus scan and receive an alert that the machine is infected with a worm virus. What should you do next?

A. Update the virus definition database.

B. Quarantine the workstation from the rest of the network.

C. Run a network scan on the workstation to identify vulnerabilities.

D. Ensure the workstation can connect to corporate servers using ping.

35. You are the network administrator for ABC, Inc. Your IT security colleagues inform you that in the past users have lost USB flash drives containing sensitive company information. You decide to implement a solution that forces all USB flash drives used on company computers to be encrypted. Which security problem are you addressing?

A. Data breach

B. Confidentiality

C. Integrity

D. Incident containment

QUICK ANSWER KEY

1. A
2. C
3. A
4. B, C
5. B
6. C
7. B
8. D
9. C

10. D
11. B
12. B, D
13. C
14. B, C
15. C
16. D
17. B
18. C

19. A, B
20. C
21. A
22. B
23. A, B, D
24. B, C
25. B
26. D
27. A, D

28. B, C
29. B, D
30. C
31. D
32. See Figure 17-3.
33. A
34. B
35. A

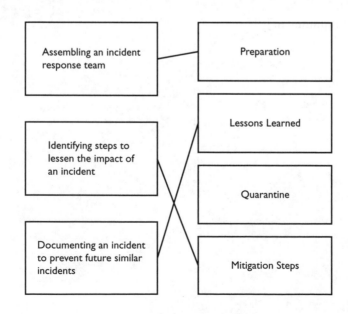

FIGURE 17-3

Incident response definitions and terms—the answer

Assembling an incident response team — Preparation

Identifying steps to lessen the impact of an incident

Documenting an incident to prevent future similar incidents

Lessons Learned

Quarantine

Mitigation Steps

IN-DEPTH ANSWERS

1. ☑ **A.** A quick assessment of the situation severity by the first responder will determine who needs to be called or what should be done next, based on the incident response policy.
   ☒ **B, C,** and **D** are incorrect. Until the severity has been determined, the first responder will not know who to call. Calculating financial loss can be done once the situation is under control. This is not the first thing that should be done; neither is pointing fingers.

2. ☑ **C.** Chain of custody has been violated. Chain of custody involves documenting evidence being collected thoroughly and legally while ensuring the evidence cannot be tampered with.
   ☒ **A, B,** and **D** are incorrect. Order of volatility determines what type of data is most easily lost, for example, data in electronic memory (RAM) versus data stored on a DVD. Damage control involves minimizing further damage in the event of an unfavorable event. Time offset is used to validate the date and time stamps of digital forensic evidence.

3. ☑ **A.** The order of volatility determines which data is most at risk of loss. Electronic memory (RAM) data is lost when a device is powered off; therefore, it must be properly collected first.
   ☒ **B, C,** and **D** are incorrect. Hard disk, USB, and CMOS data exist even without power. CMOS chips on the motherboard require a small battery to retain their configurations (boot sequence, date/time, and so on).

4. ☑ **B** and **C.** You should ensure your forensic imaging tool supports the RAID controller on the system you must image, and then you should image the disks as a single logical disk.
   ☒ **A** and **D** are incorrect. Ideally your forensic imaging tool is a separate device so you shouldn't have to modify the CMOS boot order. Unless there are problems with the RAID controller, you should not have to update the firmware to image the logical disk.

5. ☑ **B.** The mail server log will reveal SMTP activity such as excessive outbound SMTP traffic.
   ☒ **A, C,** and **D** are incorrect. Your inbox is not related to general outbound SMTP traffic unless you have configured your mail server to notify you. Mail server documentation will detail what to do to have the server function properly; it will not specifically address this issue. The web server log will not contain SMTP outbound traffic details.

6. ☑ **C.** Video surveillance provides important evidence that could be used to solve this crime.
   ☒ **A, B,** and **D** are incorrect. You must not disturb the crime scene. Because there is surveillance video, there is no need for a sketch. Never seek those who have committed a crime; leave that to law enforcement.

7. ☑ **B.** A screenshot can be acquired in many ways and can prove relevant to the particular crime since it may reveal what was happening on the system at the time.
   ☒ **A, C,** and **D** are incorrect. A picture of the motherboard would generally be useless; user data is not exposed when viewing a motherboard. A Visio network diagram is not as valuable

as a screenshot. Steganography is the art of concealing data within other data (for example, messages hidden within pictures). This would not apply in this case.

8. ☑ **D.** Digital forensic evidence must first be collected from the most fragile (power-dependent) locations such as RAM and the swap file. Swap files contain data from physical RAM that were paged to disk to make room for something else in physical RAM. Hard disks are the next most vulnerable since hard disk data can simply be deleted and the hard disk can be filled with useless data to make data recovery difficult. A DVD-R is less susceptible to data loss than hard disks since it is read-only.

☒ **A, B,** and **C** are incorrect. RAM is much more volatile (power-dependent) than hard disks and swap files. Swap files are more volatile than DVD-Rs.

9. ☑ **C.** A hash table calculates file hashes for each file. Known standard operating system file hashes can be compared to your file hashes to quickly exclude known authentic files that have not been modified.

☒ **A, B,** and **D** are incorrect. Writing a Visual Basic script is too generic; we would have to know how the script was written for this answer to be considered. Deleting files that are thought to belong to the operating system is not a thorough method of reducing files that must be analyzed. Using a script to process files is too ambiguous to simply state it will solve our problems.

10. ☑ **D.** A forensic expert witness has specialized knowledge and experience in a field beyond that of the average person, and thus their testimony is deemed authentic.

☒ **A, B,** and **C** are incorrect. The plaintiff is the party who initiates a lawsuit, and the defendant is the party against which charges are alleged. An auditor examines records of some type to ensure their thoroughness and authenticity.

11. ☑ **B.** Preserving, protecting, and documenting evidence is referred to as chain of custody.

☒ **A, C,** and **D** are incorrect. Delegation, disk imaging, and capturing memory contents are all tasks that could be performed when gathering forensic evidence, but they do not describe the entire chain of custody, which includes keeping a paper trail that shows the seizure, custody, control, transfer, analysis, and disposal of physical or electronic evidence.

12. ☑ **B** and **D.** Digitally signing an e-mail message requires a user's unique private key to which only they have access, which means they had to have sent the message. One factor used to arrive at this conclusion is how well protected user private keys are. If user private keys are simply stored on a hard disk without a password, anybody could have digitally signed the message.

☒ **A** and **C** are incorrect. Encryption is separate from verifying message sender authenticity; it scrambles data to ensure confidentiality. Public keys need not be protected; that is why they are called public keys. Their mathematically related counterpart (private keys) must be safeguarded.

13. ☑ **C.** Cell phone subscriber identity module (SIM) cards contain unique data such as a serial number, the user's contacts, text messages, and other relevant mobile subscriber data. This is used in Global System for Mobility (GSM) communication mobile devices and allows the user to use any GSM mobile device as long as their SIM card is inserted.

    ☒ **A, B,** and **D** are incorrect. IP and MAC addresses, as well as documents on a USB drive, could all be easily forged (spoofed) with freely available tools.

14. ☑ **B** and **C.** A generated file hash is unique to the file on which it was based. Any change to the file invalidates the file hash. This is a method to digitally ensure the correct version of a file is being analyzed. Data on a seized hard disk must be left intact. Forensic disk software runs on a separate device or boots using its own operating system and uses bit stream copying to copy entire hard disk contents. File hashes should never be generated on the source hard disk; it is imperative that it remain undisturbed.

    ☒ **A** and **D** are incorrect. File encryption does not ensure copied data is the same as the source; instead, it scrambles the data so only authorized persons with the correct decryption key can view it. You should never create file hashes on the original disk; its state at the time of seizure must be preserved.

15. ☑ **C.** Global System for Mobile (GSM) communication devices use subscriber identity module (SIM) cards. Code Division Multiple Access (CDMA) mobile devices do not. SIM cards contain personal user information as well as mobile account subscription information. This means you could purchase a new GSM mobile device and simply insert your SIM card without having to contact your mobile wireless service provider.

    ☒ **A, B,** and **D** are incorrect. CDMA and GSM devices use SIM cards and store user data.

16. ☑ **D.** USB write-blocking devices ensure that data can travel in only one direction when collecting digital evidence from storage media, such as a digital camera's internal memory. The fact that this tool was used must be documented to adhere to chain-of-custody procedures.

    ☒ **A, B,** and **C** are incorrect. The camera should be left in its seizure state, so you should not power it on if it is powered off. Do not flag anything on the camera as read-only; you must not disturb the state of the camera. Simply logging on to a forensic computer using an administrative account has nothing to do with not modifying data on the camera.

17. ☑ **B.** A Faraday bag is a mobile device shield that prevents wireless signals to or from the mobile device. This must be used immediately upon seizure of a wireless mobile device to ensure data on it is not modified through wireless remote communications.

    ☒ **A, C,** and **D** are incorrect. Subscriber identity module (SIM) cards contain user mobile data, but in the question you do not know whether we are inserting or removing the SIM card. Antistatic bags shield sensitive electronic components from electrostatic discharge (ESD) but do nothing to prevent wireless signals. Global Positioning System (GPS) jammers prevent unwanted GPS tracking but do not prevent normal wireless communication.

18. ☑ **C.** Ethernet switches isolate each port into its own collision domain. When capturing network traffic, this means you will not see traffic to or from other computers plugged into other switch ports, other than broadcast and multicast packets. Some switches allow you to copy all switch traffic to a monitoring port, but the scenario did not mention this.

    ☒ **A, B,** and **D** are incorrect. Promiscuous mode is required to capture network traffic, but it is not the problem in this case. Each switch port is a collision domain, but all switch ports can be grouped into virtual local area networks (VLANs); each VLAN is a broadcast domain.

19. ☑ **A** and **B.** Network Time Protocol (NTP) keeps computers synchronized to a reliable time source. Captured network traffic is time stamped and includes offset time stamps from when the capture was started.

    ☒ **C** and **D** are incorrect. Digital signatures ensure the authenticity of the message as well as the sender, but their time stamps are not guaranteed. Encryption secures data but has nothing to do with ensuring date and time stamps are authentic.

20. ☑ **C.** Thoroughly documenting the state of seized equipment is critical to adhere to chain-of-custody procedures. Failure to do so will render collected evidence inadmissible.

    ☒ **A, B,** and **D** are incorrect. Never turn on a computer that was turned off. Turning it on could destroy valuable data. Do not unplug the USB hard drive. You must not disturb the state of the equipment until it has been documented. Placing the computer in a Faraday bag might be appropriate if it has a wireless interface, but the scene must be documented first.

21. ☑ **A.** Bit stream forensic copying tools copy hard disk data at the bit level, not at the file level. When a file is deleted, it may disappear from the file system, but the file data in its entirety is intact on the hard disk until the hard disk is filled with new data. Deleted files are not copied with file-level copying, but they are with bit stream copying.

    ☒ **B, C,** and **D** are incorrect. Never log into a seized computer to copy disk contents. Use an external forensic tool instead. Do not copy data from a seized computer across the network; this will affect log entries on the target computer and will disturb the original state of the data. Viewing log files could reveal data regarding e-mail and instant messaging, but it will not reveal deleted data.

22. ☑ **B.** The existence of encrypted files implies somebody sought to protect confidential or incriminating data. The required key (file, passphrase, or physical device) must be used to decrypt the data.

    ☒ **A, C,** and **D** are incorrect. Compared to an encrypted file, they are not as likely to contain incriminating data.

23. ☑ **A, B,** and **D.** Metadata is information that describes data. For example, a JPEG picture taken with a digital camera could contain hidden data including camera settings, date and time, and so on. Microsoft Word and Portable Document Format (PDF) documents contain metadata such as the document author name, registered company name, and so on.

    ☒ **C** is incorrect. Excel documents do not record your computer's network card hardware address (MAC address).

24.   ☑ **B and C.** You must obtain proper legal permission to seize and analyze data. Perform analysis on a forensic copy of data; never work on the original data because this will render evidence inadmissible.
    ☒ **A and D** are incorrect. You should never work with the original digital data. This disturbs the data's original state, so work only on a forensic copy of the data. Your manager may not have the authority to grant permission for you to examine data; ensure proper legal permission is obtained.

25.   ☑ **B.** A packet entering interface E0 on Router A cannot have a source IP address of 200.0.0.55. A packet from 200.0.0.55 would not pass through the router; it would go directly to Server A because it is on the same subnet. A packet with 200.0.0.55 as an IP address entering from another network has been spoofed.
    ☒ **A, C, and D** are incorrect. On a destination network the source MAC address should be that of the last router on the destination network, in this case, 00:34:D6:9B:08:8C. Unless NAT or proxy servers are used, the source IP address does not change as packets travel through networks. The MAC address does, however.

26.   ☑ **D.** Annual loss expectancy (ALE) is used to calculate the probability of asset failure over a year. It is used when performing a risk assessment.
    ☒ **A, B, and C** are incorrect. Travel, man hours, and training expenses are valid IT forensic budget items.

27.   ☑ **A and D.** Once the severity of the issue has been determined, the quickest way to control the spread of a worm virus is to eliminate network connectivity.
    ☒ **A, B, and C** are incorrect. The severity would have already been discussed when talking with your IT security team. Unplugging storage area network (SAN) devices might protect data on SAN disks from infected servers, but the worm could still spread to other devices. Shutting down all servers takes longer than simply powering down network switches.

28.   ☑ **B and C.** Emptying the Windows recycle bin makes deleted files inaccessible to Windows users; however, the entire file contents are still on the disk until the disk is filled with other data. A third-party tool must be used to recover the deleted items in this case.
    ☒ **A and D** are incorrect. The files can be recovered using freely available tools, even if the recycle bin is emptied. Hard disk defragmentation has no effect on file recovery.

29.   ☑ **B and D.** A warrant should be obtained to install a keylogger on the suspect's computer. A keylogger captures everything typed in including passphrases used to decrypt hard disks.
    ☒ **A and C** are incorrect. Although many computers working together could eventually determine the encryption passphrase, this is not the best option. Capturing network traffic would not help in determining a hard disk encryption passphrase.

30. ☑ **C.** Steganography is the art of concealing data within other data, such as hiding messages within pictures. There are tools that can identify whether this is the case.
    ☒ **A, B,** and **D** are incorrect. Decrypting the USB flash drive would first be required to get to the files, but the question doesn't state that this is the case. Formatting the USB drive would be counterproductive. USB flash drives do not have logs, although the operating system might log data activity to and from the USB device.

31. ☑ **D.** Big Data analysis refers to using specialized tools or algorithms to analyze large volumes of data.
    ☒ **A, B,** and **C** are incorrect. These are not industry-standard terms.

32. ☑ See Figure 17-4. Preparing an incident response team before problems occur means problems can be dealt with in an efficient manner. Mitigation steps lessen the impact of problematic incidents. Documenting problematic occurrences and their solutions can help when similar future events occur.

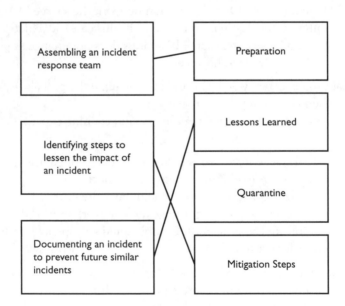

FIGURE 17-4

Incident response definitions and terms—the answer

33. ☑ **A.** Recovery and reconstitution procedures return a system to its functioning state.
    ☒ **B, C,** and **D** are incorrect. The operating system installation manual might get the system up and running after installation but not for the specific use within the organization. Acceptable use policies define how organizational assets are properly used for the interests of the organization. Service level agreements (SLAs) are contracts defining acceptable levels of service, such as the amount of guaranteed uptime for a hosted mail solution.

34. ☑ **B.** The infected system should be immediately quarantined from the networks, for example, by unplugging its network cable.

    ☒ **A, C,** and **D** are incorrect. These tasks should not be performed for fear of further infecting the network.

35. ☑ **A.** Data breach means unauthorized parties could gain access to sensitive information.

    ☒ **B, C,** and **D** are incorrect. Confidentiality and integrity are not security problems; they are security solutions. Incident containment relates to damage and loss control.

18

Security Assessments and Audits

QUESTIONS

Periodic testing of computer systems and networks over time identifies security weaknesses. Security assessments are best conducted by a third party and may be required by government regulation or to acquire business contracts. As a Security+ professional, you must know when to use various tools and how to interpret their results.

1. As part of your security audit you would like to see what type of network traffic is being transmitted on the network. Which type of tool should you use?

   A. Protocol analyzer
   B. Port scanner
   C. Vulnerability scanner
   D. Password cracker

2. A network consists of 250 computers. You must determine which machines are secure and which are not. Which type of tool should you use?

   A. Protocol analyzer
   B. Port scanner
   C. Vulnerability scanner
   D. Password cracker

3. You would like to focus and track malicious activity to a particular host in your DMZ. What should you configure?

   A. Honeynet
   B. Honeypot
   C. DMZ tracker
   D. Web server

4. Which of the following would you employ to determine which TCP and UDP ports on a host are open?

   A. Vulnerability scanner
   B. Packet sniffer
   C. Performance Monitor
   D. Port scanner

5. Which procedure identifies assets, threats, and risks and also determines methods to minimize the impact of these threats?

A. Risk analysis
B. Vulnerability assessment
C. Port scanning
D. Network mapper

6. A technician must identify deviations from normal network activity. Which task must she first perform?

A. Trend analysis
B. Baseline analysis
C. Performance monitoring
D. Risk analysis

7. A developer analyzes source code to ensure there are no errors or potential security risks. Which term best identifies this activity?

A. Risk assessment
B. Patch management
C. Debugging
D. Code review

8. A Windows computer has not been patched nor have the unnecessary services been disabled. Which of the following statements is true regarding security?

A. The computer will perform faster.
B. The computer has a large attack surface.
C. The computer has a small attack surface.
D. The computer will perform slower.

9. A network security auditor simulates various network attacks against a corporate network. Which term best defines this procedure?

A. Vulnerability analysis
B. Network mapping
C. Penetration testing
D. Risk assessment

10. Your manager asks you to configure a collection of purposely vulnerable hosts in a DMZ for the purpose of tracking hacking attempts. What term best describes what you are configuring?

- A. Honeynet
- B. Honeypot
- C. Firewall
- D. Proxy server

11. You run a vulnerability scan on subnet 192.168.1.0/24. The results state TCP ports 135 through 139 are open on most hosts. What does this refer to?

- A. File and Print Sharing
- B. Web server
- C. Mail server
- D. Remote Desktop Protocol

12. You are a network consultant in charge of creating a wireless network infrastructure for a hotel. Toward the end of the implementation your team evaluates the project to ensure it meets the original stated requirements. What is this called?

- A. Penetration testing
- B. Risk assessment
- C. Design review
- D. Code review

13. After careful log examination you realize somebody has hacked into your WEP-secured home wireless network. What can you do to further secure wireless traffic?

- A. Use WPA2 Enterprise.
- B. Use WPA2 PSK.
- C. Disable SSID broadcasting.
- D. Change the SSID name.

14. What should be done to ensure your network security is effective?

- A. Patch all operating systems.
- B. Update the BIOS on all systems.
- C. Periodically test network security controls.
- D. Upgrade to the latest version of Microsoft Office.

15. Which of the following is considered passive security testing?

- A. Capturing network traffic
- B. Brute-force password attack
- C. Dictionary-based disk decryption
- D. OS fingerprinting

16. From the following list, identify the security misconfiguration:

A. A domain administrative account is used as a service account.

B. An Active Directory account is used as a service account.

C. Windows stations receive updates from a WSUS server instead of the Internet.

D. The Windows Guest account is disabled.

17. A security auditing team has been hired to conduct network penetration tests against a network. The team has not been given any data related to the network or its layout. What type of testing will the team perform?

A. Black box

B. White box

C. Gray box

D. Blue box

18. Refer to Figure 18-1. Which of the following statements are true? (Choose two.)

A. The web server IP address is 66.220.151.75.

B. The web server IP address is 192.168.2.12.

C. The web site is not using SSL.

D. Packet 24 is going to the web site.

FIGURE 18-1   Wireshark packet capture

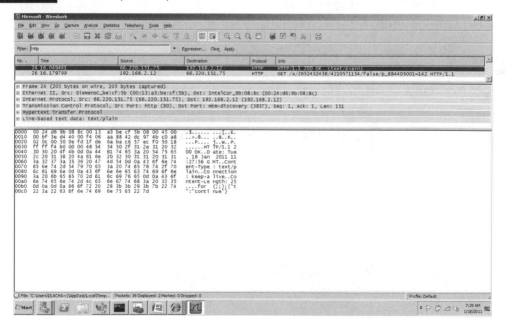

19. You are having trouble pinging host 192.168.17.45; there are no replies. One of your users must use the Remote Desktop Protocol (RDP) against the host to run an application. You cannot test RDP for the user because you are currently logged on locally to a Linux server with only a command line. What can you use to quickly determine whether RDP is running on 192.168.17.45?

   A. Packet sniffer
   B. Virus scanner
   C. Wireless scanner
   D. Port scanner

20. After conducting a security audit, you inform the network owner that you discovered two unencrypted wireless networks. Your client asks how to best secure wireless traffic. Which of the following is the most secure wireless network encryption?

   A. WEP
   B. WPA
   C. WPA2
   D. WPA3

21. Refer to Figure 18-2. What configuration error would a security audit find?

   A. The Administrator account should be deleted.
   B. The Administrator account is enabled and has not been renamed.
   C. The Guest account is enabled.
   D. The Guest account should be deleted.

FIGURE 18-2   Local user accounts on a Windows server

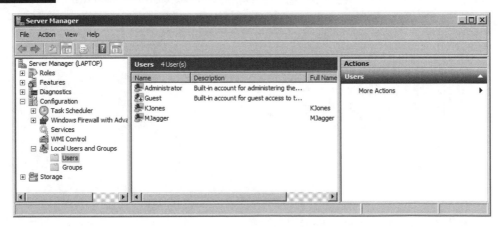

22. A security auditor must determine what types of servers are running on a network. Which type of tool should be used?

A. Network mapper

B. Protocol analyzer

C. Port scanner

D. Virus scanner

23. A security auditor discovers open wireless networks. She must recommend a secure solution. Which of the following is the most secure wireless solution?

A. 802.1x

B. WEP

C. WPA PSK

D. Disable SSID broadcast

24. Which of the following would *not* be considered during a security audit?

A. Locked server rooms

B. Wireless encryption in use

C. Patch status of all hosts

D. Price of server licensing

25. While auditing a Windows Active Directory environment, you discover that administrative accounts do not have configured account lockout policies. Which of the following are security concerns? (Choose two.)

A. If account lockout is enabled, administrative accounts could be locked out as a result of repeated password attempts.

B. If account lockout is not enabled, administrative accounts could be subjected to password attacks.

C. If account lockout is enabled, administrative accounts could be subjected to password attacks.

D. If account lockout is not enabled, administrative accounts could be locked out as a result of repeated password attempts.

26. Which type of security testing provides network configuration information to testers?

A. White box

B. Black box

C. Gray box

D. Blue box

27. You are reviewing password policies during a security audit. Refer to Figure 18-3 and identify two security problems. (Choose two.)

A. The minimum password age is 0 days.

B. The password history is set only to 5.

C. The store passwords using reversible encryption option is disabled.

D. Passwords do not meet complexity requirements.

FIGURE 18-3 Local security policy password settings on a Windows computer

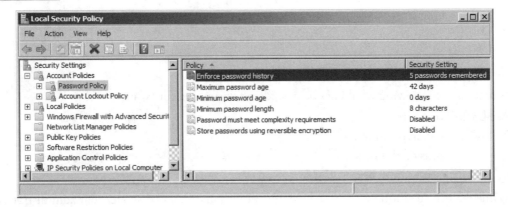

28. Which type of tool scans for known security threats on a group of computers?

A. Packet sniffer

B. Vulnerability scanner

C. Risk scanner

D. Port scanner

29. You would like an unused host to log zero-day exploit activity. What should you configure?

A. Patch server

B. Honeynet

C. Honeypot

D. Virus scanner

30. A large wireless network currently uses WPA PSK. As part of your network audit findings, you recommend a centralized wireless authentication option. What should you recommend?

A. RADIUS

B. WEP

C. WPA2 PSK

D. TKIP

31. You are performing a network penetration test for a client. From a command prompt you issue the command **telnet smtp1.acme.com 25** to see what information is returned. Which term refers to what you have done?

  A. Denial of service

  B. Port scan

  C. Banner grab

  D. Mail grab

32. Your company hired a consultant to implement a secure VPN solution using PKI certificates and smartcard authentication. Mark, your boss, has asked you to evaluate the implementation to ensure that the solution addresses the original need. Which term best describes what you will be doing?

  A. Design review

  B. Application security architecture review

  C. VPN review

  D. Network review

33. Tribbles Inc. recently hired a security consulting firm to perform a security audit of its network at its Vulcan, Alberta, location. An excerpt of the audit findings is listed here:

```
Date: March 6, 2013 4:53am EST
Task performed: Network vulnerability scan
Performed by: Lennard Kneemoy
IP Subnet: 14.65.0.0 / 16
Credential used: Tribbles\Administrator
Results: We were able to connect to most hosts without specifying a password.
Recommendation: Harden network hosts.
```

What is wrong with the audit findings?

  A. The subnet mask is incorrect.

  B. The IP address range is incorrect.

  C. The consultant ran a noncredentialed scan.

  D. The consultant ran a credentialed scan.

34. A user complains that legitimate e-mail messages from some customers are incorrectly flagged as spam by the corporate mail server. How might you explain what is happening to your user?

  A. The e-mail messages in question are generating false positives.

  B. The false positives are generating e-mail messages.

  C. The e-mail message in question are generating false negatives.

  D. The false negatives are generating e-mail messages.

35. You are a security consultant. After performing a threat assessment on a client network, you recommend actions that should be taken. In Figure 18-4, draw a line linking the requirements on the left to the correct solution on the right.

FIGURE 18-4

Security requirements and solutions

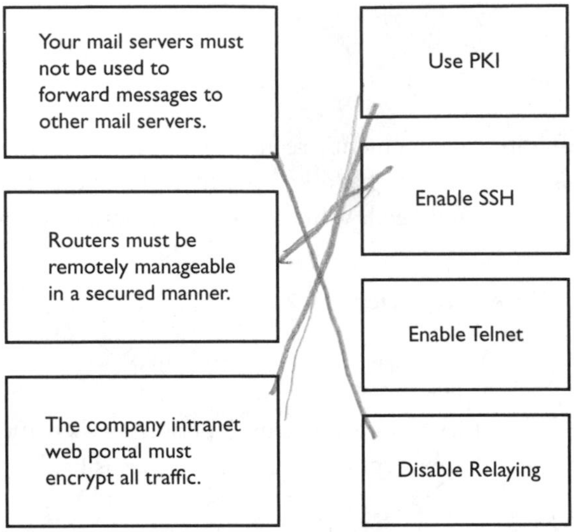

Your mail servers must not be used to forward messages to other mail servers.		Use PKI
Routers must be remotely manageable in a secured manner.		Enable SSH
		Enable Telnet
The company intranet web portal must encrypt all traffic.		Disable Relaying

36. You are the newly hired security officer for Jokers Inc. An existing network diagram for the Halifax location has been provided, as shown in Figure 18-5. Which recommendations should you make to secure the network infrastructure? (Choose two.)

A. Do not allow all outbound traffic through the firewalls.

B. Allow DNS replication traffic only between specific DNS hosts.

C. Do not place DNS servers in a DMZ.

D. Do not allow outbound TCP 443 traffic.

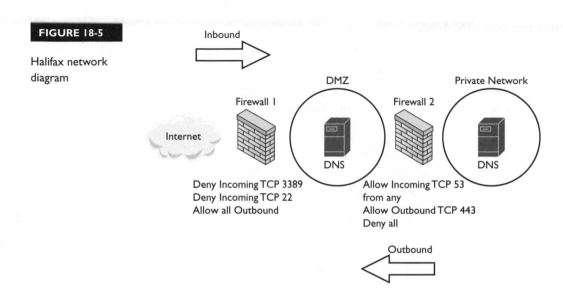

FIGURE 18-5

Halifax network diagram

Inbound

DMZ

Private Network

Firewall 1

Firewall 2

Internet

DNS

DNS

Deny Incoming TCP 3389
Deny Incoming TCP 22
Allow all Outbound

Allow Incoming TCP 53
from any
Allow Outbound TCP 443
Deny all

Outbound

37. Acme Inc. uses the 199.126.129.0/24 network address range in its DMZ. You are configuring the firewall separating the DMZ from the private network so that traffic from DMZ hosts is allowed into the private network. You issue the command **router(config)#access-list 45 permit 192.168.1.0 0.0.0.255**. What is the problem with this configuration?

   A. Access-list 55 must be used.

   B. 192.168.1.0 is a reserved private network address.   NOT   ROUTABLE

   C. The subnet mask in the router command is incorrect.

   D. The router needs to be rebooted.

38. Employee laptops must be secured when employees travel for business purposes. What can you do to harden user laptops?

   A. Set a CMOS password.

   B. Configure disk mirroring.

   C. Generate file hashes for all hard disk files.

   D. Enable verbose logging.

39. When is baseline reporting useful?

    A. When conducting a penetration test

    B. When hardening DNS servers

    C. When hardening HTTPS servers

    (D.) When comparing normal activity with current activity

40. Why are penetration tests sometimes not recommended?

    A. They can identify security threats.

    (B.) They could degrade network performance.

    C. They could generate too much logging data.

    D. They are expensive.   *HOST CRASHING Possibly*

QUICK ANSWER KEY

1. A	11. A	21. B	31. C
2. C	12. C	22. A	32. A
3. B	13. B	23. A	33. D
4. D	14. C	24. D	34. A
5. A	15. A	25. A, B	35. See Figure 18-6.
6. B	16. A	26. A	36. A, B
7. D	17. A	27. A, D	37. B
8. B	18. A, C	28. B	38. A
9. C	19. D	29. C	39. D
10. A	20. C	30. A	40. B

FIGURE 18-6

Security requirements and solutions—the answer

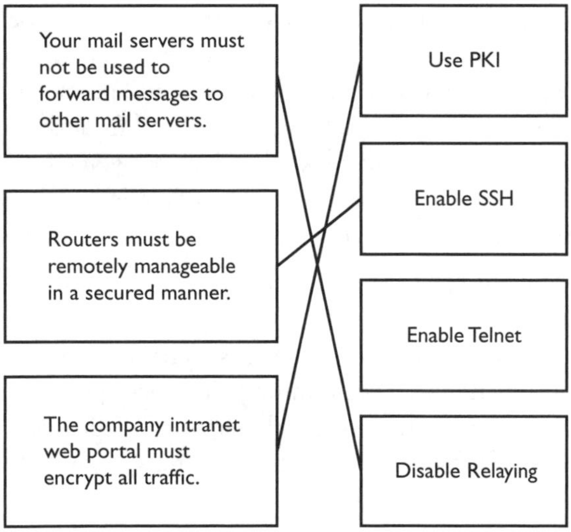

IN-DEPTH ANSWERS

1. ☑ **A.** Protocol analyzers use a promiscuous mode network card driver that allows the capture of all network traffic. Each switch port is a collision domain that prevents capturing unicast traffic related to other hosts; however, some switches allow mirroring of all switch traffic to a specific port.

   ☒ **B, C**, and **D** are incorrect. Port scanners identify running services on a host. For example, a running web server might show TCP port 80 as being open. Vulnerability scanners assess computers for weaknesses and will often generate reports. Password cracking refers to repeated attempts to guess a password and is often automated.

2. ☑ **C.** Vulnerability scanners scan computers for known security violations and weaknesses.

   ☒ **A, B**, and **D** are incorrect. Protocol analyzers capture network traffic. Port scanners list some or all open ports on one or more hosts. Password crackers repeatedly attempt to determine a password. Although port scanners and password cracking could be utilized to test system security, a vulnerability scanner provides much more data about computer security including open ports and vulnerable password settings.

3. ☑ **B.** A honeypot is an intentionally vulnerable host used to attract and track malicious activity.

   ☒ **A, C**, and **D** are incorrect. The question stated activity tracking on a single host, not a network of hosts. There is no such thing as a DMZ tracker. Web sites are not a tool to track malicious activity; web sites deliver content to web browsers.

4. ☑ **D.** Port scanners identify open ports on hosts. Personal firewall software may impede the success of port scanners. It should also be noted that port scanning can be detected.

   ☒ **A, B**, and **C** are incorrect. Vulnerability scanners can detect open ports as well as many more items; if all that is required is a list of open TCP and UDP ports, a port scanner is a better (and faster) choice. Packet sniffers capture network traffic, and from that captured traffic you can see port numbers in the TCP and UDP packet headers, but you cannot identify exactly which ports are open on a host. Performance Monitor is a Windows tool used to measure and monitor performance metrics of a Windows computer; it does not scan for open ports.

5. ☑ **A.** Risk analysis identifies and prioritizes threats while determining how to minimize their effect on business operations.

   ☒ **B, C**, and **D** are incorrect. Vulnerability assessments identify and prioritize potential threats and are performed during a risk analysis. Port scanning identifies open TCP and UDP ports; the impact of the open ports is not determined. Network mapping refers to the process of creating a map of the network layout, its configuration, and its computer systems. Threats are not identified.

6. ☑ **B.** A baseline analysis establishes what is normal on a given network. Without this data, it is difficult to determine deviations from the norm.

   ☒ **A, C,** and **D** are incorrect. Trend analysis refers to the collection of data in hopes of identifying a pattern. Performance Monitor is a tool for Windows computers that measures performance metrics such as CPU and memory utilization. Risk analysis identifies assets and related risks along with methods to minimize business disruption.

7. ☑ **D.** Code review is an examination of source code in order to uncover errors or security risks.

   ☒ **A, B,** and **C** are incorrect. Although risk assessment might involve code review, risk management also includes identifying assets and threat mitigation. Patch management involves the orderly application of software updates to hosts. Debugging implies the developer is aware of a specific problem with the code; analyzing code for errors would occur before debugging.

8. ☑ **B.** Computers with many potential vulnerabilities (software, physical) are said to have a larger attack surface than patched machines that only run software that is required. A larger attack surface means a higher degree of possibility of a machine becoming compromised.

   ☒ **A, C,** and **D** are incorrect. The question asks about security, not performing faster. Computers generally run faster with patches applied and fewer services running. Because unnecessary services have not been disabled, the machine has a larger attack surface than it otherwise should. The question refers to security, not performance; the computer might very well be performing slower since extra unnecessary services may be running.

9. ☑ **C.** Penetration testing (*pen testing*) involves simulating malicious activity against hosts or entire networks in order to assess how secure they are and to identify threats. Proper written consent must be obtained prior to performing this type of testing.

   ☒ **A, B,** and **D** are incorrect. Vulnerability analysis identifies and classifies potential threats. Network mapping plots the network layout using a discovery tool. Risk assessment does not simulate network attacks; it is used to identify business threats and how to mitigate them.

10. ☑ **A.** A honeynet is composed of two or more honeypots. These are intentionally vulnerable hosts used to track malicious activity.

    ☒ **B, C,** and **D** are incorrect. The question stated a collection of hosts, not a single (honeypot) host. Firewalls and proxy servers should never be left intentionally vulnerable.

11. ☑ **A.** Windows File and Print Sharing generally uses TCP ports 135 to 139.

    ☒ **B, C,** and **D** are incorrect. Web servers typically use TCP port 80 (clear text) or 443 (SSL). Mail servers use a variety of ports depending on their type and role. For example, Simple Mail Transfer Protocol (SMTP) servers listen on TCP port 25. Remote Desktop Protocol uses TCP port 3389.

12. ☑ **C.** Design review is a process whereby the original project objectives are compared against current progress to ensure the objectives are being met.

☒ **A, B,** and **D** are incorrect. Penetration testing simulates attacks against hosts or networks to test their security. Risk assessment determines which assets need protection from risks and how to minimize the threat impact. A code review refers to the analysis of computer source code to ensure it functions as intended and does not contain errors or security holes.

13. ☑ **B.** Wi-Fi Protected Access (WPA2) PreShared Key (PSK) is considered more secure than Wired Equivalent Privacy (WEP).
☒ **A, C,** and **D** are incorrect. WPA2 Enterprise requires a central authentication server; the average user will not have one at home. Disabling Station Set Identifier (SSID) suppresses the WLAN name from appearing in Wi-Fi beacon packets, but this is easily circumvented with freely available tools. Changing the SSID name may make it difficult for a hacker to identify what they are breaking into, but WPA2 is a much more secure solution.

14. ☑ **C.** Period network testing, perhaps even penetration testing, is valuable to ensure your network security controls remain valid over time.
☒ **A, B,** and **D** are incorrect. Patching an operating system, updating the BIOS, and upgrading Microsoft Office are all important for a single host's security, but the question asks about network security; therefore, C is the best answer.

15. ☑ **A.** Passive security testing techniques do not interfere with the normal operation of a computer system or network. Capturing network traffic simply takes a copy of network packets already being transmitted.
☒ **B, C,** and **D** are incorrect. Brute-force password attacks, disk decryption, and OS fingerprinting all must interact directly with a computer system and might affect the performance or normal operation of that host.

16. ☑ **A.** Windows services (and Unix and Linux daemons) must run under the context of a user account. Assigning a powerful domain administrative account presents a major threat in the event that the service is compromised; the hacker would then have domain administrative privileges. Service accounts should have only the rights and permissions required to function—nothing more. Many administrators do not force periodic password changes for service accounts, which presents yet another security risk.
☒ **B, C,** and **D** are incorrect. Some services run on Windows domain controller computers and must use an Active Directory account. Using Windows Server Update Services (WSUS) to update client workstations is considered ideal; this is not a security misconfiguration. The Windows Guest account is disabled by default in newer Windows versions. It should not be enabled in the interest of security and user auditing.

17. ☑ **A.** Black-box testing refers to the process by which computer software or networks are tested where the testers have no information on how the software or networks are designed.

☒ **B, C,** and **D** are incorrect. White-box testing means the testers have been given details regarding the item they are testing, for example, software source code or network diagrams. Testers have a minimal knowledge of the internals of software or network configuration when conducting gray-box testing. This allows testers to make better informed testing decisions. Blue-box testing does not exist; in the past, a blue box was a device used to make free long-distance telephone calls.

18. ☑ **A** and **C.** Packet 24 shows the packet coming from 66.220.151.75 with a source port of 80 (look at the middle of the figure at the Transmission Control Protocol, Src Port area). Since web servers use port 80, we now know the IP address of the web server. Because the packet payload (bottom-right panel) contains readable text, we know the packet is not encrypted with Secure Sockets Layer (SSL). We could determine this another way as well; SSL web servers normally use TCP port 443, not 80.

☒ **B** and **D** are incorrect. The client station IP address is 192.168.2.12 (look at the Transmission Control Protocol destination port of 3837 in packet 24). If this were the web server, traffic would be going to either port 80 or 443. Web browsing clients are assigned a dynamic port value above 1024 (such as 3837) that is used when receiving data from the web server.

19. ☑ **D.** A port scanner is a quick, simple way to determine which ports are open on a host. Even though ping packets may be blocked, RDP packets may not be.

☒ **A, B,** and **C** are incorrect. A packet sniffer captures transmitted network traffic, but it cannot determine whether RDP is available on 192.168.17.45. Virus scanners look for malicious code; they do not test for open ports on remote hosts. Wireless scanners list wireless networks within range; they do not perform port scans.

20. ☑ **C.** WPA2 is the most secure option from the presented list. Unlike WPA, WPA2 must be tested and certified by the Wi-Fi Alliance. WPA2 also uses a stronger encryption implementation.

☒ **A, B,** and **D** are incorrect. WEP encryption is easily broken sometimes within seconds with freely available tools. WPA supersedes WEP, but WPA2 is superior to WPA. WPA3 does not exist (yet).

21. ☑ **B.** Default administrative accounts must be renamed or disabled. Malicious users will try default admin accounts before moving on. Consider renaming the default admin account and creating a new administrator named account (as a regular user) with no rights or permissions. Always have more than one inconspicuous administrative account.

☒ **A, C,** and **D** are incorrect. The Windows Administrator and Guest accounts cannot be deleted because they are built-in accounts, but they can be renamed or disabled.

22. ☑ **A.** Network mapping utilities such as the open source Cheops tool can map out a network's layout and identify operating systems running on hosts.

☒ **B, C,** and **D** are incorrect. Protocol analyzers capture only transmitted network traffic; they do not scan for network hosts or network configuration. Port scanners identify listening ports. Virus scanners protect against malicious software on a host; they do not scan entire networks.

23. ☑ **A.** 802.1x requires that connecting hosts or users first authenticate with a central authentication server before even gaining access to the network. This is considered the most secure of the listed choices since WEP and WPA PSK do not require authentication to get on the network; only a passphrase is required. Neither of the two uses a centralized authentication server.
☒ **B, C,** and **D** are incorrect. WEP encryption is easily defeated with freely available tools, so it is not a secure choice. WPA PSK is more secure than WEP, but WPA2 PSK would be a more secure choice if it were listed. Disabling the SSID broadcast will stop only very inexperienced wireless hackers. 802.1x is the most secure option from the presented list.

24. ☑ **D.** The cost of licensing software is not considered during a security audit. Ensuring license compliance might be considered but not the cost of the licenses.
☒ **A, B,** and **C** are incorrect. Locked server rooms, wireless encryption, and patching status are all valid considerations during a security audit because they directly impact how secure data systems are.

25. ☑ **A and B.** These answers present a catch-22 scenario. The best solution is to authenticate admin accounts with a smartcard. This would eliminate remote attacks on admin accounts because of the requirement of possessing a physical smartcard.
☒ **C and D** are incorrect. Account lockout impedes the success of password attacks by locking the account for a time after a small number of successive incorrect passwords. Not configuring account lockout means password attacks could run against admin accounts incessantly.

26. ☑ **A.** A white-box test provides testers with detailed configuration information regarding the software or network they are testing.
☒ **B, C,** and **D** are incorrect. Black-box testing provides no information at all to system testers. Gray-box testing provides some, but not detailed, information to testers, which allows a more informed testing environment. Blue-box testing does not exist in this context.

27. ☑ **A and D.** The minimum password age prevents users from immediately changing their password a number of times (password history) to return to one they have already used that is easy to remember. Complexity requirements on Windows systems means the password cannot contain any variation of the username, it must be at least six characters long, it must contain an uppercase/lowercase character and number, and so on.
☒ **B and C** are incorrect. Compared to answers A and D, a password history of 5 is not a security issue. Storing passwords using reversible encryption is meant to be used by specific software needing the user password. Enabling this option does not store the passwords in a secure manner.

28. ☑ **B.** Vulnerability scanners normally use an updated database of known security vulnerabilities and misconfigurations for various operating systems and network devices. This database is compared against a single host or a network scan to determine whether any hosts or devices are vulnerable. Reports can then be generated from the scan.

☒ **A, C,** and **D** are incorrect. Packet sniffers are not designed to look for vulnerabilities; they simply capture transmitted network packets. There is no such thing as a risk scanner. Port scanners do not identify security threats; port scanners list open TCP and UDP ports.

29. ☑ **C.** Honeypots are intentionally exposed systems used to attract the attention of hackers or malicious code for further study.

☒ **A, B,** and **D** are incorrect. Patch servers ensure software on network hosts is kept up to date. Honeynets are a collection of two or more honeypots; the question specifically states a single host. Virus scanners would not detect zero-day exploits. A zero-day exploit is a vulnerability that has not yet been made known to the software author or virus scanner.

30. ☑ **A.** Remote Authentication Dial In User Service (RADIUS) is a central server that authenticates users connecting to a network. Failure to authenticate to the RADIUS server means access to the network is denied.

☒ **B, C,** and **D** are incorrect. WEP is not a centralized authentication mechanism; it must be configured on each access point and client station. WPA2 PSK must also be configured on each access point and client. Temporal Key Integrity Protocol (TKIP) uses key mixing and packets sequence counters to enhance security. TKIP is used with WPA to address the lack of security offered by WEP.

31. ☑ **C.** A banner grab is used to probe the listening port of a network service with the intent of learning more, such as what version of software is running.

☒ **A, B,** and **D** are incorrect. Denial-of-service attacks render a network service unavailable for legitimate use; in this case, we have nothing more than information gathering. Port scanning returns ports in use on a host; in this example, we already know that port 25 is in a listening state. There is no such term as mail grab.

32. ☑ **A.** A design review ensures a solution meets stated security requirements.

☒ **B, C,** and **D** are incorrect. Application security architecture review is focused on a particular application and not a network VPN implementation. VPN and network review do not describe the scenario as well as design review.

33. ☑ **D.** The consultant ran the vulnerability scan with administrative credentials. While this is fine, a noncredentialed scan should have also been run.

☒ **A, B,** and **C** are incorrect. The subnet mask and IP address are correct. The consultant did not run a noncredential scan; they ran a credentialed scan.

34. ☑ **A.** A false positive occurs when a harmless item or event occurs but is flagged as problematic.

☒ **B, C,** and **D** are incorrect. False positives and negatives do not generate e-mail messages, but the opposite is possible. False negatives are described as problematic security occurrences that did not generate some type of alert.

35. ☑ See Figure 18-6.

36. ☑ **A** and **B.** Firewalls should scrutinize not only incoming network traffic but also traffic leaving a network. This can prevent SMTP relaying, spam, DDoS attacks, and many more attacks initiated from your network to a victim host or network. DNS servers must replicate only with other known DNS servers to prevent replicating DNS records to rogue DNS hosts.

☒ **C** and **D** are incorrect. DNS servers can be placed in a DMZ as long as the appropriate firewall rules are in place and as long as private network DNS records are not replicated to the DMZ DNS host. HTTPS uses TCP 443, and in most cases this type of traffic should be allowed to leave a private network so users can connect to secured web sites.

37. ☑ **B.** Reserved private network addresses such as 192.168.1.0 are not routed by Internet routers and therefore should be used only on internal networks, not on a DMZ.

☒ **A, C,** and **D** are incorrect. The access-list value does not have to be 55. Cisco routers use the binary reverse subnet mask, so a /24 bit subnet mask (255.255.255.0) is expressed as 0.0.0.255; this is correct in this scenario. Rebooting a router after configuring access lists is not required.

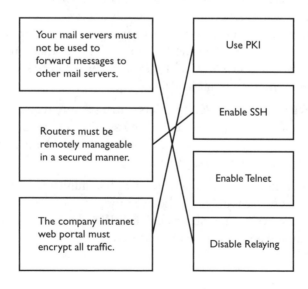

FIGURE 18-6

Security requirements and solutions—the answer

38. ☑ **A.** CMOS passwords prevent unauthorized persons from booting from USB or CD to bypass operating system security.

☒ **B, C,** and **D** are incorrect. Disk mirroring duplicates all disk writes to a separate disk; this is considered high availability, not hardening. File hashes are unique values for files that change in any way. This is useful for ensuring a file has not changed or been tampered with, but it does not make sense for traveling user laptops. Verbose logging is helpful when troubleshooting, but it does not secure a laptop.

39. ☑ **D.** A baseline establishes what system performance looks like under normal conditions. This can be compared to current conditions to determine whether anything is out of the norm.

☒ **A, B,** and **C** are incorrect. Penetration testing involves security technicians issuing common attacks against networks and hosts to identify threats. Hardening hosts is unrelated to baseline reporting.

40. ☑ **B.** Penetration testing can be risky. Many techniques are involved, but the possibility of degrading network performance or crashing hosts is a distinct possibility.

☒ **A, C,** and **D** are incorrect. Penetration tests are supposed to identify security threats; this is a good thing. Generating excessive logging and pen test costs are not as good a reason to skip a penetration test as the danger involved.

19

Understanding Monitoring and Auditing

QUESTIONS

Monitoring networks and host computers proactively can detect or even prevent the success of attacks. Network intrusion detection systems detect and report suspicious network activity. Host instruction detection systems detect and report suspicious host-based activity. Prevention systems have the ability to stop attacks once they have begun. Log files present a method of tracing activity that has already occurred. Today's networks include logs in many places; you must know which log to consult under specific circumstances.

1. Which of the following can stop in-progress attacks to your network?

    A. NIDS

    B. NIPS

    C. Proxy server

    D. Packet filtering firewall

2. Which of the following could an administrator use to determine whether there has been unauthorized use of a wireless LAN?

    A. Protocol analyzer

    B. Proxy server

    C. Performance Monitor

    D. Wireless access point log

3. You are responsible for managing an internal FTP server. A user reports that files available on the server yesterday are no longer available. Where can you look to determine what happened to the missing files?

    A. Firewall log

    B. FTP access log

    C. FTP download log

    D. FTP upload log

4. As a Windows server administrator for server ALPHA, you configure auditing so that you can track who deletes files on file share SALES. Where will you view the audit results?

    A. Security log

    B. Audit log

    C. Application log

    D. Deletion log

5. Your manager asks you to configure a honeypot to track malicious user activity. You install the host in the DMZ without any patches and configure a web site and an SMTP server on it. You have configured nothing else on the host. Identify a problem with this configuration.

    A. The honeypot needs to be patched.

    B. Honeypots should not run a web site.

    C. Forward honeypot logs to another secured host.

    D. Honeypots should not run SMTP services.

6. Which of the following are true regarding behavior-based network monitoring? (Choose two.)

    A. A baseline of normal behavior must be established.

    B. Deviations from acceptable activity cannot be monitored.

    C. New threats can be blocked.

    D. A database of known attack patterns is consulted.

7. You have configured a NIPS appliance to prevent web server directory traversal attacks. What type of configuration is this?

    A. Behavior-based

    B. Signature-based

    C. Anomaly-based

    D. Web-based

8. An administrator reports that a Windows file server is performing much slower than it normally does. The server is fully patched and has an up-to-date virus scanner. You open an RDP connection to the server to investigate the problem. Which of the following should you first use?

    A. Virus scanner

    B. Port scanner

    C. System restore point

    D. Performance Monitor

9. You have inherited the responsibility of managing an office network for which there is no documentation. As you perform desktop support duties over time, you notice many users seem to have more privileges on the network than they need. What should you do?

    A. Delete and re-create all user accounts.

    B. Conduct a user access and rights review.

    C. Check server audit logs.

    D. Enforce stronger user passwords.

10. To adhere to new corporate security guidelines, your branch offices must track details regarding visited web sites. What should you install?

    A. VPN

    B. Proxy server

    C. Packet filtering firewall

    D. NIDS

11. You would like to know when user accounts are modified in any way. What should you configure?

    A. Keyloggers on all user stations

    B. Firewall auditing

    C. User account auditing

    D. Personal firewall on all user stations

12. Which of the following are true regarding NIDS? (Choose two.)

    A. Network traffic is analyzed for malicious packets.

    B. Alerts and notifications can be configured.

    C. Malicious packets are dropped.

    D. Laptops are protected when disconnected from the LAN.

13. Which of the following is true regarding HIDS?

    A. Suspicious traffic entering the network can be blocked.

    B. Encrypted transmissions cannot be monitored.

    C. It must be installed on each system where needed.

    D. Log files are not analyzed.

14. Your company would like to standardize how long various types of documents are kept and deleted. What is needed to do this?

    A. Storage retention policy

    B. RAID 0

    C. Disaster recovery policy

    D. RAID 1

15. You are asked to analyze events in a firewall log that occurred six months ago. When you analyze the log file, you notice events go back only two months. What is the problem?

    A. You must have administrative access to the logs.

    B. The log file size is too small.

    C. Firewalls cannot keep logs for more than two months.

    D. The firewall is not patched.

16. A Windows administrator must track key performance metrics for a group of seven Windows servers. What should she do?

    A. Run Performance Monitor on each host.

    B. RDP into each host and run Performance Monitor.

    C. RDP into each host and check Event Viewer logs.

    D. Run Performance Monitor on her machine and add counters from the other seven servers.

17. You are a firewall appliance administrator for your company. Previously restricted outbound RDP packets are now successfully reaching external hosts, and you did not configure this firewall allowance. Where should you look to see who made the firewall change and when?

    A. Security log

    B. Firewall log

    C. Audit log

    D. Event Viewer log

18. In reviewing your firewall log, you notice a large number of your stations connecting to www.freetripsforyou.com and downloading an EXE file, sometimes in the middle of the night. Your users state they did not visit the web site. Your firewall does not allow any inbound packets initiated from the Internet. What does this indicate?

    A. User stations are connecting to Windows Update to apply patches.

    B. User stations have been hijacked and are downloading malware.

    C. User stations are infected with a password-cracking program.

    D. User stations are being controlled from the Internet through RDP.

19. A corporate network baseline has been established over the course of two weeks. Using this baseline data, you configure your intrusion prevention systems to notify you of abnormal network activity. A new sales initiative requires sales employees to run high-bandwidth applications across the Internet. As a result, you begin receiving security alerts regarding abnormal network activity. What are these type of alerts referred to as?

    A. False positives

    B. False negatives

    C. True positives

    D. True negatives

20. What can be done to prevent malicious users from tampering with log files? (Choose three.)

    A. Store log files on a secured centralized logging host.

    B. Encrypt archived log files.

    C. Run Windows Update.

    D. Generate file hashes for log files.

21. You have been asked to identify any irregularities from the following web server log excerpt:

```
199.0.14.202, -, 03/15/09, 8:33:12, W3SVC2, SERVER, 192.168.1.1, 4502
12.168.12.79, -, 03/15/09, 8:34:09, W3SVC2, SERVER, 192.168.1.1, 3455
12.168.12.79, -, 03/15/09, 17:02:26, W3SVC2, SERVER, 192.168.1.1, 4302
192.16.255.202, -, 03/15/09, 17:03:11, W3SVC2, SERVER, 192.168.1.1, 4111
```

   A. 199.0.14.202 is not a valid IP address.
   B. 192.16.255.202 is not a valid IP address.
   C. Web servers cannot use 192.168.1.1.
   D. The log is missing entries for a long period of time.

22. You are the Windows server administrator for a clothing outlet in Manhattan, New York. There are six Windows Server 2008 Active Directory computers used regularly. Files are being modified on servers during nonbusiness hours. You would like to audit who makes the changes and when. What is the quickest method of deploying your audit settings?

   A. Configure audit settings using Group Policy.
   B. Configure each server with the appropriate audit settings.
   C. Configure one server appropriately, export the settings, and import them to the other five.
   D. Delegate the audit configuration task to six other administrators.

23. What is the difference between a packet sniffer and a NIDS?

   A. There is no difference.
   B. Packet sniffers put the network card in promiscuous mode.
   C. NIDS puts the network card in promiscuous mode.
   D. Packet sniffers do not analyze captured traffic.

24. Your manager has asked you to identify which internal client computers have been controlled using RDP from the Internet. What should you do?

   A. Check the logs on each computer.
   B. Check the logs on your RDP servers.
   C. Check your firewall log.
   D. Contact your ISP and have them check their logs.

25. What is a potential problem with enabling detailed verbose logging on hosts for long periods of time?

   A. There is no problem.
   B. Performance degradation.
   C. Network bandwidth is consumed.
   D. Verbose logging consumes a user license.

26. A user, Jeff, reports his client Windows 8 station has been slow and unstable since last Tuesday. What should you first do?

    A. Use System Restore to revert the computer state to last Monday.

    B. Check log entries for Monday and Tuesday on Jeff's computer.

    C. Run Windows Update.

    D. Re-image Jeff's computer.

27. User workstations on your network connect through NAT to a DMZ where your Internet perimeter firewall exists. On Friday night a user connects to an inappropriate web site. You happened to have been capturing all network traffic on the DMZ at the time. How can you track which user workstation visited the web site? (Choose two.)

    A. View logs on the NAT router.

    B. View logs on the perimeter firewall.

    C. View your packet capture.

    D. View all workstation web browser histories.

28. An administrator is scheduling backup for Windows servers. She chooses to back up system state as well as user data folders on drive D:. What else should she have included in the backup?

    A. Drive C:

    B. Log files

    C. Wallpaper images

    D. Registry

29. Using Figure 19-1, match the requirements listed on the left with the solutions listed on the right.

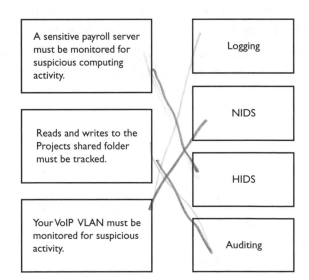

FIGURE 19-1

Security requirements and solutions

30. You are monitoring the performance on a Unix server called Alpha. Alpha is used to host concurrent remote sessions for users. You notice that long periods of intense server disk activity on Alpha coincide with remote users working with large documents stored on a separate Unix server called Bravo. What might be causing the degraded performance on Alpha?

A. There is too much network traffic.

B. The CPU is too slow.

C. The disks are too slow.

D. There is not enough RAM.

31. A server, Charlie, runs a mission-critical database application. The application encrypts all data from connected client workstations. You would like to monitor Charlie for suspicious activity and prevent any potential attacks. What should you deploy?

A. Honeypot

B. HIPS

C. NIDS

D. PKI

32. You are reviewing forwarded log entries for your Internet-facing firewall appliance. Last year, your company did some IP restructuring and began using the 172.16.0.0/16 address space internally. You notice abnormally large amounts of traffic on the firewall appliance's public interface within a short time frame coming from 172.16.29.97 destined for UDP port 53. Which of the following might you conclude from this information?   *DNS*

A. 172.16.29.97 is an invalid IP address.

B. 172.16.29.97 is a spoofed IP address.

C. The logs on the firewall appliance have been tampered with.

D. An HTTP denial-of-service attack was in progress.

33. A user complains that their machine performance has degraded ever since they downloaded a free file recovery utility. You would like to rule out the possibility of any malicious network services running in the background by viewing active port numbers on the machine. Which Windows command should you use to do this?

_____ *netstat* _____

34. How do logging and auditing differ?

A. Logging tracks more than just security events; auditing tracks specifically configured security events.

B. Auditing tracks more than just security events; logging tracks specifically configured security events.

C. Logging can track hardware events; auditing cannot.

D. Auditing can track hardware events; logging cannot.

QUICK ANSWER KEY

1.	B	**10.**	B	**19.**	A	**28.**	B
2.	D	**11.**	C	**20.**	A, B, D	**29.**	See Figure 19-2.
3.	B	**12.**	A, B	**21.**	D	**30.**	D
4.	A	**13.**	C	**22.**	A	**31.**	B
5.	C	**14.**	A	**23.**	D	**32.**	B
6.	A, C	**15.**	B	**24.**	C	**33.**	netstat
7.	B	**16.**	D	**25.**	B	**34.**	A
8.	D	**17.**	C	**26.**	B		
9.	B	**18.**	B	**27.**	A, C		

FIGURE 19-2

Security requirements and solutions—the answer

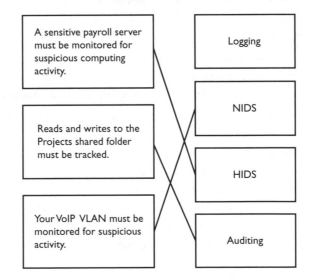

IN-DEPTH ANSWERS

1. ☑ **B.** A network intrusion prevention system (NIPS) analyzes network traffic patterns. Some implementations have a database of known attack patterns while others can take notice of abnormal traffic for a specific network. Measures can then be taken to stop the attack, such as by simply dropping the offending packets.

   ☒ **A, C,** and **D** are incorrect. A network instruction detection system (NIDS) can detect network anomalies, but they don't stop them; instead, they raise an alert or notify an administrator. Proxy servers retrieve Internet content on behalf of users; they do not analyze network traffic at all. Packet filtering firewalls analyze packet headers only to determine whether traffic should be allowed or denied, and they are not designed to stop in-progress network attacks; a NIPS is.

2. ☑ **D.** A wireless access point log can reveal all wireless LAN activity. Some access points may require you to enable logging.

   ☒ **A, B,** and **C** are incorrect. Protocol analyzers capture network traffic; the question asks whether unauthorized WLAN usage in the past can be determined. Proxy servers have nothing to do with wireless LANs. Performance monitoring measures various metrics of a computer system.

3. ☑ **B.** File Transfer Protocol (FTP) access logs list file activity on FTP servers including file deletions or renames.

   ☒ **A, C,** and **D** are incorrect. Firewall logs can list traffic to or from an FTP site, but unless the firewall logs all packet payloads (this is rare because of performance and space reasons), it cannot reveal who deleted or renamed files on the FTP site. FTP download and upload logs are just that: records of who downloaded files from the FTP server and who uploaded files to the FTP server, respectively.

4. ☑ **A.** Windows machines write audit data to the Event Viewer security log.

   ☒ **B, C,** and **D** are incorrect. Windows machines do not have an audit or deletion log. The application log lists events related to specific applications, not audit data.

5. ☑ **C.** The honeypot host is unpatched and is therefore vulnerable. Storing the only copy of log files on a honeypot is self-defeating.

   ☒ **A, B,** and **D** are incorrect. The honeypot does not need to be patched; this creates an easy target for malicious users and malicious code. Honeypots can run web or SMTP mail services if you want to track related malicious activity.

6. ☑ **A** and **C.** Behavior-based monitoring detects activity that deviates from the norm. A baseline is required to establish what normal is. Because of this, new attacks could potentially be stopped if they do not conform to normal network usage patterns.

☒ **B** and **D** are incorrect. With behavior-based monitoring, deviations from normal acceptable activity are detected. Signature-based monitoring uses a database of known attack patterns to compare against current network activity.

7. ☑ **B.** Comparing known attacks against current activity is called *signature-based detection*.
☒ **A**, **C**, and **D** are incorrect. With behavior-based monitoring, deviations from normal acceptable activity are detected. A deviation from normal behavior is referred to as an *anomaly*. Web-based is a fictitious detection method in this context.

8. ☑ **D.** Windows machines include Performance Monitor to measure which aspect of the software or hardware is not performing as well as it should.
☒ **A**, **B**, and **C** are incorrect. The question states the virus scanner is up to date, so running a virus scan is pointless since modern virus scanners watch all activity in real time. Port scanners show only open ports; they cannot identify why a system is slowing down. System restore points can sometimes revert the computer to a previous (and faster) state to solve these types of problems, but Windows servers do not support system restore points.

9. ☑ **B.** A user access and rights review identifies the rights and permissions users must have compared against what they have been given. In this case, the review would reveal what needs to be changed so users have only the rights needed to do their jobs.
☒ **A**, **C**, and **D** are incorrect. There is no reason to delete and re-create user accounts; existing account permissions and rights could be configured properly instead. Server audit logs could reveal how and when users got so many rights, but this will not help you solve the problem, nor will stronger user passwords.

10. ☑ **B.** Proxy servers can track detailed web surfing activity including site visited, time of day, user account name, and so on.
☒ **A**, **C**, and **D** are incorrect. Virtual private networks (VPNs) allow secure connections to a private LAN across an untrusted network, but they do not track web surfing activity. Packet filtering firewalls cannot track details, although they can log general network traffic allowed to pass through the firewall. A NIDS does not track visited web sites; they instead analyze network traffic for irregularities and then trigger alarms or notifications.

11. ☑ **C.** Enabling auditing of user account administrative activities will log any modifications made to user accounts.
☒ **A**, **B**, and **D** are incorrect. Keyloggers capture all keystrokes on a given host; this is not what is required in this case. Firewall auditing would apply to firewall activity, not specifically to user account modifications. Personal firewalls do not track changes to user accounts.

12. ☑ **A** and **B.** A NIDS does analyze network traffic for malicious packets, and it then triggers an alarm or notification.

☒ **C** and **D** are incorrect. A NIPS has the ability to drop malicious packets; a NIDS does not. A NIDS does absolutely nothing to protect laptops disconnected from the LAN. A HIDS could, though.

13. ☑ **C.** A HIDS is a host-based solution and thus must be installed on hosts where you would like this protection. A HIDS has the benefit of being very application specific.

☒ **A, B,** and **D** are incorrect. A HIDS cannot block suspicious traffic from entering the network; this is the job of a NIPS. Because a HIDS resides on a host, encrypted network traffic is no longer encrypted by the time a HIDS analyzes it (if it does at all). D in incorrect since a HIDS will normally analyze various host log files.

14. ☑ **A.** Storage retention policies are sometimes mandated by government regulation. Even if they are not, this type of policy states how and where data is stored, how it is backed up, how long it must be kept, and how it is to be disposed of.

☒ **B, C,** and **D** are incorrect. Redundant Array of Inexpensive Disks (RAID) 0 increases disk performance by striping data writes across multiple physical disks. RAID 1 provides fault tolerance (disk mirroring); data written to one disk is automatically immediately written to the second disk. Disaster recovery policies outline what is done by whom in the event of a catastrophe.

15. ☑ **B.** The firewall is probably configured to overwrite the oldest log entries first once the maximum log size has been reached. Even if this is the case, there are normally log archival options available for configuration.

☒ **A, C,** and **D** are incorrect. Administrative rights are definitely required to access firewall logs, but you wouldn't be able to see any entries if you did not have this privilege. Most firewalls can keep logs as long as you configure them to (log archiving). Failure to patch a firewall (software or firmware) would not be the cause of the problem stated in the question.

16. ☑ **D.** Like many Microsoft administrative tools, Performance Monitor can run locally but display data (performance counters) added from remote hosts.

☒ **A** and **B** are incorrect. Running Performance Monitor on or RDPing into each host is not an efficient solution. You generally cannot monitor system performance with Event Viewer log data.

17. ☑ **C.** Audit logs differ from regular activity logs because they record administrative configuration activities, such as modifying firewall rules.

☒ **A, B,** and **D** are incorrect. On Windows machines, the security log shows security events including Windows auditing events. Firewall logs display normal usage firewall activity, not administrative configuration activity. Windows Event Viewer logs would not display anything related to firewall appliance configurations.

18. ☑ **B.** If a computer is visiting a web site and downloading an EXE file without the user's knowledge, the machine is under malicious control. It would appear the malware is trying to download a Trojan of some kind.

    ■ A, C, and D are incorrect. Windows Update does not use the listed URL. Password-cracking programs try to guess passwords; they do not download EXE files without user consent. Since the firewall blocks connections initiated from the Internet, being controlled via RDP is unlikely.

19. ☑ **A.** False positives report there is a problem when in fact there is none, such as in this case. The alert should still be checked to ensure an attack is not coinciding with this new network activity.
    ■ **B, C,** and **D** are incorrect. Not reporting a problem when there is one is referred to as a false negative. True positives and true negatives are fictitious terms.

20. ☑ **A, B,** and **D.** Log files should be encrypted and stored on secured centralized hosts, so if a machine is compromised, there is still a copy of the log. File hashes ensure files have not been tampered with in any way; a modified file generated a different hash.
    ■ **C** is incorrect. Windows Update would not prevent log file tampering.

21. ☑ **D.** There is a long time discrepancy between the second and third lines. Almost nine hours of log activity are unaccounted for. This could mean somebody cleared incriminating log entries.
    ■ **A, B,** and **C** are incorrect. The IP addresses listed are valid. Web servers can use 192.168.1.1.

22. ☑ **A.** In an Active Directory environment Group Policy can be used to deliver settings to domain computers, such as audit settings for servers.
    ■ **B, C,** and **D** are incorrect. Each listed solution would work, but they take much more time to implement than using Group Policy would.

23. ☑ **D.** Packet sniffers (protocol analyzers) capture network traffic, but they do not analyze it in any way.
    ■ **A, B,** and **C** are incorrect. There is a difference between a packet sniffer and NIDS. Packet sniffers capture network traffic passively, nothing more. A NIDS analyzes traffic looking for suspicious activity. Promiscuous mode allows the station to analyze more network traffic than it otherwise would.

24. ☑ **C.** Since RDP connections from the Internet would go through the firewall, it would be quickest and easiest to consult your firewall log.
    ■ **A, B,** and **D** are incorrect. Checking logs on each computer is too time-consuming. Your RDP servers would not be involved with somebody from the Internet RDPing to one of your internal client stations. There is no need to contact your ISP; your own firewall would have this information.

25. ☑ **B.** Detailed verbose logging presents much more log data than normal logging; therefore, performance is affected. Depending on what is being logged and how much activity there is will determine how much of a performance degradation there will be.
    ■ **A, C,** and **D** are incorrect. Verbose logging is useful for troubleshooting but not for long periods of time because performance is degraded. Network bandwidth is not affected by verbose logging (unless forwarding log data to a central logging host). Changing logging levels does not consume a user license.

26. ☑ **B.** Before jumping the gun and re-imaging or applying a restore point, first check the log files for any indication of what changed before the machine became slow and unstable.

    ☒ **A, C,** and **D** are incorrect. System restore and re-imaging should normally not be performed immediately (unless your corporate policy states to); check logs first. Windows Update would most likely not make a difference on Jeff's computer.

27. ☑ **A** and **C.** NAT router logs will list which internal addresses were translated and at what time. This could be used in correlation with captured packet time stamps to establish who visited the web site.

    ☒ **B** and **D** are incorrect. The perimeter firewall most likely will list only the IP address of the NAT router's public interface; all outbound packets assume this IP address. Viewing all client browsing histories would take longer than viewing the NAT log or your packet capture.

28. ☑ **B.** Log files must be backed up along with user data and system configuration data.

    ☒ **A, C,** and **D** are incorrect. Drive C: normally contains the operating system files, and these are replaceable. Wallpaper images are not considered critical data that must be backed up. Backing up system state already includes the registry.

29. ☑ See Figure 19-3. Host intrusion detection (HID) software could be installed on the payroll server to detect suspicious activity and alert security professions. Tracking reads and writes to a folder is accomplished with auditing. Network intrusion detection systems monitor networks for suspicious activity.

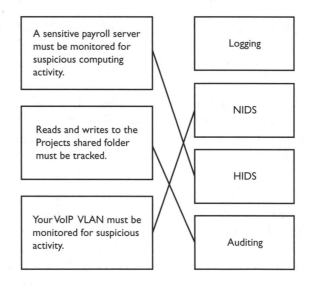

FIGURE 19-3

Security requirements and solutions—the answer

30. ☑ **D.** Lack of RAM causes the oldest used data in RAM to be swapped to disk to make room for what must now be placed in RAM (many large documents). This sometimes makes it appear as if the disk is the problem.

☒ **A**, **B**, and **C** are incorrect. The server network connection, CPU, and disks seem fine other than when remote users work with large documents.

31. ☑ **B.** To monitor specific apps running on host computers and prevent potential attacks, you should deploy a HIPS.

☒ **A**, **C**, and **D** are incorrect. Honeypots are hosts left intentionally vulnerable for the purpose of tracking or studying malicious code. A NIDS analyzes network packets looking for suspicious traffic. Public Key Infrastructure (PKI) is a hierarchy of certificates containing public and private keys for securing data.

32. ☑ **B.** From the list of choices, the most likely answer is that 172.16.29.97 was a spoofed IP address. IP addresses used on the internal network should not be coming into the network from the outside.

☒ **A**, **C**, and **D** are incorrect. 172.16.29.97 is a valid IP address. The question states you are reviewing forwarded log entries, not entries on the firewall appliance itself, so log file tampering would not affect you in this case. HTTP uses TCP port 80; the question states UDP port 53 (DNS).

33. ☑ **netstat.** This built-in Windows command can display local listening ports that can accept connections, as well as which network services (and ports) you are connected to.

34. ☑ **A.** Logging tracks many different types of events related to hardware and software, but auditing specifically tracks security-related events that have been preconfigured.

☒ **B**, **C**, and **D** are incorrect. Auditing focuses on tracking access to a specific resource for security purposes. Both logging and auditing could track hardware-related events. For example, logging can track the activity related to a printer, whereas auditing could track smartcard authentication.

A

Pre-assessment Exam

QUESTIONS

This pre-assessment exam will gauge your knowledge of security-related concepts that you are expected to understand to pass exam SY0-401. When you take your real exam, you will have 90 minutes to answer up to a maximum of 100 questions. This pre-assessment includes 40 questions, so you should allow yourself a maximum of 40 minutes to complete all 40 questions. To mimic the real exam environment, make sure you are in quiet place where you will not be interrupted. Afterward, refer to the self-grading section that appears after the answer section to determine your best course of action to ensure your success in passing exam SY0-401.

1. Which TCP/IP protocols use encryption to secure data transmissions?
   A. SCP, DNS, SSH
   B. SSH, SCP, Telnet
   C. HTTPS, FTP, SSH
   D. SSH, SCP, FTPS

2. While troubleshooting connectivity to your remote file server, you realize that a firewall is preventing you from pinging the server. Which type of firewall rule should you create to allow ping traffic?
   A. UDP
   B. IGMP
   C. TCP
   D. ICMP

3. You are a guest at a hotel offering free Wi-Fi Internet access to guests. You connect to the wireless network at full signal strength and obtain a valid TCP/IP configuration. When you try to access Internet web sites, a web page displays instead and asks for a code before allowing access to the Internet. What type of network component is providing this functionality?
   A. DHCP server
   B. NAT
   C. Proxy server
   D. Switch

4. You are configuring a wireless router at a car repair shop so that waiting customers can connect to the Internet. You want to ensure wireless clients can connect to the Internet but cannot connect to internal computers owned by the car repair shop. Where should you plug in the wireless router?
   A. LAN
   B. Port 24 on the switch
   C. Port 1 on the switch
   D. DMZ

5. What will detect network or host intrusions and take actions to prevent the intrusion from succeeding?

   A. IPS
   B. IDS
   C. IPSec
   D. DMZ

6. You must purchase a network device that supports content filtering and virus defense for your LAN. What should you choose?

   A. NAT router
   B. HIPS
   C. Web security gateway
   D. Packet filtering firewall

7. A router must be configured to allow traffic from certain hosts only. How can this be accomplished?

   A. ACL
   B. Subnet
   C. Proxy server
   D. NAT

8. Your company issues smart phones to employees for business use. Corporate policy dictates that all data stored on smart phones must be encrypted. To which fundamental security concept does this apply?

   A. Confidentiality
   B. Integrity
   C. Availability
   D. Accountability

9. To quickly give a contractor network access, a network administrator adds the contractor account to the Windows Administrators group. Which security principle does this violate?

   A. Separation of duties
   B. Least privilege
   C. Job rotation
   D. Account lockout

10. Complex passwords are considered which type of security control?

   A. Management

   B. Technical

   C. Physical

   D. Operational

11. You are responsible for completing an IT asset report for your company. All IT-related equipment and data must be identified and given a value. What term best describes this action?

   A. Asset identification

   B. Risk assessment

   C. Risk mitigation

   D. Threat analysis

12. An insurance company charges an additional $200 monthly premium for natural disaster coverage for your business site. What figure must you compare this against to determine whether to accept this additional coverage?

   A. ALE

   B. ROI

   C. Total cost of ownership

   D. Total monthly insurance premium

13. Which of the following physical access control methods do not normally identify who has entered a secure area? (Choose two.)

   A. Mantrap

   B. Hardware locks

   C. Fingerprint scan

   D. Smartcard

14. Turtle Airlines has hired you to ensure their customer reservation system is always online. The software runs and stores data locally on the Linux operating system. What should you do?

   A. Install two Linux servers in a cluster. Cluster the airline software with its data being written to shared storage.

   B. Install a new Linux server. Ensure the airline software runs from the first server. Schedule airline data to replicate to the new Linux server nightly.

   C. Configure the Linux server with RAID 5.

   D. Configure the Linux server with RAID 1.

15. Juanita uses the Firefox web browser on her Linux workstation. She reports that her browser home page keeps changing to web sites offering savings on consumer electronic products. Her virus scanner is running and is up to date. What is causing this problem?

    A. Firefox on Linux automatically changes the home page every two days.

    B. Juanita is experiencing a denial-of-service attack.

    C. Juanita's user account has been compromised.

    D. Juanita's browser configuration is being changed by adware.

16. What type of malware dynamically alters itself to avoid detection?

    A. Chameleon malware

    B. Polymorphic malware

    C. Changeling malware

    D. Armored virus

17. A user on your network receives an e-mail from the bank stating that there has been a security incident at the bank. The e-mail continues by asking the user to log on to her bank account by following the link provided and verify that her account has not been tampered with. What type of attack is this?

    A. Phishing

    B. Spam

    C. Dictionary attack

    D. Spim

18. Which of the following refers to unauthorized data access of a Bluetooth device over a Bluetooth wireless network?

    A. Bluejacking

    B. Bluesnarfing

    C. Packet sniffing

    D. Port scanning

19. What type of attack involves the hacker inserting client-side script into the web page?

    A. XSS

    B. Watering hole attack

    C. ARP poisoning

    D. SQL injection

20. The process of disabling unneeded network services on a computer is referred to as what?

    A. Patching

    B. Fuzzing

    C. Hardening

    D. Debugging

21. How can you prevent rogue machines from connecting to your network?

    A. Deploy an IEEE 802.1x configuration.

    B. Use strong passwords for user accounts.

    C. Use IPv6.

    D. Deploy an IEEE 802.11 configuration.

22. You would like to focus and track malicious activity to a particular host in your DMZ. What should you configure?

    A. Honeynet

    B. Honeypot

    C. DMZ tracker

    D. Web server

23. A security auditor must determine what types of servers are running on a network. Which tool should be used?

    A. Network mapper

    B. Protocol analyzer

    C. Port scanner

    D. Virus scanner

24. Which type of security testing provides network configuration information to testers?

    A. White box

    B. Black box

    C. Gray box

    D. Blue box

25. The web developers at your company are testing their latest web site code before going live to ensure that it is robust and secure. During their testing they provide malformed URLs with additional abnormal parameters as well as an abundance of random data. What term describes their actions?

    A. Cross-site scripting

    B. Fuzzing

    C. Patching

    D. Debugging

26. You are the founder of Acme Data Mining. The business focuses on retrieving relevant consumer habits from various sources, and that data is then sold to retailers. Because of the amount of data that must be processed, you must implement the fastest possible solution. Which type of technology should you implement?

    A. SQL
    B. NoSQL
    C. SATA
    D. NoSATA

27. What can be done to protect data after a handheld device is lost or stolen?

    A. Enable encryption.
    B. Execute a remote wipe.
    C. Enable screen lock.
    D. Disable Bluetooth discovery.

28. Which of the following correctly identifies an operating system that meets specific government or regulatory security standards?

    A. Hardened OS
    B. Trusted OS
    C. Security OS
    D. Patched OS

29. Which standard is a firmware solution for drive encryption?

    A. TPM
    B. DLP
    C. EFS
    D. NTFS

30. Your company has issued Android-based smart phones to select employees. Your manager asks you to ensure that data on the smart phones is protected. How do you address your manager's concerns?

    A. Implement SCADA, screen locking, device encryption, and anti-malware, and disable unnecessary software on the phones.
    B. Implement PKI VPN authentication certificates, screen locking, device encryption, and anti-malware, and disable unnecessary software on the phones.
    C. Implement screen locking, device encryption, patching, and anti-malware, and disable unnecessary software on the phones.
    D. Implement HTTPS, screen locking, device encryption, and anti-malware, and disable unnecessary software on the phones.

31. What type of server authenticates users prior to allowing network access?

   A. File server

   B. Active Directory

   C. RADIUS

   D. Domain controller

32. You are the network administrator for a UNIX network. You are planning your network security. A secure protocol must be chosen to authenticate all users logging in. Which is a valid authentication protocol choice?

   A. TCP

   B. Telnet

   C. Kerberos

   D. AES

33. Which of the following is considered three-factor authentication?

   A. Building access card/voice recognition scan

   B. Building access card/username/password

   C. Username/password/smartcard

   D. Username/password/smartcard/PIN

34. You are evaluating public cloud storage solutions. Users will be authenticated to a local server on your network that will allow them access to cloud storage. Which identity federation standard could be configured to achieve this?

   A. LDAP

   B. SSL

   C. PKI

   D. SAML

35. A network administrator must grant the appropriate network permissions to a new employee. Which of the following is the best strategy?

   A. Give the new employee user account the necessary rights and permissions.

   B. Add the new employee user account to a group. Ensure the group has the necessary rights and permissions.

   C. Give the new employee administrative rights to the network.

   D. Ask the new employee what network rights they would like.

36. You are a security auditing professional. After evaluating Linux server usage, you determine that members of the IT administrative team regularly log in to Linux servers using the root account while performing regular computer tasks. Which recommendations should you make based on your findings? (Choose three.)

   A. Do not allow multiple users to use generic credentials.
   B. Conduct periodic user access reviews.
   C. Monitor Linux server use continuously.
   D. Encrypt all files on Linux servers.

37. Which term describes the process of concealing messages within a file?

   A. Trojan
   B. Steganography
   C. Encryption
   D. Digital signature

38. You are a developer at a software development firm. Your latest software build must be made available on the corporate web site. Internet users require a method of ensuring they have downloaded an untampered version of the software. What should you do?

   A. Generate a file hash for the download file and make it available on the web site.
   B. Make sure Internet users have antivirus software installed.
   C. Configure the web site to use TLS.
   D. Make sure the web server has antivirus software installed.

39. Which cryptographic approach uses points on a curve to define public and private key pairs?

   A. RSA
   B. DES
   C. ECC
   D. PKI

40. Your colleagues report that there is a short time frame where a revoked certificate can still be used. Why is this?

   A. The CRL is published periodically.
   B. The CRL is published immediately but must replicate to all hosts.
   C. The CRL lists only revoked certificate serial numbers; it is not used in any way.
   D. The CRL is dependent on network bandwidth.

QUICK ANSWER KEY

1. D	11. A	21. A	31. C
2. D	12. A	22. B	32. C
3. C	13. A, B	23. A	33. D
4. D	14. A	24. A	34. D
5. A	15. D	25. B	35. B
6. C	16. B	26. B	36. A, B, C
7. A	17. A	27. B	37. B
8. A	18. B	28. B	38. A
9. B	19. A	29. A	39. C
10. B	20. C	30. C	40. A

IN-DEPTH ANSWERS

1. ☑ **D.** Secure Shell (SSH), Secure CoPy (SCP), and File Transfer Protocol Secure (FTPS) encrypt data transmissions.

   ☒ **A, B**, and **C** are incorrect. Domain Name System (DNS), Telnet, and File Transfer Protocol (FTP) do not encrypt data. DNS normally resolves fully qualified domain names to IP addresses, Telnet is used for remote command-line management, and FTP is used to transfer files between hosts.

2. ☑ **D.** Internet Control Message Protocol (ICMP) is the transport used by the ping command.

   ☒ **A, B**, and **C** are incorrect. User Datagram Protocol (UDP) is a best-effort transport protocol. Internet Group Management Protocol (IGMP) is used for multicast applications. Transmission Control Protocol (TCP) is a reliable connection-oriented transport protocol.

3. ☑ **C.** Proxy servers retrieve content for connected clients and can also require authentication before doing so.

   ☒ **A, B**, and **D** are incorrect. Dynamic Host Configuration Protocol (DHCP) provides clients with a valid IP address, subnet mask, default gateway, Domain Name System (DNS) server, and so on; there is no mechanism for authentication. Network Address Translation (NAT) uses a single public IP address to represent all internal computers. Like DHCP, NAT does not authenticate connections. Switches isolate network conversations between hosts and track which computers are plugged into which switch port using the machine's MAC address.

4. ☑ **D.** A demilitarized zone (DMZ) is a network allowing external unsecure access to resources while preventing direct access to internal resources. If the wireless router is plugged into the DMZ, this will provide Internet access to customers while disallowing them access to internal business computers. Plugging the wireless router into the internal LAN would also allow Internet access but would place customers on a business LAN.

   ☒ **A, B**, and **C** are incorrect. A LAN would allow customer access to internal computers and is therefore incorrect. Ports 24 and 1 on a switch generally have no special DMZ meaning any more than any other port does, although some network devices do have special designated DMZ ports.

5. ☑ **A.** An intrusion prevention system (IPS) actively monitors network or system activity for abnormal activity and also takes steps to stop it. Abnormal activity can be detected by checking for known attack patterns (signature-based) or variations beyond normal activity (anomaly-based).

   ☒ **B, C**, and **D** are incorrect. Like an IPS, an intrusion detection system (IDS) monitors network or system activity for irregular activity but does not attempt to stop this activity. IP Security (IPSec) provides data confidentially and integrity to network transmissions and does not detect or prevent intrusions. A DMZ does not detect or prevent attacks; it is a network segment hosting services (and ideally an IPS) that are accessible to an untrusted network.

6. ☑ **C** is correct. Web security gateways can perform deep packet inspection (content) to filter network traffic. They also include the ability to detect and deal with malware.
☒ **A, B,** and **D** are not correct. NAT does not support content filtering or virus protection; it merely analyzes and modifies packet headers. A host intrusion prevention system (HIPS) detects and stops attacks on a host computer and does not monitor the content of LAN network traffic. Packet filtering firewalls look only at packet headers to allow or deny traffic; they do not analyze packet payloads.

7. ☑ **A.** Access control lists (ACLs) are router settings that allow or deny various types of network traffic from or to specific hosts.
☒ **B, C,** and **D** are incorrect. A subnet cannot restrict network traffic. Routers can be used to divide larger networks into smaller subnets. The question specifically states configuring a router, and proxy hosts should have routing disabled. Proxy servers do have the ability to limit network access from certain hosts, though. NAT routers do not restrict network traffic from certain hosts; instead, they use a single external IP address to allow many internal computers access to an external network.

8. ☑ **A.** Confidentiality ensures that data is accessible only to those parties that should be authorized to the data. Encrypting data stored on smart phones protects that data if the phone is lost or stolen.
☒ **B, C,** and **D** are incorrect. Integrity ensures that data comes from the user or device it appears to have come from and that the data has not been altered. Making sure data is available when needed is referred to as availability. Accountability makes people accountable for their actions, such as modifying a file. This is accomplished most often with auditing.

9. ☑ **B.** The least privilege principle states users should be given only the rights needed to perform the duties and nothing more. Adding a contractor to the Administrators group grants too much privilege to the contractor.
☒ **A, C,** and **D** are incorrect. Separation of duties requires multiple people to perform a specific job. Job rotation is a strategy that exposes employees to various facets of a business and has nothing to do with security. Account lockout relates to security but is not violated by giving a user too many permissions.

10. ☑ **B.** Technical security controls are put in place to protect computing resources such as files, web sites, databases, and so on. Passwords prevent everybody from accessing network resources.
☒ **A, C,** and **D** are incorrect. Management controls are written policies that determine acceptable activities and how they should be conducted. Physical controls such as door locks and fences protect organizational assets from threats. Operational controls such as data backups ensure business continuity.

11. ☑ **A.** Asset identification involves identifying assets (including data) and associating a value with them. This can then be used to justify expenditures to protect these assets.

☒ **B, C,** and **D** are incorrect. Risk assessment is the identification of threats, but the next step in this case is asset identification. Risk mitigation minimizes the impact of perceived risks. Threat analysis does not involve identifying IT hardware with a cost.

12. ☑ **A.** The annual loss expectancy (ALE) value is used with quantitative risk analysis approaches to prioritize and justify expenditures that protect from potential risks. For example, an ALE value of $1,000 might justify a $200 annual expense to protect against that risk.

☒ **B, C,** and **D** are incorrect. The return on investment (ROI) calculates how efficient an investment is (does the benefit of a product or service outweigh the cost?). Total cost of ownership exposes all direct and indirect dollar figures associated with a product or service. Using the total monthly premium value to determine whether to accept the additional insurance coverage would be meaningless; it must be compared against the probability of natural disasters in your area.

13. ☑ **A** and **B.** Mantraps are designed to trap trespassers in a restricted area. Some mantrap variations use two sets of doors, one of which must close before the second one opens. Traditional mantraps do not require access cards. Hardware locks simply require possession of a key. Neither reveals the person's identity.

☒ **C** and **D** are incorrect. Fingerprints identify the user via biometric authentication. Smartcard authentication identifies the user through a unique code or PKI certificate in a smartcard.

14. ☑ **A.** Clustering software between two servers will allow the customer reservation system to function even if one server fails because the data is not stored within a single server; it exists on shared storage that both cluster nodes can access.

☒ **B, C,** and **D** are incorrect. Scheduling nightly data replication does not ensure the airline software is always online. RAID 1 (mirroring) and RAID 5 (striping with distributed parity) are useless if the server fails because, in this case, RAID 1 and RAID 5 would use multiple hard drives within a single server.

15. ☑ **D.** Adware attempts to expose users to advertisements in various ways including through pop-ups or changing the web browser home page. Spyware often analyzes user habits so that adware displays relevant advertisements. Some antivirus software also scans for spyware but not in this case.

☒ **A, B,** and **C** are incorrect. Firefox on Linux does not change the home page every two days. Denial-of-service attacks prevent legitimate access to a network resource; Juanita is not being denied access. The presence of spyware or adware does not imply the user account has been compromised. Often these types of malware are silently installed when visiting web sites or installing freeware.

16. ☑ **B.** Polymorphic malware dynamically adjusts itself to avoid detection while maintaining its original functionality.

☒ **A, C,** and **D** are incorrect. There are no such things as chameleon malware and changeling malware. Armored viruses prevent software engineers from decompiling the program to reveal the programming code that makes it run.

17. ☑ **A.** Phishing is when the hacker e-mails a victim and hopes she clicks the link that leads her to a fake site (typically a bank). At this point, the hacker hopes the user types information into the fake site (such as bank account information) that he can use to gain access to her real account.

☒ **B, C,** and **D** are incorrect. Spam is an unsolicited e-mail you receive that tries to encourage you to buy a product or a service. Dictionary attacks read a text file and use all words in the text file as password attempts. Spim is spam-type messages sent through instant messaging instead of e-mail.

18. ☑ **B.** Bluesnarfing is the act of connecting to and accessing data from a device over a Bluetooth wireless connection. It is considered much more invasive than packet sniffing or port scanning.

☒ **A, C,** and **D** are not correct since bluejacking does not access data from a Bluetooth device; instead, bluejacking sends an unsolicited message to another Bluetooth device. The question specifies accessing data. Packet sniffing captures network traffic; it does not access data from a wireless device. Port scanning enumerates running services on a host, but it does not access data stored on the host.

19. ☑ **A.** Cross-site scripting (XSS) is an attack that involves the hacker inserting script code into a web page so that it is then processed and executed by a client system.

☒ **B, C,** and **D** are incorrect. A watering hole attack is when a hacker plants malicious code on a site you may visit so that when you navigate to the site, the code attacks your system from a site you trust. ARP poisoning is when the hacker inserts incorrect MAC addresses into the ARP cache, thus leading systems to the hacker's system. SQL injection is inserting SQL code into an application in order to manipulate the underlying database or system.

20. ☑ **C.** Hardening includes actions such as disabling unneeded services to make a system more secure.

☒ **A, B,** and **D** are incorrect. Patches fix problems with software. Fuzzing refers to testing your own software for vulnerabilities. Debugging is the methodical testing of software to identify the cause of a flaw.

21. ☑ **A.** The IEEE 802.1x standard requires that devices be authenticated before being given network access. For example, this might be configured for VPN appliances, network switches, and wireless access points that adhere to the IEEE 802.1x standard.

    ☒ **B, C,** and **D** are incorrect. Strong passwords might prevent the compromising of user accounts, but it will not prevent rogue machines from connecting to the network. IPv6 does not prevent rogue machine network connections. IEEE 802.11 defines the Wi-Fi standard; this does not prevent rogue machine network connections.

22. ☑ **B.** A honeypot is an intentionally vulnerable host used to attract and track malicious activity.
    ☒ **A, C,** and **D** are incorrect. The question stated activity tracking on a single host, not a network of hosts. There is no such thing as a DMZ tracker. Web sites are not a tool to track malicious activity; web sites deliver content to web browsers.

23. ☑ **A.** Network mapping utilities such as the open source Cheops tool can map a network's layout and identify operating systems running on hosts.
    ☒ **B, C,** and **D** are incorrect. Protocol analyzers capture only transmitted network traffic; they do not scan for network hosts or network configuration. Port scanners identify listening ports. Virus scanners protect against malicious software on a host; they do not scan entire networks.

24. ☑ **A.** A white-box test provides testers with detailed configuration information regarding the software or network they are testing.
    ☒ **B, C,** and **D** are incorrect. Black-box testing provides no information at all to system testers. Gray-box testing provides some, but not detailed, information to testers, which allows a more informed testing environment. Blue-box testing does not exist in this context.

25. ☑ **B.** Fuzzing is a means of injecting data into an application that it does not expect to ensure there are no weaknesses.
    ☒ **A, C,** and **D** are incorrect. Cross-site scripts do not ensure applications are secure; they are a type of attack. Patching would occur after flaws were discovered. Debugging implies software flaws are already known.

26. ☑ **B.** NoSQL is a simplified database standard (nonrelational) designed for quick retrieval when processing large volumes of data.
    ☒ **A, C,** and **D** are incorrect. SQL databases are relational databases that do not scale well when processing enormous amounts of data. The SATA standard relates to data storage and not directly to data mining.

27. ☑ **B.** Remote wipe is an option administrators can exercise to remotely wipe the contents of a handheld device.
    ☒ **A, C,** and **D** are incorrect. These settings would have to be either set before the device was lost or stolen or pushed out the next time the device was connected.

28. ☑ **B.** A trusted OS is a secured operating system that meets or exceeds stringent security standards.

☒ **A, C,** and **D** are incorrect. These terms do not apply in the context of the question. A security OS provides security tools. There are many Linux distributions built for this purpose. A hardened OS is the process of securing an OS by disabling or removing unnecessary services and software. A patched OS is one that has had OS and application patches applied.

29. ☑ **A.** Trusted Platform Module (TPM) chips can store cryptographic keys or certificates used to encrypt and decrypt drive contents. If the drive were moved to another computer (even one with TPM), the drive would remain encrypted and inaccessible.

    ☒ **B, C,** and **D** are incorrect. Data loss prevention (DLP) refers to fault tolerance and related mechanisms for ensuring data is safe, such as preventing sensitive data from being copied while it is being viewed (data in use). Encrypting File System (EFS) is purely software, not a firmware chip. NTFS uses ACLs to control access to data, but the data is not encrypted.

30. ☑ **C.** Hardening a smart phone includes configuring automatic screen locking, encrypting data on the device, patching the OS and required apps, installing and updating anti-malware, and disabling unnecessary features and software.

    ☒ **A, B,** and **D** are incorrect. Supervisory Control And Data Acquisition (SCADA) is a special system used in industrial environments to monitor operations and to provide alarms if any system is tampered with. The question asks about securing data on the phone, not through the network with a VPN. HTTPS will not protect data on the phone, only data in transit between the web browser and secured website.

31. ☑ **C** is correct. Remote Authentication Dial In User Service (RADIUS) servers are central user or device authentication points on the network. Authentication can occur in many ways including Extensible Authentication Protocol (EAP) and Challenge Handshake Authentication Protocol (CHAP).

    ☒ **A, B,** and **D** are incorrect. File servers host shared file and folder resources; they rely on users and devices already having network access. Active Directory is a replicated network database of network resources in a Microsoft domain environment, and it does not control network access; it partially controls network resource access. Domain controllers partake in Active Directory database replication.

32. ☑ **C.** Kerberos is an authentication protocol used by many vendors, including Microsoft with Active Directory Services. Clients and servers must securely prove their identity to each other by way of a central third party referred to as a key distribution center (KDC).

    ☒ **A, B,** and **D** are incorrect. TCP is a connection-oriented reliable TCP/IP transport protocol, but it does not perform authentication. Telnet transmits data in clear text, so it is not secure. It is used to allow administrative remote access to hosts running a Telnet daemon, usually in UNIX or Linux environments. Advanced Encryption Standard (AES) is a symmetric key encryption algorithm; it encrypts data transmissions, but it does not authenticate users on a network.

33. ☑ **D.** The username and password combination is considered single-factor authentication. It coupled with possessing a smartcard and knowing the PIN to use the smartcard results in three-factor (or multifactor) authentication.

    ☒ **A, B,** and **C** are incorrect because they are only two-factor authentication.

34. ☑ **D.** Security Assertion Markup Language (SAML) is an XML standard that defines how authentication and authorization data can be transmitted in a federated identity environment.

    ☒ **A, B,** and **C** are incorrect. Lightweight Directory Access Protocol (LDAP) is a protocol defining how to access a replicated network database. Secure Sockets Layer (SSL) provides a method to secure application-specific network transmissions. A public key infrastructure (PKI) is a hierarchy of digital security certificates that can be used with computing devices to provide data confidentiality, authentication, and integrity services.

35. ☑ **B.** The best strategy for assigning rights and permissions is to add users to groups. Working with rights and permissions for individual users becomes unmanageable beyond a small number of users. New employees can then simply be added to the appropriate group to acquire the needed access to network resources.

    ☒ **A, C,** and **D** are incorrect. Granting individual user rights and permissions becomes difficult to manage as the number of users grows. Granting new employees administrative rights to the network is a violation of all network security best practices—grant only the rights needed. Users may not know what rights they need, or they may ask for rights they do not need to perform their job.

36. ☑ **A, B,** and **C.** Each member of the IT team should use their own user account when performing regular computer tasks. Periodically reviewing user access and server usage will ensure security controls are effective for the Linux servers.

    ☒ **D** is incorrect. Encrypting files increases file security, but it is not related to the security audit findings stated in the question.

37. ☑ **B.** Steganography hides messages within files. For example, a message could be hidden within an inconspicuous JPEG picture file.

    ☒ **A, C,** and **D** are incorrect. A Trojan is malware masking itself as a useful file or software. Encryption makes no attempt to hide the fact that data is encrypted. Digital signatures are used to verify the integrity and authenticity of data. No attempt is made to conceal a message.

38. ☑ **A.** File hashing performs a calculation on a file resulting in what is called a hash. Changing a file in some way and then performing the same calculation would result in a different hash. This is one way to verify that file is the correct version.

    ☒ **B, C,** and **D** are incorrect. As a software developer, you cannot control whether Internet users have antivirus software installed. Antivirus software on a server is always important but is not related to file hashing. While Transport Layer Security (TLS) could be used to secure the Internet traffic to the web site, it cannot check for file tampering.

39. ☑ **C.** Elliptic Curve Cryptography (ECC) is public key cryptography based on points on an elliptic curve.

☒ **A, B,** and **D** are incorrect. RSA is an asymmetric cryptographic standard. DES is incorrect because it is a symmetric standard. PKI does involve public and private key pairs but has nothing specifically to do with elliptic curve points.

40. ☑ **A.** The CRL is not published immediately; it is published either manually or on a schedule, so there may be a small time frame where revoked certificates can still be used.

☒ **B, C,** and **D** are incorrect. The CRL is not published immediately when a certificate is revoked; it is published on a periodic interval. Once the CRL is published, it is referenced by clients. Network bandwidth does not affect when the CRL is published.

CREATE YOUR STUDY PLAN

Congratulations on completing the Security+ pre-assessment! You should now take the time to analyze your results with two objectives in mind.

1. Identifying the resources you should use to prepare for the Security+ exam

2. Identifying the specific topics you should focus on in your preparation

Review Your Score

Use the following table to help you gauge your overall readiness for the Security+ exam. Total your score from the pre-assessment questions for an overall score out of 40.

Number of Answers Correct	Recommended Course of Study
1–25	We recommend you spend a significant amount of time reviewing the material in the *Security+ Study Guide* before using this book.
26–30	We recommend you review your scores in the specific functional areas shown in the next table to identify the particular areas that require your focused attention and use the *Security+ Study Guide* to review that material. Once you have done so, you should proceed to work through the questions in this book.
31–40	We recommend you use this book to refresh your knowledge and prepare yourself mentally for the actual exam.

Security+ Exam SY0-401

Domain	Weight	Question Numbers in Pretest	High Priority for Additional Study	Medium Priority for Additional Study	Low Priority for Additional Study
1.0 Network Security	20 percent	1–8	0–2 correct	3–4 correct	5–8 correct
2.0 Compliance and Operational Security	18 percent	9–16	0–2 correct	3–4 correct	5–8 correct
3.0 Threats and Vulnerabilities	20 percent	17–24	0–2 correct	3–4 correct	5–8 correct
4.0 Application, Data and Host Security	15 percent	25–31	0–2 correct	3–4 correct	5–6 correct
5.0 Access Control and Identity Management	15 percent	32–37	0–2 correct	3–4 correct	5–6 correct
6.0 Cryptography	12 percent	38–40	0–1 correct	2 correct	3 correct

B

About the CD-ROM

The CD-ROM included with this book comes complete with Total Tester customizable practice exam software with a pool of 300 practice exam questions, enough for three practice exams, and a PDF copy of the book.

SYSTEM REQUIREMENTS

The software requires Windows XP or higher and 30MB of hard disk space for full installation. To run, the screen resolution must be set to 1024 × 768 or higher. The PDF copy of the book requires Adobe Acrobat, Adobe Reader, or Adobe Digital Editions.

TOTAL TESTER PREMIUM PRACTICE EXAM SOFTWARE

Total Tester provides you with a simulation of the CompTIA Security+ exam. You can also create custom exams from selected domains or chapters. You can further customize the number of questions and time allowed.

The exams can be taken in either Practice Mode or Exam Mode. Practice Mode provides an assistance window with hints, references to the book, explanations of the correct and incorrect answers, and the option to check your answer as you take the test. Exam Mode provides a simulation of the actual exam. The number of questions, the types of questions, and the time allowed are intended to be an accurate representation of the exam environment. Both Practice Mode and Exam Mode provide an overall grade and a grade broken down by domain.

To take a test, launch the program and select Sec+ PE from the Installed Question Packs list. You can then select either Practice Mode, Exam Mode, or Custom Mode.

INSTALLING AND RUNNING TOTAL TESTER PREMIUM PRACTICE EXAM SOFTWARE

From the main screen you may install the Total Tester by clicking the Total Tester Practice Exams button. This will begin the installation process and place an icon on your desktop and in your Start menu. To run Total Tester, navigate to Start | (All) Programs | Total Seminars, or double-click the icon on your desktop.

To uninstall the Total Tester software, go to Start | Settings | Control Panel | Add/Remove Programs (XP) or Programs And Features (Vista/7/8), and then select the Total Tester program. Select Remove, and Windows will completely uninstall the software.

PDF COPY OF THE BOOK

The entire contents of the book are provided in PDF format on the CD-ROM. This file is viewable on your computer and many portable devices. Adobe Acrobat, Adobe Reader, or Adobe Digital Editions is required to view the file on your computer. A link to Adobe's web site, where you can download and install Adobe Reader, has been included on the CD-ROM.

Note: For more information on Adobe Reader and to check for the most recent version of the software, visit Adobe's web site at www.adobe.com and search for the free Adobe Reader or look for Adobe Reader on the product page. Adobe Digital Editions can also be downloaded from the Adobe web site.

To view the PDF copy of the book on a portable device, copy the PDF file to your computer from the CD-ROM, and then copy the file to your portable device using a USB or other connection. Adobe offers a mobile version of Adobe Reader, the Adobe Reader mobile app, which currently supports iOS and Android. For customers using Adobe Digital Editions and an iPad, you may have to download and install a separate reader program on your device. The Adobe web site has a list of recommended applications; McGraw-Hill Education recommends the Bluefire Reader.

TECHNICAL SUPPORT

Technical Support information is provided in the following sections by feature.

Total Seminars Technical Support

For questions regarding the Total Tester software or operation of the CD-ROM, visit www.totalsem.com or e-mail support@totalsem.com.

McGraw-Hill Education Content Support

For questions regarding the PDF copy of the book, e-mail techsolutions@mhedu.com or visit http://mhp.softwareassist.com.

For questions regarding book content, e-mail customer.service@mheducation.com. For customers outside the United States, e-mail international_cs@mheducation.com.

Stop Hackers in Their Tracks

Hacking Exposed, 7th Edition

Hacking Exposed:
Mobile Security

Hacking Exposed: Computer
Forensics, 2nd Edition

Hacking Exposed: Wireless,
2nd Edition

Hacking Exposed:
Web Applications, 3rd Edition

Hacking Exposed:
Malware & Rootkits

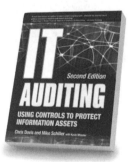

IT Auditing,
2nd Edition

IT Security Metrics

Gray Hat Hacking,
3rd Edition

Available in print and ebook formats

 @MHComputing

 Mc Graw Hill Education

Learn More. Do More.
MHPROFESSIONAL.COM

Complete coverage of today's top IT SECURITY certification exams

0-07-176026-1 • $60.00 • Available now

0-07-183648-9 • $50.00 • May 2014

0-07-183873-2 • $30.00 • Aug 2014

0-07-183557-1 • $70.00 • Oct 2014

0-07-183156-8 • $50.00 • July 2014

0-07-183976-3 • $60.00 • Sept 2014

0-07-183179-7 • $60.00 • Aug 2014

Available in print and as e-books.

 Follow us @MHComputing

Mc Graw Hill Education

Learn more. Do more.
MHPROFESSIONAL.COM

LICENSE AGREEMENT

THIS PRODUCT (THE "PRODUCT") CONTAINS PROPRIETARY SOFTWARE, DATA AND INFORMATION (INCLUDING DOCUMENTATION) OWNED BY McGRAW-HILL EDUCATION AND ITS LICENSORS. YOUR RIGHT TO USE THE PRODUCT IS GOVERNED BY THE TERMS AND CONDITIONS OF THIS AGREEMENT.

LICENSE: Throughout this License Agreement, "you" shall mean either the individual or the entity whose agent opens this package. You are granted a non-exclusive and non-transferable license to use the Product subject to the following terms:

(i) If you have licensed a single user version of the Product, the Product may only be used on a single computer (i.e., a single CPU). If you licensed and paid the fee applicable to a local area network or wide area network version of the Product, you are subject to the terms of the following subparagraph (ii).

(ii) If you have licensed a local area network version, you may use the Product on unlimited workstations located in one single building selected by you that is served by such local area network. If you have licensed a wide area network version, you may use the Product on unlimited workstations located in multiple buildings on the same site selected by you that is served by such wide area network; provided, however, that any building will not be considered located in the same site if it is more than five (5) miles away from any building included in such site. In addition, you may only use a local area or wide area network version of the Product on one single server. If you wish to use the Product on more than one server, you must obtain written authorization from McGraw-Hill Education and pay additional fees.

(iii) You may make one copy of the Product for back-up purposes only and you must maintain an accurate record as to the location of the back-up at all times.

COPYRIGHT; RESTRICTIONS ON USE AND TRANSFER: All rights (including copyright) in and to the Product are owned by McGraw-Hill Education and its licensors. You are the owner of the enclosed disc on which the Product is recorded. You may not use, copy, decompile, disassemble, reverse engineer, modify, reproduce, create derivative works, transmit, distribute, sublicense, store in a database or retrieval system of any kind, rent or transfer the Product, or any portion thereof, in any form or by any means (including electronically or otherwise) except as expressly provided for in this License Agreement. You must reproduce the copyright notices, trademark notices, legends and logos of McGraw-Hill Education and its licensors that appear on the Product on the back-up copy of the Product which you are permitted to make hereunder. All rights in the Product not expressly granted herein are reserved by McGraw-Hill Education and its licensors.

TERM: This License Agreement is effective until terminated. It will terminate if you fail to comply with any term or condition of this License Agreement. Upon termination, you are obligated to return to McGraw-Hill Education the Product together with all copies thereof and to purge all copies of the Product included in any and all servers and computer facilities.

DISCLAIMER OF WARRANTY: THE PRODUCT AND THE BACK-UP COPY ARE LICENSED "AS IS." McGRAW-HILL EDUCATION, ITS LICENSORS AND THE AUTHORS MAKE NO WARRANTIES, EXPRESS OR IMPLIED, AS TO THE RESULTS TO BE OBTAINED BY ANY PERSON OR ENTITY FROM USE OF THE PRODUCT, ANY INFORMATION OR DATA INCLUDED THEREIN AND/OR ANY TECHNICAL SUPPORT SERVICES PROVIDED HEREUNDER, IF ANY ("TECHNICAL SUPPORT SERVICES"). McGRAW-HILL EDUCATION, ITS LICENSORS AND THE AUTHORS MAKE NO EXPRESS OR IMPLIED WARRANTIES OF MERCHANTABILITY OR FITNESS FOR A PARTICULAR PURPOSE OR USE WITH RESPECT TO THE PRODUCT. McGRAW-HILL EDUCATION, ITS LICENSORS, AND THE AUTHORS MAKE NO GUARANTEE THAT YOU WILL PASS ANY CERTIFICATION EXAM WHATSOEVER BY USING THIS PRODUCT. NEITHER McGRAW-HILL EDUCATION, ANY OF ITS LICENSORS NOR THE AUTHORS WARRANT THAT THE FUNCTIONS CONTAINED IN THE PRODUCT WILL MEET YOUR REQUIREMENTS OR THAT THE OPERATION OF THE PRODUCT WILL BE UNINTERRUPTED OR ERROR FREE. YOU ASSUME THE ENTIRE RISK WITH RESPECT TO THE QUALITY AND PERFORMANCE OF THE PRODUCT.

LIMITED WARRANTY FOR DISC: To the original licensee only, McGraw-Hill Education warrants that the enclosed disc on which the Product is recorded is free from defects in materials and workmanship under normal use and service for a period of ninety (90) days from the date of purchase. In the event of a defect in the disc covered by the foregoing warranty, McGraw-Hill Education will replace the disc.

LIMITATION OF LIABILITY: NEITHER McGRAW-HILL EDUCATION, ITS LICENSORS NOR THE AUTHORS SHALL BE LIABLE FOR ANY INDIRECT, SPECIAL OR CONSEQUENTIAL DAMAGES, SUCH AS BUT NOT LIMITED TO, LOSS OF ANTICIPATED PROFITS OR BENEFITS, RESULTING FROM THE USE OR INABILITY TO USE THE PRODUCT EVEN IF ANY OF THEM HAS BEEN ADVISED OF THE POSSIBILITY OF SUCH DAMAGES. THIS LIMITATION OF LIABILITY SHALL APPLY TO ANY CLAIM OR CAUSE WHATSOEVER WHETHER SUCH CLAIM OR CAUSE ARISES IN CONTRACT, TORT, OR OTHERWISE. Some states do not allow the exclusion or limitation of indirect, special or consequential damages, so the above limitation may not apply to you.

U.S. GOVERNMENT RESTRICTED RIGHTS: Any software included in the Product is provided with restricted rights subject to subparagraphs (c), (1) and (2) of the Commercial Computer Software-Restricted Rights clause at 48 C.F.R. 52.227-19. The terms of this Agreement applicable to the use of the data in the Product are those under which the data are generally made available to the general public by McGraw-Hill Education. Except as provided herein, no reproduction, use, or disclosure rights are granted with respect to the data included in the Product and no right to modify or create derivative works from any such data is hereby granted.

GENERAL: This License Agreement constitutes the entire agreement between the parties relating to the Product. The terms of any Purchase Order shall have no effect on the terms of this License Agreement. Failure of McGraw-Hill Education to insist at any time on strict compliance with this License Agreement shall not constitute a waiver of any rights under this License Agreement. This License Agreement shall be construed and governed in accordance with the laws of the State of New York. If any provision of this License Agreement is held to be contrary to law, that provision will be enforced to the maximum extent permissible and the remaining provisions will remain in full force and effect.